HAIG:
A Reappraisal 70 Years On

HAIG

A Reappraisal 70 Years On

Edited by Brian Bond and Nigel Cave

LEO COOPER

First published in Great Britain in 1999
by
LEO COOPER
an imprint of
Pen & Sword Books Ltd,
47 Church Street,
Barnsley, South Yorkshire S70 2AS

A CIP record for this book is available from the British Library

ISBN 0 85052 698 1

Typeset in Sabon by Phoenix Typesetting, Ilkley, West Yorkshire.

Printed in Great Britain by Redwood Books Ltd,
Trowbridge, Wilts

For John Terraine, Douglas Haig's
most stalwart defender

Contents

Acknowledgements

The editors wish to thank the contributors for taking time from busy schedules to write for this book. For the sake of space and convenience the acknowledgements to the copyright holders of sources used by contributors have been gathered here.

Grateful thanks are due, therefore, to Earl Haig; the Trustees of the National Library of Scotland; the Warden and Fellows of New College, Oxford; the Earl of Derby; Countess Deidre de Roany; Mr M A F Rawlinson; Lord Robertson; the Trustees of the Liddell Hart Centre for Military Archives; the Trustees of the Public Record Office and the Controller of HM Stationery Office; the Trustees and Keeper of the Liddle Collection at Leeds University; Colonel 'Rundy' Kiggell OBE and Mr David Kiggell; the Trustees of the Imperial War Museum; Mr P M Lee. Every effort has been made by contributors to locate current holders of copyright in text, but the editors apologise for any omissions which may have occurred in this respect and would welcome information so that amendments can be made in future editions.

The Contributors

Stephen Badsey is a Senior Lecturer in the Department of War Studies at the Royal Military Academy Sandhurst. He has written extensively, including collaborating with John Pimlott on *The Gulf War Assessed* and Andrew Lambert on *The War Correspondents: The Crimean War*.

Niall Barr is a Senior Lecturer in the Department of War Studies, Royal Military Academy Sandhurst. He studied at St Andrews University for both his degree and his dictorate. He is an expert in the development of the British ex-service movement and has a deep interest in the military history of both World Wars. He is currently researching the Alamein campaign of 1942.

Ian Beckett is a Professor and Head of the Department of History at the University of Luton. He has written exclusively on the British Army and is the author of the biography, *Johnnie Gough VC*. He is the Secretary of the Army Records Society.

Brian Bond is Professor of Military History at King's College, London and President of the British Commission for Military History.

John Bourne is the author of *Great Britain and the First World War*. He has contributed numerous articles to books and periodicals and is working on a computer-based study of all the British Western Front generals in the First World War.

Nigel Cave is engaged in doctoral research at King's College, London, on staff officers in the Great War. He is a contributor to, and general editor of, the *Battleground Europe* series.

Michael Crawshaw was commissioned into the Royal Engineers in 1960 and retired from the Active List in 1992, after which he took up his present post as Editor of the British Army Review. During his tenure he has made a point of encouraging the study of the Great War by the military community – which initiative is beginning to show results as the relevance of that war becomes more appreciated by today's serving officers.

Gerard J DeGroot is a Senior Lecturer and Chairman of the Department of Modern History, University of St Andrews. He is the author of numerous books, including *Douglas Haig: 1861–1928* (1988) and *Blighty: British Society in the Era of the Great War* (1996) and *Noble War. America and the Viernam War* (1999).

Keith Grieves is a Reader in History at Kingston University. He is the author of *The Politics of Manpower 1914–18* and the biography of Sir Eric Geddes.

Paul Harris gained both his bachelor's degree in History and PhD in War Studies at King's College, London. He is a Senior Lecturer in War Studies at the Royal Military Academy Sandhurst, and is author of *Men, Ideas and Tanks* (1995) and *Amiens to the Armistice* (1998).

John Hussey OBE read History at Cambridge and then served for thirty years with British Petroleum in various parts of the world; ten of them managing companies in Africa. Since retirement in 1987 he has developed his life-long interest in military and naval history and has published some forty articles on subjects ranging from Marlborough at the Ne Plus Ultra Lines, Wellington and the Prussians before Waterloo, aspects of Haig's career, Churchill in the Boer War, to studies of command problems in the First World War.

John Peaty is engaged in doctoral research at King's College, London, studying the British Army's manpower problems in the twentieth century and particularly the Second World War. He worked for many years at the Ministry of Defence and before that at the Public Record Office. He is International Secretary of the British Commission for Military History.

William Philpott lectures in European history at London Guildhall University. He is the author of *Anglo-French Relations and Strategy on the Western Front, 1914–18*.

Gary Sheffield is Chair of Research and Academic Development, Department of War Studies, Royal Military Academy Sandhurst. He is a former Secretary-General of the British Commission for Military History.

Peter Simkins has recently retired after more than thirty-five years at the Imperial War Museum, where he was Senior Historian from 1976 to 1999. The author of *Kitchener's Army* – which was awarded the Templer Medal by the Society for Army Historical Research – he is now an Honorary Professor in the School of Historical Studies at the University of Birmingham.

David R Woodward is a Professor of History at Marshall University in Huntington, West Virginia. He is the author of *Lloyd George and the Generals* and *Field Marshal Sir William Robertson, Chief of the Imperial General Staff in the Great War*.

Editors' Foreword

Last year, 1998, marked the seventieth anniversary of the death of Field Marshal Earl Haig, and since his reputation continues to arouse as much interest and controversy as ever, this seemed an appropriate occasion for a scholarly reappraisal as the twentieth century draws to a close.

This volume represents the collaboration of two historical societies; namely the British Commission for Military History (BCMH) and the Douglas Haig Fellowship, from one or both of which all but two of the contributors are drawn. Four of the papers published here were presented at a conference jointly staged at the Imperial War Museum on 26 September, 1998, which also provided a platform for a wider discussion of various aspects of Sir Douglas Haig's career. All but one of the contributors were simultaneously commissioned by the editors from leading authorities on their subjects and, as such, familiar with the relevant archival sources. Michael Crawshaw, equally authoritative, was co-opted at a later stage to provide wider coverage of the equally important aspect of technological innovation, and to complement Paul Harris' contribution on Haig and the development of tanks.

A glance at the list of contents will show that no claim is made to cover every aspect of Haig's military career. There is room , for example, for further studies of his pre-1914 experience of combat and work as an Army reformer during Haldane's tenure of the War Office; and his performance as a Corps and Army commander in France in 1914–1915 before his promotion to Commander-in-Chief. The editors also hoped to include a contribution on Haig's relations with the monarchy, and perhaps also with the military leaders of the Dominions' forces – though to have included some but not others would have been impolitic to say the least. Consequently one contributor has been given the task of covering Haig's relations with Britain's allies and co-belligerents on the Western Front.

What we do claim, however, is that the collection as a whole represents a fair and reasonably comprehensive survey of the most significant and most frequently debated aspects of Haig's career, and especially those relating to his term as Commander-in-Chief between December 1915 and the end of the war. These topics comprise: Haig's relations with the British and French Governments (and with Lloyd George in particular); with his loyal Chief of the Imperial General Staff, Sir William Robertson; and with the Press; his attitude to technical innovation in general and, most importantly, to the tank; and his role in the gigantic operations of 1916, 1917 and 1918. Less often the subject of public controversy, but equally interesting, are the contributions on Haig and the historians, the spiritual and practical significance of religion to Haig the military commander, and his concern with ordinary soldiers as well as officers both during the war and after it in his work on behalf of the British Legion.

This volume is unapologetically 'pro-Haig' in the sense that the editors and a majority of contributors believe that he has been misunderstood, misrepresented and excessively criticized in numerous books, plays, television documentaries and newspaper articles, ranging in time from the Lloyd George *Memoirs* in the 1930s, via the anti-establishment polemics of the 1960s to the recent press campaign (in November 1998) proposing to demolish his equestrian statue in Whitehall. But the volume is 'pro-Haig' in a wider sense in that scholarly opinion – with some notable exceptions – is generally moving towards a more favourable interpretation of Haig's achievements – reflecting those of the vast forces he commanded, based on a wider range of sources than those available to earlier polemical writers such as Liddell Hart – and from a more understanding approach derived from a longer perspective and access to a proliferating array of specialist studies. This more sympathetic, or at least non-partisan, approach among the majority of First World War scholars has not so far percolated down to some of the most influential shapers of pubic opinion, for whom the simplistic myth of 'butchers and bunglers' exemplified by the egregious 'General Melchett', in the Blackadder television series, continues to exert an irresistible appeal. It is the editors' hope that this collective reappraisal will reach beyond readers already 'converted' to others who are open to reasoned analysis based on careful documentation from a wide range of evidence.

Clearly, revisionism in directions broadly favourable to Haig can take two very different forms. The first, direct, approach is to show that Haig has been wrongly or excessively criticized on specific issues: for example that he appointed a disproportionate number of cavalry officers to the highest commands; opposed or obstructed technical innovation; was callous or indifferent towards casualties; and cut himself off from combat conditions by taking refuge in his general headquarters remote from the front line. Secondly, and indirectly, historians – following the trail blazed by John Terraine – have increasingly come to appreciate the enormous difficulties experienced in expanding from the original British Expeditionary Force of some 220,000 troops to the vast Army of over two million soldiers (mostly conscripts) organized in some sixty divisions and five Armies during the culmination of the British war effort on the Western Front in 1917 and 1918. Few historians who have studied this unique British military achievement now question the impressive developments in material and war-fighting efficiency embodied in the term 'learning curve'. Indeed the debate among these historians has moved on to consider the timing and steepness of the 'curve' and to assess the level at which improvements were introduced, codified and implemented. There is, not surprisingly, some disagreement about how much credit Haig deserves for developments in such matters as staff work, training, operational planning and all-arms co-operation in combat. But since he remained in the top command throughout and displayed a close day-to-day interest in many facets of this vast military organization, he must surely be given some of the credit, if only to offset the bitter criticisms he has received for the conduct of the attritional campaigns of 1916 and 1917. The problem, as John Bourne points out, is that the Commander-in-Chief's name has become synonymous with the huge organization and its complex operations for which no single person can realistically be held responsible, whether in the allocation of blame or the bestowal of praise. Furthermore, as Dr Bourne remarks, "In future there seems little doubt that Haig's reputation will be finally determined, not by studies of the man himself, but of the man in context of the armies which he commanded, and especially by detailed operational analyses at the army, corps, divisional, brigade and even battalion level".

A final note on editorial policy and practice may be in order. Despite the earlier comment that we are, in broad terms, 'pro-Haig', there has been no editorial intervention or pressure to suppress contrary views or enforce uniformity on any particular issue. In pursuance of their own researches and independent judgements several contributors, including John Hussey, John Bourne, Bill Philpott, Gary Sheffield and Peter Simkins take positive views of Haig's achievements in various roles but others such as Gerry deGroot, Ian Beckett and Keith Grieves remain – in varying degrees – critical. However, what we all have in common is a belief that, given the long lapse of time and the availability of a vast amount of new documentary evidence, the British Army's part in the

First World War, and Haig's role in particular, should at last be placed in a full historical context where there will be less need for emotional partisanship on either side and more dispassionate concern with the complexity of events and the limited scope for the decisive influence of individuals even at the highest level of command.

Brian Bond and Nigel Cave

Chapter 1

Haig and the Historians

J.M. Bourne

Haig and the historians. Haig versus the historians. Haig and me. History and me. Whenever I write or (more rarely) speak about Haig it always becomes personal. 'What's the matter?' my wife asked as I sat slumped over my desk with my head in my hands. 'It's this article I'm writing on "Haig and the Historians",' I replied, 'it's depressing me.' Writing and speaking about Haig always depresses me. This is because, despite my best intentions, I nearly always become far more strident in Haig's defence than is proper and more than the evidence permits. Stridency has no place in the repertoire of a respectable historian. But, in Haig's case it is difficult to avoid. My own painful journey of discovery about the true nature of the First World War and Haig's role in it has been described elsewhere.[1] Public discussion of the war surrounding the eightieth anniversary of the Armistice, in November 1998, made it abundantly clear how few of my fellow countrymen have followed me down the road to Damascus. On 6 November, 1998, a national newspaper, *The Express*, under the banner headline 'He led a million men to their deaths', launched a campaign for Haig's statue in Whitehall to be removed because of the 'shadow' it cast over the Cenotaph and the memory of Britain's war dead. Its extraordinary editorial deployed the full panoply of anti-Haig prejudice. He was an 'ambitious cavalryman' 'who did not share the sufferings and deprivations of his men'. His view of strategy and tactics was 'blinkered'. 'Hundreds of thousands of men died needlessly as a result of his orders.' The situation in our schools appears to be little better. A recent GCSE 'Revision Guide' explains how 600,000 British troops were *killed* on the Somme, that Haig ordered 400,000 men to advance up to their waists in mud at Passchendaele (close your eyes and imagine the scene), and that he did not understand the use of tanks because he was 'used to cavalry charges'.[2] In this atmosphere it is difficult not to succumb to the temptation of joining the 'angry band of revisionists', who, 'hopelessly outnumbered', are driven to the 'opposite extreme, transforming the senior commanders from butchers into saints'.[3] Brian Bond's hope that one day the Great War would be studied 'simply as history without polemic intent or apologies' still seems a long way from realization.[4]

The gulf between popular understanding of the war and the burgeoning academic scholarship on the British Army's performance on the Western Front remains vast. 'After the work of the last ten years,' wrote Ian Beckett, 'it might be argued that we have broken the Hindenburg Line, we are somewhere around the end of October 1918 and we can see those green fields beyond. It is only a pity that, back in Blighty, it is still 1 July, 1916. Clearly, we need a superior breed of conducting officers when the war correspondents arrive to visit the 'Old Front Line'.'[5] This conducting officer is beginning to wonder whether he is up to the task.

The gulf between popular understanding of the war and academic scholarship on the British Army has affected views of Haig in a particular way. Haig is absolutely central to the popular view of the war. His 'stupidity' and 'indifference' to the sufferings of his men provide an explanation for the war's horrors which people can readily grasp. Those who lecture to 'extra-mural' audiences on the Great War will know how impossible it is to keep Haig out of the discussion. No matter what the subject of the lecture, questions always return to the first day on the Somme and Passchendaele, which continue to exercise a firm grip not only on popular memory but also on popular historiography. This is in marked contrast to the revisionist academic literature of the last fifteen years, which has begun to transform our understanding of how the British Expeditionary Force actually planned and executed military operations, and which is becoming increasingly concerned with 1918, the war's 'forgotten year'. Haig has all but disappeared from this literature. Some of the leading figures in the renaissance have been quite blunt about the matter. 'We need no more books devoted exclusively to Sir Douglas Haig,' declared Robin Prior and Trevor Wilson in their devastating review of Denis Winter's *Haig's Command*, 'and least of all to trivialities such as his spitefulness or noble character, his callousness or grim forbearance, his sexual deviance or marital uprightness. There are large issues crying out to be explored: among them, how first world war battles were devised and organized and waged and supplied and commanded and made to serve a purpose, or caused to serve no purpose. A book like *Haig's Command* is more than an impediment to the exploration of real issues. It helps to preserve historical writing about the Great War in its ridiculously protracted adolescence.'[6] In practice, this means that popular opinion holds Haig responsible for the British Expeditionary Force's bloody failures but academic revisionist history has not credited him with responsibility for its bloody successes.

There is a certain irony in the personal demonization of Haig, because his doughtiest champions over the years have undoubtedly been found among his biographers. These have been numerous.[7] Haig's predecessor, Sir John French, has not enjoyed such lavish attention. Neither have Haig's immediate subordinates, all of whom commanded at a level comparable with Bernard Montgomery in the Second World War. Only Rawlinson has been the subject of a truly distinguished and enlightening study.[8] Gough has, perhaps, fared next best.[9] Plumer and (more particularly) Byng have been the subject of adequate accounts.[10] But there is little of value on Allenby and virtually nothing has been written about the seemingly unknowable Horne.[11] This is not simply because Haig is more important than the others, but because it is more practical to write about him. The distinctiveness of history as a subject is that it is about documents. In Haig's case, there is no shortage of documents, especially material of a personal kind. Haig kept a diary and wrote copious letters to his wife. These provide ideal material for painting a portrait of Haig. In the case of his most recent biographers, however, the portrait has been far from flattering.[12]

Haig emerges from the pages of Gerard De Groot as a man of awesome self-assurance, with a religious sense of mission and a direct line to God, whose military 'education' had revealed to him the road to victory but closed his mind to any thoughts of an alternative route, a dabbler in spiritualism and a self-obsessed valetudinarian who surrounded himself with sycophants, a man of calculating ambition, petty-minded, devious and disloyal. To this, Denis Winter, self-appointed Witchfinder General of the Great War, has added the charge of fraud. Haig is accused of deliberately falsifying his diary, setting in train an international conspiracy of official historians and archivists designed to protect his reputation and render a true explanation of the war's operational history impossible from the official record. Refutation of these charges would take up more space than is available here. Suffice it to say, that Winter's perceived conspiracy would appear to be one of the least successful in history, judging by the state of Haig's public reputation in Britain. The falsification of his diary seems equally inept, given the frequency with which its contents are held against the author's competence, integrity and humanity, not least by Winter himself.

There are, however, wider and more serious problems with the personal approach. Haig's papers provide abundant evidence about Haig. They offer a splendid platform from which to observe their author, but they lack the altitude for a comprehensive survey of the war as a whole. Those who see the war on the Western Front as little more than a working out of Haig's pre-war (mis)conceptions have a dilemma. How do they explain the eventual British and Allied victory? In Winter's case the dilemma is avoided by the classic psychological ploy of denial. There was no military victory on the battlefield in 1918, therefore there is nothing to explain. Except, perhaps, why the German military leadership asked for an Armistice. There are often major disjunctions between what Haig thought should happen, would happen and even had happened and what *did* happen. Nowhere, perhaps, is this clearer than in the case of Haig's 'cavalry obsession'.

Haig's origins as a cavalry officer are frequently cited against him. Cavalry officers were supposedly incapable of understanding technology. Why this should be is rarely explained. Horse management was certainly complex and technical: horses were in an important sense muscle-powered machines. Haig's private papers provide abundant evidence of his devotion to the cavalry. His pre-war writings are optimistic about its utility on modern battlefields. During the war he did his best to emphasize the cavalry's successes. After the war he lent his support and encouragement to maintaining the arm.

Given this evidence, one might expect certain things to follow: a British Army in which cavalry was a major component; the widespread appointment of cavalry officers to key posts; a low level of mechanisation. None of these things was true during Haig's command of the BEF. By September 1916 there were only five cavalry divisions on the Western Front, two of them Indian Army, less than three per cent of the BEF's total strength. By September 1918 the number of cavalry divisions on the Western Front had fallen to three compared with sixty infantry divisions. During the war the cavalry grew by some 80 per cent, a growth accounted for largely by Yeomanry, which did find an effective use in Palestine. But the infantry grew by 469 per cent, the artillery by 520 per cent, the engineers by 1,429 per cent and the army service corps by 2,212 per cent.[13] Both the artillery and engineers grew to a size larger than the whole of the British Regular Army in August 1914. The BEF also boasted the world's first Tank Corps, which had 22,000 officers and other ranks by September 1918, equal to the size of the cavalry in August 1914. It was also supported by the world's first independent air force, an organization much sponsored by Haig, and many of whose officers had transferred from the cavalry. Appointment to general officer rank in the BEF was not dominated by cavalrymen. Haig showed no preference for appointing cavalrymen either to senior appointments (with the exception of Gough) or to his circle of 'syco-phants'. And by the end of the war the BEF was not only awash with horses and mules but also with lorries, motor-cars, armoured cars, tanks and motor-bikes.[14] It was the most mechanized army in the world. Haig's 'cavalry obsession' therefore seems to have had little practical effect.

De Groot's biography provides an interesting account of the evolution of Haig's pre-war ideas as well as a ruthless dissection of his character and personality, but ultimately it fails to convince because it does not sufficiently engage with the most important issues of Haig's wartime command, of what actually happened to the BEF on the Western Front and why. De Groot offers us his understanding of Haig, but little of his understanding of the war. The two are clearly connected but to understand one is not necessarily to understand the other. John Terraine's *Douglas Haig, the Educated Soldier* remains formidable precisely because it does engage with these issues.[15] Terraine has always insisted that his view of Haig was determined by his view of the war and not the other way round.[16] This appears to be the sounder method-ological approach. In future there seems little doubt that Haig's reputation will be finally determined not by studies of the man himself, but of the man in the context of the armies which he commanded, and especially by detailed operational analyses at the army, corps, divisional, brigade and even battalion level. It is equally clear that the day has not yet arrived.

Despite the transformation of our understanding of the conduct of war on the Western Front by an impressive body of work published by British and Commonwealth historians since 1982, the year in which Shelford Bidwell and Dominick Graham's seminal study *Firepower* appeared, there has been no fundamental re-assessment of Haig.[17] This is, to some extent, unsurprising. Bidwell and Graham deliberately shifted the academic historiography of the Great War from an increas-ingly sterile debate about a handful of leading military and political leaders (especially Haig), based largely on gossip, to an increasingly fruitful consideration of the British Army as an instrument of war, based largely on contemporary archive sources, especially the 4,500 boxes of operational records contained in the Public Record Office's WO 95 series of unit war diaries and after-action reports. Although valuable and much-needed at the time, the long-term consequence of this shift has been to disembody the BEF's evolution. It is now time, perhaps, to restore some individuality to the process.

Although a few unreconstructed traditionalists, such as John Keegan, refuse to accept that the BEF underwent a 'learning curve' during the war, there is little disagreement among scholars about the nature of the military transformation. In August 1914 the British soldier might have passed for a gamekeeper in his soft cap, puttees and pack.[18] He walked into battle. He was armed with little more than a rifle and bayonet. For support he could call only on the shrapnel-firing field guns of the Royal Artillery. His commanders were often elderly and unfit, with little relevant pre-war experience of any level of command above the battalion. By September 1918 he was dressed like an industrial worker in a safety helmet, with a respirator protecting him against gas close to hand. He was just as likely to be armed with a Lewis gun, grenade or rifle grenade as a simple rifle. He was trucked into battle. His appearance on the battlefield was preceded by a deception campaign based on sophisticated signals intelligence. He was supported by an high explosive artillery barrage of crushing density, by tanks, armoured cars, machine-guns, smoke and gas. Enemy guns were identified and attacked using leading-edge technologies of sound-ranging and flash-spotting, in which specially-recruited scientists played a key role. His commanders had emerged from the 'tougher and younger core of natural leaders among surviving officers' and, in some cases at brigade level and below, from Kitchener volunteers and Territorials.[19] Many possessed in good measure the military leadership qualities of courage, boldness, judgement, flexibility and integrity. They abandoned strategic grandiosity in favour of the tactically possible in a war where tactical possibilities were determined principally by the covering fire of artillery. They no longer re-inforced failure or hung on to captured ground for the sake of it. The importance of thorough planning and preparation was accepted. Individual enterprise and initiative was encouraged. By 1918 the BEF had adopted a 'modern style of war',[20] very different from that of 1914 or 1916 or even 1917, something which popular and media opinion seemingly finds it impossible to grasp and which, during the Armistice commemorations, was totally ignored.

There is no consensus, however, about the speed or quality of the BEF's learning or of the role of high command in the process. The Canadian historian, Tim Travers, remains an influential critic not only of the army but also of Haig. In a series of articles and two major books, Travers has investigated the British Army's weaknesses during the Great War in managerial terms.[21] His 'villain' is not one individual, not even Haig, but the pre-war Regular Army itself.

He deploys three main arguments. The first concerns the 'ethos' of the pre-war officer corps. He describes this as 'strangely personalized', a glorified old-boy network, hierarchical and riven with favouritism, whose principal intellectual activity was the dishonest preservation of individual and collective reputations. This had important consequences. It meant that the army was poorly adapted to meeting some of the war's most important challenges. It was rigid and inflexible. Initiative and independent judgement were not encouraged. Intellectual honesty and curiosity were lacking. The historical record was deliberately distorted. Failure was disguised and tolerated. The second theme is that the army's ethos was conducive to the persistence throughout the war of pre-war ideas. These emphasized a 'human' image of the battlefield at the expense of a disregard for the tactical implications of new technology. The fire-power lessons of the Russo-Japanese war were ignored in favour of a 'human-centred' model of battle in which mass, concentration of force, the 'offensive spirit', morale and the idea of 'breakthrough' were key elements. As a result senior commanders, especially Haig, pursued tactics which were often inappropriate and beyond the capabilities of the weapons systems employed. Travers' third argument is the propensity of senior commanders to regard battle as an ordered and regular activity. Haig, in particular, saw his role as that of 'master planner' issuing generalized instructions. In the inevitable chaos of war, top-down control was abandoned and a command vacuum created. Too often during major offensives the lights were on at GHQ but there was no one at home.

As an explanation, Travers' account explains too much. Given the severity of his strictures, the pre-war Regular Army ought not to have been able to adapt at all, even slowly and inadequately, to the challenge of defeating the German Army on the Western Front. It is tempting to accuse him of the same failure as he does Haig: that of becoming trapped in a rigid pre-war model and of trying to force reality to submit to his preconceptions. In particular, it is difficult to square his account of the pre-war army, based largely on personal papers and 'court gossip', with the army as a practical instrument of empire. The army's role as a colonial police force has often been regarded as a source of institutional weakness. It produced an army which fought in 'penny packets', lacked operational doctrine, was weak in staff work and undergunned in heavy artillery. But the wars of empire also produced an officer corps with vast combat and active service experience. The intensity and range of professional opportunity offered by the pre-war British Army was enormous. It is difficult to reconcile the fit, adaptable, energetic, resourceful men who emerge from the pre-war Army's multi-biography, and who were its battalion, battery, brigade and divisional commanders in 1918, with the somnolent, dogma-ridden, unprofessional, unreflecting institution depicted by Professor Travers. The British Army in the Edwardian period was then, as now, essentially a pragmatic, empirical institution. Pragmatism and empiricism also have their limitations but they are different from the ones which

Travers depicts. He also gives far too little attention in his work to the second half of 1918, when the BEF finally succeeded in integrating infantry, artillery, armour and aircraft, something it could hardly have achieved had it been as 'traditional' and hostile to 'technological solutions' as he claims.

Where does all this leave Haig? Travers is one of the few modern, archival historians concerned with operational history to give much consideration to Haig at all. His portrait is again critical. As a manager in a managerial war, Haig was not a success. He too often left his subordinate commanders to their own devices in a fog of uncertainty about GHQ's real intentions. At other times, he interfered unnecessarily. These inconsistencies produced neither a coherent doctrine nor a decentralized, initiative-taking system. Haig demanded absolute loyalty. His GHQ engendered an atmosphere of fear which discouraged productive dialogue and made operational analysis difficult. The achievements of the BEF in 1918 are, again, difficult to reconcile with this view. Travers' explanation is that Haig's attempts to control the BEF from above broke down under the strain of the German offensives. A system of 'constructive chaos' ensued, in which subordinate formations, by now much more experienced and better equipped, simply got on with the job in their own way. Some units did this better than others and the BEF's performance remained patchy to the end.

Other historians who take a more positive view of the BEF's evolution than Travers, notably Prior and Wilson and Griffith, give less systematic attention to Haig's role, though Prior and Wilson are hardly admirers. This brings us to a final problem with regard to Haig and the historians, the inadequacies of the historiography. Despite the great advances of the last few years in the analysis of operations on the Western Front there are still huge gaps. There are no good modern archival studies of the battles of Loos or of Cambrai or of Arras. The huge battles, with their equally huge casualties, in the late summer and autumn of 1918, the greatest battles ever fought by the British Army, remain scandalously under-studied, though much important work is going on. There are no modern studies of communications, a fundamental problem during the war, or of that despised body of men, the staff. The Canadian historian Ian Brown has made an important start with his recent book on logistics, but much remains to be done in this area, as well.[22] There are no modern studies of the corps level of command, other than John Baynes's biography of Ivor Maxse,[23] and few on divisional command, though several divisions are currently the subject of postgraduate scrutiny. The role of some of Haig's closest subordinates, notably his long-serving chief of staff Launcelot Kiggell, are poorly understood. And finally, little is known of how general and other officers were appointed during the war, though Travers has thrown some light on how and why they were replaced. The role of the Military Secretary's office in identifying men for promotion has never been analysed: the department's papers were destroyed in the disastrous German air raid of 8 September, 1940. How the Military Secretary's staff operated and what qualities they looked for can only be inferred. The statistical evidence suggests that promotion had little to do with 'cap badge' patronage or the operation of regimental mafias,[24] but beyond that it is difficult to speculate. The managerial aspects of command (which mainly concern Travers) and the technical aspects (which mainly concern Prior and Wilson) are clearly intimately connected and brought together by the BEF's command and control and promotions systems. Haig's role remains obscure, especially for later stages of the war, but it is clear from his diary that he spent a great deal of time visiting subordinate formations and his comments display detailed knowledge of his 'middle' and 'junior' managers, which does not give the impression of a man cut off from reality either physically or mentally. Until these historiographical gaps are filled it is difficult to see how a properly rounded, critical account of Haig and Haig's command will emerge. Prior and Wilson were surely right when they dismissed the need for any more books 'devoted exclusively to Sir Douglas Haig', but there is a need for a new study which places him properly in the context of the much changed landscape of Western Front operational historiography, a replacement indeed for Terraine's *Educated Soldier*. It is doubtful whether much fresh illumination will emanate from Haig's private papers, though there is surely a case for a fuller publication of them than that achieved by Lord Blake's edition of 1952. This would not be a cheap operation for a conventional publisher, but in the age of the Internet perhaps the time has come to be unconventional. Otherwise, Haig's admirers will find much to admire in his diary and letters. His detractors will find much to censure. Haig does not fit the traditional view of a military hero, one of the 'Great Captains' so admired by Liddell Hart. He was no Alexander or Napoleon. Few commanders are and perhaps none in modern war, with its remorseless materialism, weapons of mass destruction and creeping bureaucracy. We live in a confessional culture. Strength, reticence, privacy, religious faith, devotion to duty are no longer much admired. Our society admires the ability to confess weakness and to be seen to be struggling to overcome it. Historians of the operational history of the Western Front may hold out some hope for a proper restoration of Haig's reputation, but his best bet is probably to come back from the dead, appear on the *Oprah Winfrey Show*, explain how he was abused as a child, admit to being gay and – above all – cry for the men he 'killed'.

Notes

1   J.M. Bourne, *Britain and the Great War* (London: Edward Arnold, 1989), pp. ix-x, 173–74.
2   I should like to thank Mr Peter Lawrence for bringing this guide to my attention. The publishers have since removed some of its more absurd assertions.
3   Gerard J. De Groot, *Douglas Haig, 1861–1928* (London: Unwin Hyman, 1988), p. 1.
4   Brian Bond, 'Introduction', in Brian Bond, ed., *The First World War and British Military History* (Oxford: Clarendon Press, 1991).
5   Ian Beckett, 'Revisiting the Old Front Line. The Historiography of the Great War since 1984', *Stand To! The Journal of the Western Front Association*, 48 (April 1995), p. 13.
6   Robin Prior and Trevor Wilson, 'Review of Denis Winter, *Haig's Command: A Reassessment*', *Australian War Memorial Journal*, 23 (October 1993), p. 57.
7   For a full discussion of Haig's treatment by his biographers, see Keith Simpson, 'The Reputation of Sir Douglas Haig', in Bond, ed., *First World War and British Military History*, pp. 141–62.
8   Robin Prior and Trevor Wilson, *Command on the Western Front. The Military Career of Sir Henry Rawlinson* (Oxford: Blackwell, 1992).
9   Anthony Farrar-Hockley, *Goughie. The Life of General Sir Hubert Gough* (London: 1975).
10 Geoffrey Powell, *Plumer. The Soldiers' General* (London: 1990) and Jeffery Williams, *Byng of Vimy* (London: 1983).
11 A collection of Horne's papers has recently been deposited in the Imperial War Museum. Whether these throw more light on his command of First Army remains to be seen.
12 De Groot, *Douglas Haig*; Denis Winter, *Haig's Command: A Reassessment* (London: Viking, 1991).
13 Figures are based on Statistics of the Military Effort of the British Empire during the Great War (London: HMSO, 1922), section 26.
14 Bourne, *Britain and the Great War*, p. 178, gives the figures.
15 John Terraine, *Douglas Haig, the Educated Soldier* (London: Hutchinson, 1963; 1990).
16 Terraine, *Haig*, 1990 edn., p. xiii.
17 Shelford Bidwell and Dominick Graham, *Firepower. British Army Weapons and Theories of War, 1904–1945* (London: Allen & Unwin, 1982). See also, Peter Simkins, *Kitchener's Army* (Manchester: Manchester University Press, 1988); Bill Rawling, *Surviving Trench*

Warfare. Technology and the Canadian Corps, 1914–1918 (Toronto: 1992); Paddy Griffith, Battle Tactics of the Western Front (London: Yale University Press, 1994); and Shane B. Schreiber, *The Shock Army of the British Empire. The Canadian Corps in the Last 100 Days of the Great War* (Westport: Praeger, 1997).

18 I owe this illustration to Keith Simpson.

19 Ian Beckett, 'The Military Historian and the Popular Image of the Western Front, 1914–1918', The Historian, (Spring 1997), p.13.

20 See Jonathan Bailey, The First World War and the Birth of the Modern Style of Warfare (Camberley, Strategic and Combat Studies Institute, 1996).

21 Tim Travers, 'A Particular Style of Command: Haig and GHQ, 1916–1918', *Journal of Strategic Studies*, 10 (1987), pp. 363–76; 'The Evolution of British Strategy and Tactics on the Western Front in 1918: GHQ, Manpower and Technology', *Journal of Military History*, 54 (1990), pp. 173–200; *The Killing Ground* (London: Allen & Unwin, 1987); and *How the War Was Won* (London: Routledge, 1992).

22 Ian Malcolm Brown, *British Logistics on the Western Front* (Westport: Praeger, 1998).

23 John Baynes, *Far From a Donkey. The Life of General Sir Ivor Maxse* (London: Brassey's, 1995). Andy Simpson's London PhD thesis on corps command is eagerly awaited.

24 J.M.Bourne, 'British Divisional Commanders during the Great War: First Thoughts', *Gun Fire. A Journal of First World War History*, 29 (n.d.), p. 26.

Chapter 2

Portrait of a Commander-in-Chief

John Hussey

'I have never understood history other than in terms of human relationships; and I have attempted to judge individuals in their own terms and
from what they say about themselves in their own language. . . .
Historians should not "intellectualize" about people less sophisticated
than themselves, and about societies less complicated than those in which
we live'.

Richard Cobb[1]

PLANS AND REALITIES, 1916

Ten days before the start of the great 1916 offensive a conversation was
recorded by an infantryman-novelist, which provides a good introduction to a chapter on Chief Command in the First World War. An
artillery officer told this battalion commander:

It will not be an offensive, only a promenade for your infantry. There
has never been in military history such a gigantic expenditure of guns
and ammunition. . . . We know from air photographs every earthwork,
every blockhouse, every wire entanglement – not to speak of the forts.
We shall crumple them all up, stamp them into the ground. You will only
have to take possession of corpses and ruins. A promenade for you
infantry, a promenade.

The outcome was somewhat different. In the first days of the attack
this infantry officer's 850 men were reduced to 107 due to machine-
gun fire, and their successors, he says, were 'shot to pieces'. Of this
carnage one of the Army commanders there grimly noted in his diary,
'too great a task undertaken with insufficient means'. How typical it
all seems: the unprecedented logistical achievement which enabled the

mass armies to function; the reliance upon artillery power – and in 1916 upon artillery 'destruction' rather than the more sophisticated 'neutralization'; the General Staffs' careful preparations and confident assumptions for the impending battle; the dreadful reality and horrific casualties.

One might think it an all-too-familiar Somme story, another instance of Laffin's *British Butchers and Bunglers*, but it is not to be found there, nor in Martin Middlebrook's fine study *The First Day of the Somme*; and there is something a little un-English about the artilleryman's phraseology. For we are hearing words spoken between German officers just before Falkenhayn's onslaught against Verdun in February 1916, launched nine weeks after Haig became C-in-C of the BEF in France; and the diarist Army commander was General von Gallwitz, commanding on the west bank of the Meuse.[2] I begin with it because it marks the reality of the Western Front and the German attempt to achieve a decision – actually to win the war – in 1916; and because it indicates the compulsions in the minds of the Commanders-in-Chief on both sides.[3]

The proper study of any single Commander-in-Chief in a World War needs to examine not merely the man and the functioning of his General Headquarters, his Army's doctrine, his relations with subordinate generals, and his bond with his men. It must place him within the context of his country's policy and the political leaders who define, support and (when necessary) circumscribe his role[4], who create (or ought to create) the framework within which he must work with his allies and they with him. But even that is not enough. The extract from the German novel I have just quoted implies the comparative question: how did the other side perform? These are the factors for a full consideration of Sir Douglas Haig's forty months as C-in-C of the BEF, from December, 1915 until April, 1919, and they would require yet another massive book. All that can be offered in this chapter is something less – a miniature sketch of a vast subject.[5]

SOME PERSONAL FACTORS

Douglas Haig's mental and physical robustness was so great during the World War and in his subsequent ten year campaign for ex-servicemen, that we forget that he was not born with a strong constitution and that his boyhood was badly affected by asthma. He conquered this mysterious killer disease by the classic methods of light diet, daily exercise (riding had been found beneficial for the disease as long ago as the 18th Century) and by thought control when attacks threatened; it was rare for him to suffer attacks in later life, though during the crisis of Spring 1918 his breathing was again a problem.

There are two points of significance here: first, asthma forced Haig constantly to watch his general health and diet (quite different from the 'hypochondria' sometimes alleged against him), and take regular outdoor exercise; secondly, as Adler has pointed out, asthmatics tend to excessive self-control and to 'over-achievement', and such traits are not lacking in Haig's mature personality. [6]

Haig always insisted in doing the work of the day within the day. He was not fluent in speech and wherever possible left telephone communication to his senior staff. Except among a chosen few he preferred to remain as silent as was consistent with good manners. His chosen method of work was by close study of the written word backed by concise verbal reports from his staff, by his own rapid composition of letters and memoranda, and by personal observation. He had early trained himself to write with great clarity and directness; he had studied closely military history and theory; and he was by nature firm and confident. In a deeply perceptive appreciation John Charteris, who had known Haig well wrote:

> He had deep confidence in his own judgment on facts within his own knowledge or which (lacking knowledge) he accepted from others; but he never closed his mind to an addition to these facts and was always ready to amend his previous judgments in the light of further facts. He did not resent, in any way, the expression of a judgment contrary to his own from those he trusted; but while he did not resent it it rarely altered his own confidence in his own judgment. But this confidence was only in his own *judgment*. He made no claim to knowledge above other people's. Indeed he drew the line of his own limitations of knowledge far lower than was necessary or justified. One saw therefore the queer blend of confidence in *judgment*, diffidence in *claim to knowledge*. This made him very (unusually so) open to new ideas.[7]

If Haig's mind was not of an inherently speculative cast dreaming up revolutionary new concepts, it did possess in large measure the ability to see the practical possibilities in the ideas of others. Without the febrility of J F C Fuller (or 'Chink' Dorman-Smith in the next war), he was always ready to study the practicability of the ideas thrown up, to push for them and to persist with their implementation in the face of considerable opposition or scepticism: his enthusiasm for tanks is the most famous instance, but in fact it is only one example among the plethora of inventions and developments which so mark these four years and so interested him as a means of shortening the road to victory – not excluding in 1916 a 'medical ray' which also was claimed to be a 'death-ray'.[8]

His quiet courtesy and self-control were proverbial: Edmund Ironside thought him 'a man with the most courteous manner. I never saw him once lose his temper', a point confirmed by Clement Armitage, a personal liaison officer, who never heard Haig lifting his voice in any discussion. An ADC remarked that 'what he was thinking about the war as it stood on any particular day, no one, not even his Chief of Staff, could fully make out'. When a sudden crisis blew up in April, 1918, Churchill who was present heard Haig quietly remark as he received the news, 'the situation is never so bad or so good as first reports indicate' but he sent off his Chief of Staff post-haste to find out more.[9] He was always fortified by his personal religious belief and his positive and optimistic nature, but underneath there was immense and continuous strain. It comes out in the remark Haig made to Trenchard that 'it was the greatest strain of any man always to be planning how others were to get killed'; in a letter to his wife after a few days' leave at the start of 1918 he confessed 'it was everything having nothing to do, except do what I could to amuse you and the children'. And many soldiers noted the strain in his face, as well as his courtesy, as he made his visits.[10]

He had very definite ideas on what was acceptable conduct and he was by nature quick to notice such failings in others: although he was clannish, his own family's eccentricities or failings were dryly, if humorously, noted down. Yet he was only intermittently self-critical and the contrast between his diary's criticisms of the unacceptable conduct of others and the lack of awareness when his own conduct fell short of those same standards has created a degree of personal hostility towards him among some historians.[11] On the other hand, he had all the Scottish admiration for hard work and 'canniness', so that when he visited Australia in 1891 he was much impressed by these qualities among the population there. And so this product of Clifton and Oxford and the socially exclusive 7th Hussars formed a high opinion of, and excellent relations with, the Australian Jewish civil-engineer militiaman John Monash, and the Canadian real-estate agent and militiaman Arthur Currie and with others whose backgrounds and experience in life were far from his. Time and again during the war he records appreciative things of them, and the reason is simple: like him they were entirely committed to the main task in hand.[12]

It was with no intention of pandering to popular sentiment but with genuine pride in his men that in his Final Despatch Haig listed among brigadiers a taxi-cab driver, among battalion commanders a railway signalman and a coalminer, and among staff officers 'the under-cook of a Cambridge College' and an insurance clerk. A favourite saying of his was 'it is the spirit that quickeneth' and Churchill recalled that on telling Haig that a naval officer had failed to engage the enemy with determination the light kindled in Haig's eye and he repeated Winston's phrase: bending the whole spirit to the task, engaging the enemy – that was the way by which many failings could be forgiven. Charteris remarked on his 'very real generosity in mind and in dealing with others, a generosity that was limitless *until it impinged on the "cause"* as he saw it. Then it was cut off as by a guillotine'. [13] That opinion seems essentially true to me. Haig's 'cause' was to lead the British Armies in France to victory over the Germans and every moment of his day and everyone else's day had to be devoted to it.

THE WORKING DAY

Haig's principal quarters were in a simply furnished country house just outside Montreuil-sur-Mer, served by his personal staff and visited by his departmental heads. Montreuil itself housed the many GHQ working branches, and although it was Haig's habit after Sunday service at the Presbyterian church hut to visit the staff at their offices in town, his main contact was necessarily through his Chief of the General Staff, Director of Military Operations, Adjutant General, QMG, Director of Medical Services, as well as through the useful 'grapevine' of his ADCs and personal liaison officers.

Of course, during the frequent periods of battle his office moved to Advanced GHQ – often a house close to a particular battle-zone, or in his special train parked on a siding – and kept in touch with main GHQ through telephone and despatch-rider. Again, if he was on one of his extended inspections of hospitals, base areas, etc., or visiting one of his Army commands, or attending meetings in London or Paris, the same system applied. The C-in-C was constantly in touch.

Each day for Haig had a similar pattern, save that Sundays (and Christmas day) entailed attendance at church and a more relaxed lunchtime. In the middle years of the war, on first rising he took a run round the grounds of his quarters before breakfast, though later on this became a walk. [14] He checked the meteorological conditions and recorded the details meticulously. After breakfast he went to his office and (if he had not done so the previous night) wrote up his daily diary in a duplicate notebook and penned a short letter to his wife: if a King's Messenger was going to London a bundle of diary pages would be sent to Lady Haig, he himself retaining the carbon copy for reference.

He would next study and annotate the files on operations, the requirements of the BEF, correspondence between London and GHQ, position papers, tabulations and recommendations. He spent a considerable time listening to the AG, QMG, CGS and others. His Artillery Adviser Noel Birch, his DMO the rifleman 'Tavish' Davidson, the

Intelligence chief the sapper Charteris, and the head of the RFC Hugh Trenchard, were always closely questioned, and their views later recorded in his diary.

The decisions reached on the day's matters, documents would then be drafted by the Staff and issued in his name over the signature of the relevant head: an instance is the DMO's analysis of tactics (OB.2089) which the CGS issued to Army Commanders on the authority of the 'FM C-in-C' on 7 August, 1917. But in addition Haig himself either wrote a considerable number of letters or reviewed his staff's drafts and produced his own final version, many of these being for the CIGS or the War Cabinet.

If there were important 'business visitors', such as the Secretary of State for War, railway experts, foreign delegations, or clerics, a part of the morning would have to be made over to seeing them. So far as possible the less important ones were handled by the departmental heads so that the C-in-C was left undisturbed until they came to him at lunchtime. Although he himself ate sparingly it was necessary that his guests should be properly entertained and their views listened to; on many occasions this was something of a trial for this busy man, but his invariable courtesy masked any inward feelings of impatience or irritation. With the coffee he would excuse himself and leave.

Nearly every afternoon was spent out of doors and if he was fortunately free of visitors he began before lunch, taking a snack from his luncheon box somewhere along the road. Haig would drive to inspect a formation or unit, meet its senior officers and (when possible) its junior leaders, talk over plans and prospects, equipment problems, morale and all the other things that indicated its efficiency and spirit. Usually he visited several such formations, and might take tea with some of the officers or have a few words with senior NCOs. His diary is full of comments on what he saw, the names of officers whom he considered good, and judgements on the brigadiers and major generals in command. He had an excellent memory for the men he had met and so possessed an ever-growing mental 'data bank' (backed by the diary) on potential leaders and their qualities. After these visits were completed he would meet one of his ADCs with the horses and they would gallop home several miles across country to reach quarters at sunset; if the ground was too frozen Haig would walk the last few miles home.[15] In the summer of 1918 when victory was coming within sight, by then a tired man and a little bowed, he occasionally played a round of golf in the afternoon.

After a glance at the afternoon's information he would prepare for the inevitable hospitality to be offered at dinner. He was to some extent shielded by his ADCs if conversation with his guests flagged: they were ready to bring up topics in which the C-in-C was known to be interested, and as his table was well supplied with good wines and brandy, the Asquiths, Churchills and others who invited themselves to GHQ were able to indulge themselves in talk, speculation and copious reinforcement; the most important of them would be invited by Haig for a private talk afterwards. At about 9.30 p.m. the C-in-C would return to his office and deal with late evening reports and any matters brought to him then by the CGS. It was a time when he would put thoughts and questions to Kiggell (or Lawrence later), seeking views, testing for other insights: in Kiggell's words, 'as always, thinking much and saying d—d little', after which he would silently come to his own conclusions. If there was time he would write his diary, his daily letter to Lady Haig. Then he went to bed and read a Psalm or two (in difficult times, Psalm 91, *qui habitat*), the Bible or the *Pilgrim's Progress*.

This was his habitual regime from December 1915 until the war's end. Only one member of his staff possessed the power to break this routine: his physician Colonel Ryan (often with covert advice from Haig's servant, Secrett) would order him to stop work or go to bed, in a way undreamt of by the remainder of his staff, and DH would obey.[16]

UNDERSTANDING A 'DURATION ONLY' ARMY

Haig's intense thirty-year application to the often dull routine of pre-1914 soldiering has been deemed 'limiting'. Yet his work as an adjutant and squadron commander, as a Staff College student, as a staff officer and unit commander in the Sudan and South Africa meant that he acquired an intimate and exact knowledge of how troops live, are fed, what are their needs and how they should be controlled and led.[17] His studies of the wars of the past century were thorough and gave him a theoretical foundation for his incessant and energetic teaching. He had no experience of commanding one of the new (1907) 'big' divisions, but he learned at Aldershot (as GOC-in-C, 1912–14) about the command and deployment of a corps. By 1914 he was regarded as destined for the highest posts in any war. To pre-eminence in the professional Army he added another advantage. His work for Haldane on the General Staff, on the Army's first *Field Service Regulations* (1909), and on the establishment of the Territorial Force ensured that he had not only vast experience of the administration of an army but also understanding of the peculiar problems of a *citizen* army.[18]

If some of his ideas on future war proved wrong (as did those of many others, whether trained at Balliol, the *École Polytechnique*, Camberley or the *Kriegsakademie*) yet his grasp of how an army works was strong and possibly unsurpassed in the British Army, and this is of vital importance, since, as Wavell has said, it is 'the matter of administration' that is the crux of generalship.[19]

'THE MATTER OF ADMINISTRATION'

No British officer then under sixty years of age had commanded in war a force much in excess of 20,000 men. The prewar concept of the Expeditionary Force was for a 120,000-man six-division army to fight a six-month Continental campaign, backed by stocks on a scale fixed by the Mowatt committee in the light of the South African War. By December, 1915 this tiny force had risen to 986,000 men, to 1.5 million by July 1916 and stood above 1.8 million throughout 1918, with new functions demanding budgets, staff, space, materials and co-ordination while the demands of war continually altered the nature of work currently being done.[20] Such demands went far beyond the usual 'A and Q' functions, though the administration of discipline, promotion, leave, movements of units, bath-houses, mail, supplies of boots, whale-oil, plum and apple jam, barbed wire, planks for roads and trenches, forage and fodder, placed an administrative burden on the staff beyond anything imagined before 1914.[21] The extraordinarily good health and sanitary standards of the BEF in the difficult living conditions imposed by static trench warfare were due to constant medical and administrative effort. The C-in-C was thus principal director of Britain's newest and greatest corporate enterprise, comparable in size to the administration of the largest city in the Kingdom (with the sole exception of London), the governance of which was the more delicate since it was based within a jealous and suspicious foreign state. To make the BEF run as smoothly as it did is an achievement as remarkable as it is under-praised.[22] Much of the daily administration inevitably went on at low levels of command, but Haig's knowledge and constant stimulus, his tireless visits and the awe in which he was held by his departmental heads ensured that standards were maintained or improved. For this reason, *and alone among the armies which entered the war in 1914,* the BEF never mutinied.

I spoke of 'tireless visits': it is often complained that Haig was a 'château' general stuck permanently behind his desk, invisible to the troops, not giving his full attention to planning and operations, and letting his subordinates behave likewise. Such a complaint ignores the vast amount of business that could not be dealt with except inside an office. But is the complaint true? That excellent infantryman-historian Cyril Falls insisted that Haig spent a great deal of time on field visits: 'Grumblers have said that Haig should have spent more time minding his business in his office and less on visits . . . I think it likely that Foch was even more open to that reproach, if such it is'.[23].

'If such it is'. For Haig was endeavouring personally to keep touch on the BEF's pulse and well-being, to understand its experience and thinking. A random sample for a quiet fortnight 17–30 April, 1916 shows that in addition to visiting battalions of the 6th Division, XIV Corps HQ, Canadian and South African units, an RFC unit, a sniping school, and also holding an Army Commanders' conference, he inspected base camps, hospital wards, recreation facilities, and a military prison. Fully aware that a modern army depends on the efficient back-up of the ancillary services he paid special attention to the morale and efficiency of the rear echelons: he insisted, for instance, that clerks he saw working at boring and mindless form filling should be got out and given more fresh air and exercise.

Another sample for the month of May 1917 is highly instructive. It was the month when Lloyd George came to Paris to insist on a continued effort by the French, when Pétain replaced Nivelle as French C-in-C, and the Arras-Aisne offensives came to an end. For much of the time Haig was at Advanced GHQ but even there was obliged to entertain visitors on six days; he had to join the Prime Minister for the Paris meetings; later in the month he went to Amiens to meet Pétain and learn of his plans (and would have gone to a third inter-Allied meeting had it not been cancelled at a few hours' notice, thus wasting the hours spent in preparation for it); he also had meetings with the King of the Belgians who was concerned about the role of his army and its relations with the Allies; and he was with Plumer at Cassel for five days. All that in itself demanded a considerable time in preparation and travel, but during the month Haig also visited eight Corps HQs and those of 23 Divisions, and he recorded the names of 68 British and Dominion officers whom he met, ranging from Lieutenant-General to Captain, often with brief comments on their abilities. He discussed plans with the operational commanders and he followed up these discussions with his Staff on returning to his office.

FEELING THE PULSE

Thus insofar as the head of a great enterprise ever can, Haig sought to find out and see for himself. But it went farther than this. Though it is an innovation usually claimed for Montgomery in the next war, Haig used a team of majors and lieutenant-colonels as his personal liaison officers, men whose war service had shown them as fine fighting men and also skilled at staff matters, Armitage, Lord Gort, 'Guffin' Heywood, Osborne, Bernard Paget and others. Armitage stated that on at least one occasion his verbal report on the problems of a planned Fifth Army operation led Haig to cancel it, and Osborne later testified that during Third Ypres his adverse report on ground conditions was carefully and courteously listened to by the C-in-C, who thanked him.[24] This daily information was backed up by Haig's more trusted field commanders (from divisional commanders upwards) who were invited to working lunches and given the opportunity to open up on their thoughts, ideas and problems.

So far as morale was concerned, the censorship of letters made it possible to gauge the feelings in the trenches with reasonable accuracy, and though too little is known about such exercises a very significant survey was undertaken in 1918: the high command was given very unvarnished summaries and quotations of what Tommy was thinking.[25] So despite the apparent quiet at Montreuil, I think it difficult to maintain that either GHQ or Advanced GHQ was an ivory tower. The reports came in and they were studied attentively. There was discussion of the conclusions and there were recommendations. The decisions were sometimes right and sometimes not, but they were based upon careful study and much thought.

THE OPERATIONAL CONTEXT

The task laid upon Sir Douglas Haig on 19 December, 1915 was to lead his citizen army to final victory in 1916 over the greatest military Power in the world – or if that proved impossible in 1916, then as early as possible thereafter – and in doing this he was to co-operate fully with his French allies, to recognize that his role was necessarily that of junior partner in France but to protect British interests from being subordinated to those of France. The growing size of his armies meant that he would inevitably take a greater share of the fighting and would have to find a solution to the problem of breaking through the deeply defended and flankless trench-lines behind which lay imprisoned large parts of France and Belgium. Had he advocated a strategy which was defensive, had he suggested that cautious 'nibbling' at the German defences might eventually bring the Allies to the Rhine in about 1925 or 1930, he would have deserved to be replaced at once. The essence of his Instructions from Kitchener was to carry the war to the enemy, to overthrow him, and to liberate occupied territory.[26] This Haig achieved in 1918.

The old 'drum and trumpet' school of military historians tended to write of 'Great Captains', their insights and their inspirational switches of attack. Such an approach to the great industrial conflicts – where railways, coal, steel output and chemical production were the material foundations – is not only inappropriate but actually misleading. The dominance of these industrial factors in 1914–18 ensured that armies could be assembled, fed, equipped and munitioned as never before (on both sides of the wire), but thereafter operational mobility was limited to the speeds of man or horse or the one-mile-per-hour infantry tank. Until the fledgling internal combustion engine enabled motor- and air-transport to approach the carrying capacity and surpass the flexibility of trains and horses, and until the internal cohesion of the major armies on one or other side began to collapse, the possibility of strategic surprise and deception leading to decisive results was a matter of doubt and bloody experiment. When the German commanders in 1916–17 bemoaned the *'Materialschlacht'* as the way the war was going, they were in reality lamenting that their studies of Napoleon's and the elder Moltke's classic campaigns (the manna of generations of Great General Staff officers) could provide no operational answers to the dilemmas of the (industry-fed) Western Front, that the GS side was unable to match the Q side, and that Ludendorff and von Kuhl were less important to their armies than Wilhelm Gröner.[27] And this was true of both sides, for the more one considers the essential policy for the Entente Powers (the liberation of occupied territory), the technical state to which warfare had developed by winter 1914–15 when trench warfare set in, and the dreadfully inadequate base for war industries in France (after the loss of the Briey basin) and Britain, the more intractable become the *strategical* and *operational* problems which 'General Staffs' were expected to handle.

These problems were worsened, if anything, by the inability of commanders to communicate with their tactical units in battle in the way that Lee could at Gettysburg half a century earlier or the Second World War generals were able to through their walkie-talkies. A comparison of the gigantic strides in logistical art, of motor transport, armoured fighting vehicles, aircraft and air mobility – *as against the progress of communication* – in August 1914 and August 1918 would confirm this point.

In the space available I must limit discussion to a few comments on logistics, on the learning process that everyone without exception had to undergo, and on the tension between vision and pessimism, and I shall deliberately concentrate on the middle years before mobile warfare enabled Haig once more to practice 'classical generalship' with such success.

LOGISTICS

The BEF relied upon French-run ports and the French *Nord* Railway. Over-stretch, manning problems, wear, and exhaustion of facilities, resulted in congestion in the French Channel ports by mid–1916, with the average rate of discharge about half the 'normal minimum' and thus clogging railway turn-round. Moreover, artillery ammunition cargoes, often stowed in England with regard to ship stability rather than end use, had to be re-sorted after discharge, thus increasing the general port congestion. These problems had their effect on the BEF's planning and operations in 1916 and their solution went beyond the skills available in France: the dispatch of Eric Geddes to France as 'transport supremo' may have been Lloyd George's idea but it was one readily accepted by Haig, and the relationship between Haig and Geddes was harmonious and fruitful. It could not, however, prevent the *Nord* railway's exhaustion and near-collapse in the winter of 1916–17. That, and the shipping accident which blocked Boulogne harbour for *twenty-six days* in December and January, 1916–17, were disasters outside the BEF's control. Haig personally involved himself in the solutions to these problems – thus initiating the transport conference which resulted in the infamous Calais meeting of February 1917. Geddes' reforms lasted until the interference in BEF transport matters in mid–1918 by Milner and Henry Wilson, by then War Minister and CIGS respectively[28], undermined a good system at a time when mobile warfare was to make extra demands upon this service: Haig's views were largely ignored, and the result was a self-inflicted deterioration in efficiency just as victory came in sight.[29]

How this railway factor dominated the war may be seen from a curiosity in Liddell Hart's *History of the First World War*, where he remarks that after the 1 July, 1916, setback on the Somme, Haig should immediately have switched his attack to Messines, sixty miles to the north, which was indeed one of the several alternatives approved by Haig in January 1916. We need not ask whether the crisis at Verdun had ruled out such possibilities by 30 June, 1916, or what Joffre and the French government would have said about breaking off a joint Anglo-French attack (in some places disastrous but in others highly successful) after one day – for the logistics tell it all. To mount the Somme the BEF had laid fifty-five miles of new railway track, leaving only ten miles of unused rail stock on 1 July. 'Messines, 1917' was eventually to require ninety miles of new railway. Moreover, of the twenty mines dug under Messines and essential to the plan, only six had been fully dug by 1 July, 1916, (though a further ten were completed by November) but the roadworks and transport links were not ready and could not be ready without a massive switch of non-available labour. Then compare the artillery and ammunition available at the Somme and Messines: only 808 18-pdrs at the start of the Somme against 1314 at Messines (double the number per yard), with other sizes in proportion; and the ammunition fired in one week: 1,733,000 of all natures and 3,258,000 respectively – *all of which was carried by rail*. That was the simple and unavoidable logistical reality.

Nothing that any general wished or ordered could have created an instantaneous Messines.[30]

THE LEARNING CURVE

The effect of this war of continuous innovation on thinking and doctrine can be seen most easily in artillery and air power. In 1898 British artillery considered direct fire at 1200 yards the correct doctrine, and direct fire was still advocated by several Gunner officers at Le Cateau in 1914; indirect fire, though in the manuals, was not adopted without some lingering reluctance. Equipments for British field artillery were among the best in the world by 1914 (the 4.5" howitzer and the 18-pdr), but their tactical employment in war was still a matter of theory and not direct experience.[31] The 18-pdr field gun (Mark I, with pole trail), carefully designed by specialist artillerymen, had a 6500-yard range and proved the workhorse of the war, first to last firing over 99 million rounds on the Western Front (or 58% of all ammunition expenditure by the BEF). It was fully adequate for the battles of 1914, but by 1916 its defect was becoming clear: lack of range sufficient to reach the great depths of the German trench defences – 9000 yards. The pole trail limited breech depression (necessary for increased range). A box trail would overcome this, but the trials on a new carriage in 1916–17 failed, and it was 1918 before a satisfactory carriage and 9000-yards range was given to the BEF. It was a hard-learned discovery to which the solution was not tactical or in the hands of a general, but depended entirely on engineering and design managers.[32]

The combined-arms learning process was not easy in a 'cap badge' Army within which the Royal Artillery cherished its independence. In 1915 Colonel Trenchard, ex-Royal Scots Fusiliers and now RFC, was told by the Gunner generals that they were too busy fighting a war to bother with the reports from 'your toys in the air'. They mistook their man. He went to First Army Commander (Haig) who told them that he would not tolerate 'early Victorian methods. He was going to use the air in this war, and they had to use it'. The cavalryman thus backed the airman's vision and continued to back it throughout the war to the great benefit of the artillery. Incidentally, these two men created a doctrine for the future RAF: that in air-fighting the work should be over enemy lines, whether in good times or bad, leaving the air above the British trenches comparatively untroubled, and establishing 'dominance'.[33]

To complaints that artillery doctrine in 1916 was one of 'destruction' and not 'neutralization' the answer is that until air-ground and ground-ground referencing and communication was better, until sound-ranging and flash-spotting enabled gunners to develop 'predicted' shooting (in late 1917) there was no other way perceived by the Royal Artillery – or its opponents. The artillery generals could not provide Haig with an ideal instrument until Cambrai (November, 1917) and the campaign of 1918. If the Gunner Birch warned in 1916 that the Somme plan stretched artillery resources too thinly for the length of front, he and his staff offered no solution but left the dilemma for Haig to solve:[34] for the alternative, a dense destructive bombardment of a narrower front left the attack vulnerable to counter-attack from the flanks – which is what befell Falkenhayn at Verdun. It may be that in the circumstances of 1916 – inadequate factory production, a high proportion of dud ammunition, a semi-trained British citizen army – there was no solution to this artillery-density versus width-of-front dilemma, yet the Somme campaign could not therefore be abandoned: agreement among all the Allies, pressure on Verdun, ending the war as quickly as possible, precluded that. The learning curve of the Somme was costly to Haig, to the Gunners, above all to the men; yet they ended the year worn and experienced but still victors by a small margin.[35]

THE SLIDE RULE AND THE LONG VIEW

In 1916 and 1917, as we have seen, the BEF required constant supervision in all aspects of its work, and in static warfare with endless experiment in new techniques and weaponry this led to over-management, a concentration on detail, on the next hundred feet of trench – in staff terms the 'slide rule' factor. Yet a Commander-in-Chief's job is also to push his Army Commanders,[36] to see beyond the next trench, and watch for the signs of enemy collapse. How far 'adrift' the reports of Haig's Intelligence chief were is still open to question, but Haig was in any case an optimist and his search for the 'break', for the 'unlimited' opportunity seems to me right and necessary at his level . That by constant study and calculation he and his staff came to optimistic conclusions as to the forthcoming great offensive may be regrettable,[37] but his confidence in those plans and in his *sure knowledge* that Falkenhayn had thrown away decisive victory at First Ypres through a failure of will, are factors that are a part of the man, and to remove them from the assessment of Haig's generalship is to remove Haig himself. He believed in the 'wearing out' fight leading to the eventual disintegration of the German Army – and his vision went beyond.

General Sir David Fraser, in his fine study of the British Army in the Second World War noted a most significant instance of this vision in Montgomery. The occasion was the unsuccessful 'Goodwood' operation in July, 1944, designed as a limited battle, but with surprisingly distant final objectives. In a letter to the CIGS before 'Goodwood' began Monty wrote: 'The possibilities are immense: with 700 tanks loosed to the south-east of Caen and armoured cars operating far ahead anything may happen'. Sir David comments:

> If language means anything, those words far transcend the concept of a strictly limited attack, a gesture to attract the German armour. Monty, *quite rightly*, was ready for anything.[38]

That could also stand for Haig.

HAIG AND HIS MEN

Because it is so 'undemonstrative' and its language so cool, Haig's diary almost conceals his depth of feeling towards his men; and in addition he was by nature and training a man averse to expressing strong emotion. That feeling for the men can be heard in his reply to his chaplain's congratulations after Messines, 'its you: its you *all*', and in his dedication of his *Collected Despatches* to 'the valour of the British soldier and the character of the British nation' .[39] Above all, it is pencilled privately with no thought of publication, at the back of Haig's 1921 pocket diary:

> If one considers how small an amount of success is due to one's individual self, and thro' what weak instruments God manifests his greatness, it is a simple matter to be modest. The Chief credit is due to the gallant troops who know how to win victory wherever one sends them.[40]

'Wherever one sends them' recalls to me Charteris's judgement of the supremacy of 'the cause' – that Haig possessed 'a very real generosity in mind and in dealing with others, a generosity that was limitless until it impinged on the "cause" as he saw it. Then it was cut off as by a guillotine'. It was his ability to shoulder responsibility for savage operations, heavy casualty lists, disappointments – and to go on believing in and working for 'the cause' that marks Douglas Haig out as a man of quite exceptional strength. He never gave up. On the terrible sixth morning of the Ludendorff offensive, desperately short of reserves and with French assistance much slower than expected, before the statesmen and commanders had met at Doullens to seek a solution, and with his colleague Pétain openly saying that the British were beaten and that the French would likewise be within a fortnight, Haig wrote to his only confidant, 'we must go through with the business, and try and keep the war going . . .' – not the words of a cowed man.[41] It was recognised also by his men in their differing measure.

Here are some representative judgements from field officers, a sergeant and a private on Haig's strength, and the reliance they placed on it. As the German offensive continued to batter away in April 1918 and the bad news seemed endless, Lieutenant-Colonel William Fraser, DSO and two bars, MC, noted in his diary: 'I have arrived at the stage of a blind faith in the C-in-C because any other course would mean absolute dismay'. Lieutenant-Colonel E D Jackson, DSO and two bars, who commanded 7/Middlesex and 14/London (1/London Scottish) in the final two years of war in France, wrote in old age that 'we felt that as our Commander-in-Chief we had a rocklike personality on whom we could always rely'. Major-General Sir John Kennedy (Alan Brooke's DMO in 1941–44), a young Brigade Major by the end of the First World War, referring to the trust in a general that troops acquire through victories, remarked that 'it is much harder in stalemate conditions. Yet somehow Haig managed to convey to every man who served under him his own resolution and singleness of purpose'. Sergeant Wilfred Williams, MM, who enlisted in the Worcesters at 16½ in 1914 and went through to the end, wrote: 'At Ypres, Arras, the Somme, Cambrai, "the March retreat", and again in the great final advance Tommy invariably thought of "Douggie" – "Douggie" knows what he is doing. On two occasions I have been cheered up on seeing his quiet, resolute face as he watched us "coming out". He was not only our leader and commander-in-chief but our friend'. A Tommy commented 'when one thinks of the awful load of responsibility there is on his shoulders, I don't know how he can bear it. But it fills one with respect for him just to look at him'. [42]

'A HUNDRED PALESTINES'

Many of those comments refer to the period of the 'wearing out struggle' and not to the months of successive victories in 1918. We are sometimes told these days that though Haig was responsible for the bloody struggles of 1916 and 1917, he was not responsible for these victories – he was just there, an irrelevancy. That is to misunderstand the growth in maturity of the BEF and the development of a very modern all-arms integrated battle doctrine, the German Army's decline, the new techniques which restored a degree of mobility and strategic surprise to the war,[43] all of which meant that the former style of 'management' was less necessary and that Haig could return to the 'classical' tradition of generalship. He saw as clearly as anyone (and more clearly than most) that the conditions of 1918 enabled him to bypass a resolute German defence by thrusting at its weaker flanks in a way impossible against the still-flankless defences of 1917, thus sustaining mobility and accelerating German disintegration. The BEF took hitherto 'impregnable' positions and Haig's belief that war could be won in 1918 (a belief which Foch in July – and Lloyd George until much later – did not share [44]) was confirmed by his strategy and won by his men. Nineteen-eighteen was the pay-off for the years of slogging, partial success or drawn battles. He and his armies did what Kitchener had asked of them.[45]

On 7 October, 1918, Walter Braithwaite, a man who had seen at Gallipoli the reality of British military unpreparedness, whose only child had been killed on the Somme, who had trained and led the unshowy 62nd Division on the Western Front for two years and was now commanding IX Corps which had just carried the St Quentin canal, the main Hindenburg position and the Beaurevoir Line, wrote to a friend:

> Had a long visit from Lawrence [Haig's Chief of Staff] today who told me that when DH went to see Foch yesterday the latter had in his hand the Boche proposal for an armistice, and said to DH "This is the result of the splendid fighting of the British Army".

Did the Army consider that Haig was irrelevant to these great victories of 1918? Braithwaite – whose record and personal knowledge I think entitled him to speak on that matter – was in no doubt, and his verdict may conclude this chapter on Haig as Commander-in-Chief. For Braithwaite continued:

> Well Foch may say it. Why doesn't our own Damned Government say something to DH and the Army he commands? They thank Allenby and rightly [for his victory at Megiddo in September 1918]. *But why leave DH out who has done more in France since August 8 than a hundred Allenbys in a hundred Palestines.*[46]

Notes

1   R Cobb, *A Second Identity , Essays on France and French History* (Oxford, 1969), p.17.

2   From Walter Bloem's novel *Das Ganze Halt* (The Complete Halt), reviewed in *Army Quarterly*, vol 32, No 1, April 1936, pp. 96–103. Bloem's unit was the first battalion of the 12th Brandenburg Grenadiers, it was succeeded by the 52nd Regiment.

3   John Terraine once remarked that if the entire BEF and its commanders and staff had never joined the war in 1914, the *nature* of this war of railways, mass armies, vast industrial production and constant technological innovation, would have remained unaffected. See his outstanding one-volume survey *White Heat , the new warfare 1914–18* (Sidgwick and Jackson, 1982). In a brilliant short chapter elsewhere, he correctly notes that 'in much British writing about the war there are two conspicuous absentees: the enemy and the Allies' (in H Cecil and PH Liddle eds, *Facing Armageddon, the First World War Experienced*, Pen and Sword, 1996, p.13).

4   This is less true of Germany. From before the war and until late 1916 Germany's military leaders never paid much attention to the opinions of the Reichstag or Imperial Chancellors. Once Hindenburg and Ludendorff attained the supreme command they paid none – and later even reduced the Kaiser's power and influence to nothing. It was indeed a case of *hubris*.

5   Other contributors are providing detailed chapters on Haig and his Commanders, and his allies, and the Government; I have perforce left these topics alone, though they are not unimportant to the role of C-in-C. May I therefore record the opinion that he acted towards them with generally good sense, some charity, and with considerable restraint when provoked.

6   Haig passed his Army medicals and despite serving in total ten years in India (inevitably contracting enteric and malaria) his general health remained good. In the dry heat of the Sudan and South Africa it was excellent and the only years when his health deteriorated were 1906-09 when, cooped up in the War Office by day and spending evenings talking through matters with Haldane, he missed regular exercise. For asthma and exercise, diet and the reference to Adlerian theories see D J Lane and A Storr, *Asthma, the facts* (OUP, 1979), esp pp.3–17, 45–6, 67, 150–53.

7   Brigadier-General J Charteris to Liddell Hart, 11 Oct, 1935, LHCMA, LH 1/162/1, also quoted but with some slips in Major General E K G Sixsmith (*Douglas Haig*, Weidenfeld and Nicolson, 1976), p.183.

8   See Terraine's *White Heat, passim*, for the stream of innovations. An article of mine in the *British Army Review*, No 112, April 1996, pp.78–97, gives the full account of Shearer's bogus medical-cum-death-ray.

9   FM Lord Ironside's note in his copy of R Blake's *Private Papers of*

Douglas Haig 1914–1919 (Eyre and Spottiswood, 1952), NLS, Acc.3155/347/65 and General Sir C Armitage, memorandum, 19 March, 1969, Acc.3155/337G ; Major Sir Desmond Morton to Liddell Hart, 17 July, 1961, LHCMA Liddell Hart papers 1/531; W S Churchill, *The World Crisis, 1916–1918* (Thornton Butterworth, 1927), p.445 (29 April, 1918).

10 His Chief of Staff Kiggell said, 'He doesn't show it one bit, but by God doesn't he feel it', as reported by the Rev G S Duncan, diary 18 Sept, 1917, in *Military Miscellany 1* (Army Records Society, Sutton Publishing, 1997), p. 382 [all further references to Duncan's diary are to this edition]; Trenchard's autobiographical notes, quoted in M Occleshaw, *Armour against Fate* (Columbus, 1989), p.10; Haig to his wife, 15 Jan, 1918, NLS Acc.3155/149; Monash thought Haig 'looked grey and old' by the end of the Somme: F M Cutlack [ed], *The War Letters of General Monash* (Angus and Robertson, Melbourne, 1935), p. 151 (dated 21 Dec, 1916: it should be 22nd). Major N M McLeod, DSO, MC, RA (a Brigade-Major in 25th Division) noted in Feb, 1918 that the visiting C-in-C 'looked done up. I thought he looked dejected and old and no wonder. He is very nice of course' (letter to his wife, 6 Feb, 1918, McLeod papers 19/18, Liddle archive, Leeds).

11 Likewise, Labouchère once remarked of Gladstone that he did not object to him always having the ace of trumps up his sleeve, merely to Gladstone's belief that God Himself had put it there. We may share that opinion and yet, now that so many of the great 19th Century political debates seem as remote as the Norman conquest, recognise more truly what an outstanding man Gladstone was, for all his faults. In another fifty years I believe that will be true of Douglas Haig.

12 Of course he was not in *constant* contact with them. The ex-ranker and great CIGS, Wully Robertson, tended to grate upon him in their continual dealings as the months passed. Haig privately called him 'Iron Rations', and was quick to note any failings in that much-beset man as he struggled to defend the Western strategy from Lloyd George's schemes. This least pardonable of Haig's attitudes may possibly stem in part from Wully's Lincolnshire earthiness: so he remained always 'my dear Robertson' whereas the Irish gentleman, that lightweight CIGS, Wilson, was 'my dear Henry'. Nonetheless during a short visit to London to discuss armistice terms Haig made time to visit and talk with the displaced ex-CIGS Wully at his quarters (20 Oct, 1918).

13 Charteris to Liddell Hart, 11 Oct, 1935; Sixsmith, p.183.

14 On pre-breakfast exercise in 1916 or 1917 see Haig's long-time friend the old Indian commander Sir Pratap Singh's account in R B Van Wart, *The Life of Sir Pratap Singh* (Oxford, 1926), pp.209–10 and for July, 1918 Sir Sam Fay, *The War Office at War* (Hutchinson, 1937), pp.157 and 186.

15 See Haig to Gen Sir George Greaves (1831–1922; his old chief in 1891–92), 12 June, 1918: 'Y'day I was over 2 hours in the saddle, so I do pretty well. I hate the long motor drives which I have to take now and then. Last Friday I left early for a Conference in Paris at 3 p.m., and returned here early next morning. The roads are very rough now in most parts' (NLS Acc.3155/337L). Instances of walking home are in Haig's diary, e.g. January, 1917: 'five miles' (27th), 'the last few miles' (30th).

16 The foregoing derives from Haig's own diary, together with a valuable passage in Brigadier-General J Charteris, *Field Marshal Earl Haig* (Cassell, 1929), pp.204–7, part of which deals with Ryan telling off Haig '"If you don't sleep you won't last", Ryan would say sternly. "I told you to go to bed at eleven". And the Chief would reply mildly – though with the suspicion of a twinkle in his eye: "All right, I'll be good"'.

17 Haig's 1891 pamphlet on demolition duties for pioneers, his notes on canteen management, his Staff College notebooks and working papers on matters such as embarkation duties, and the recollections of contemporaries such as John Vaughan, *Cavalry and Sporting Memories* (Bala Press, 1954), (with its story of Major Haig dashing round Norwich to find enough fish and chips for the regimental canteen) all confirm that there was little of regimental soldiering that this outstanding staff officer did not know.

18 The recognition that his was a deeply civilian, 'duration only' force led to Haig's concentration on educational schemes for his men. He had instituted 'university extension lectures' for officers in 1916; on 8 March, 1918, he initiated a major education programme '(a) to give men a wider view of their duties as citizens of the British Empire, (b) to help men in their work *after the war*'. The vision, foresight and practicality of this – and we know how it fared post-war for too many of these men in that 'land fit for heroes' – was not that of a small or narrow military mind. See the Rev G S Duncan's diary for 8 July, 1917, p. 362; the 1918 scheme in Lord Gorell, *Education and the Army* (Oxford, 1921), pp. 24–6, 69–70; Haig's words (my italics) are given in Fourth Army note, 22 June, 1918, in PRO.WO.95/436.

19 Wavell's 1939 Lees-Knowles lectures set down three of the principal requirements of generalship as 'the matter of administration, which is the real crux of generalship' and 'practical sense' and 'energy'. However, he held that 'the first essential of a general [is] the quality of robustness, the ability to stand the shocks of war', the strength to endure, which he insisted was not the same as good health. The most important of mental qualities he termed 'common sense, knowledge of what is and is not possible . . . based on a really sound knowledge of the "mechanism of war", i.e. topography, movement and supply. These are the real foundations of military knowledge, not strategy and tactics'. Field-Marshal Earl

Wavell, *The Good Soldier* (Macmillan, 1948) p.6, where with all his Second War experience behind him he reconfirmed his 1939 opinions.

20 'Tim' Harington noted that at Camberley under Wilson in 1907 'we never, even in theory, dealt with or thought of a force exceeding our Expeditionary Force of six divisions. A corps of four divisions had seemed enormous [his Staff post in 1915]. But here was I [June 1916] confronted with the Staff work of [Plumer's Second] Army which, two or three times in my tenure, exceeded thirty divisions!' (*Tim Harington Looks Back* (Murray, 1940, p. 53). A 'Q' officer who served with 'citizen soldier' formations summed up their consequential staff needs thus: 'Nothing impressed me more at conferences or on occasional reliefs than the unconcern with which [the Guards Division] staff treated details. *Whereas every particular had to be most carefully considered by us, and every unit fed with a spoon*, my opposite number in the Guards passed on the barest orders, knowing they would be adequately dealt with by the many trained Regular officers and NCOs of all his units'. (Col W N Nicholson psc, *Behind the Lines*, (Cape, 1939, repr 1988) pp.183–84, italics mine).

21 Three instances of necessary, unspectacular development: a mapping service whereby the few and out-of-date 1/80,000-scale maps of France and Belgium were replaced by an entirely new survey employing aerial photography and resulting in a modern, gridded 1/10,000-scale coverage of the entire front, continually updated; the development of a first class meteorological service under a Cambridge future FRS; the production of a steady stream of Intelligence, tactical, training and instructional pamphlets from the printing section under General Staff auspices. For the mapping initiative see S Bidwell and D Graham, *Fire-Power* (Allen and Unwin, 1983), pp. 101–8; for meteorological developments my chapter 10 in P Liddle [ed], *Passchendaele in Perspective* (Leo Cooper, 1997); for the printing service, Paddy Griffith, *Battle Tactics on the Western Front* (Yale, 1994), chapter 10.

22 Apart from J H Boraston [ed], *Sir Douglas Haig's Despatches* (Dent, 1919), esp. pp. 335 onwards, the QMG to the Forces' [Sir John Cowans], note in *Statistics of the Military Effort of the British Empire, 1914–1920* (HMSO, 1922, and London Stamp Exchange, 1992), pp. 833–80, 'GSO' (the Australian, Major Sir F Fox), *GHQ* (P Allan, 1920), and Nicholson's *Behind the Lines* , the subject has been sadly neglected. For the many small but intractable problems that arose in France see RH Mottram's novel *The Crime at Vanderlynden's* (Chatto, 1926), the final part of the *Spanish Farm* trilogy.

23 C Falls, 'A Meditation on Two Wars', *The Illustrated London News*, 22 Nov, 1958, p.886.Falls wrote an underrated short biography of Foch (Blackie, 1939) which still repays study.

24 Lieutenant-General (in 1917 a Major and one of Haig's junior liaison officers) E A Osborne, *The Spectator*, 10 January, 1958, p. 47 on briefing Haig during Third Ypres, also given in Terraine, *The Road to Passchendaele* (Leo Cooper, 1977), p.339.

25 John Terraine examines this neglected subject in his *Impacts of War 1914 and 1918* (Hutchinson, 1970), chapter 12, pp. 170–76: he comments that the censorship staff did not 'paint rosy pictures or decorate with whitewash' the findings sent to GHQ.

26 'The special task laid upon you is to assist the French and Belgian governments in *driving the German Armies from French and Belgian territory . . . The defeat of the enemy* by the combined Allied Armies must always be regarded as the *primary object* . . . and to achieve that end the closest co-operation of French and British *as a united Army* must be the governing policy; but I wish you distinctly to understand that your command is an independent one, and that you will in no case come under the orders of any Allied General further than *the necessary co-operation with our Allies* already referred to'. *OH 1916*, vol. i (Macmillan, 1932), App. 5, paras 1 and 3, italics mine.

27 Gröner, born 1867 to a Württemberg military official, enlisted in the ranks for a commission, later passed the *Kriegsakademie* and served in the General Staff, becoming head of the Railway Section in 1912. He commanded the Field Railway Section 1914–16 and was then made head of the *Kriegsamt* and responsible for the economic programme. In 1918 he was made responsible for satisfying German food needs out of the conquered Russian territories. He succeeded his long-time rival Ludendorff as First QMG on 29 Oct, 1918, and had to advise the Kaiser to accept the Armistice. He was Minister of Communications in 1923 and *Reichswehr* Minister 1928–31; despite his outstanding record in maintaining Germany in the war the nationalists (and later the Nazis) accused him of 'stabbing the Army in the back' in 1918.

28 Milner's performance as War Secretary was below that of his predecessor Derby, partly because the Prime Minister had saddled him with an unsatisfactory new CIGS, partly because he was always being distracted from his duties by odd jobs the Premier wished on him, partly because he evinced little interest in or understanding of how an army works and would not attend to his Army Councillors' expert advice. He passed the entrance to Gough's HQ in Amiens on 26 March, 1918, but would not see him to learn first-hand of the battle and its problems, preferring the opinion of L S Amery in Versailles. Although Kitchener's instructions to Haig needed revision after Foch became Allied generalissimo in March 1918, no new instructions were issued: Haig had eventually to ask for them, and even then there followed a two week delay, to 21 June. It may be that Milner's greatest contributions to the war were his prescient 1915

reports on Britain's over-dependence on foreign foodstuffs and the urgent need for agricultural changes.

29 K Grieves, *Sir Eric Geddes* (Manchester U P 1988), pp.36–9. All biographies of Haig contain accounts of the logistical problems during winter 1916–17 and the Calais conference, though the reality and effect of the problems are still not always recognised (e.g. by J Turner in *Passchendaele in Perspective*, pp.17–8); for the 1918 re-structuring see the wartime Army Councillor and professional railwayman Sir Sam Fay's mordant chapter 21 ('Disintegration of Transport on the Western Front') in *The War Office at War* .

30 Liddell Hart, op cit (Faber, many editions since 1934), pp.318–9, drawing on an ill-judged comment in *OH 1916*, i, p.265. For railway details see Colonel A M Hennicker, *Transportation on the Western Front* (HMSO, 1937), pp.119, 125 (though *OH, 1917*, ii, 39, HMSO, 1948, speaks of 115 miles being laid for Messines), for mine construction *OH 1916*, i, p.32 and ii, p.545, and for artillery and ammunition *OH 1916*, i, pp.300–1. The old-fashioned 'Great Captains' approach is not the least of the weaknesses of Liddell Hart's book.

31 The revolution was not only in artillery pieces; the artillery manual of 1896 was rewritten in 1902 (twice), 1906, 1908, 1912 (provisional) and 1914, each time with new concepts and modifications: in 1908 the telephone featured, in 1914 so did aircraft. The Royal Artillery had traditionally been somewhat wary of sending officers to the Staff College, and this apartness, together with the rapidity of change 1902–14, meant that true inter-arm co-operation had painfully to be learnt – under fire.

32 Although Haig backed new inventions such as the tank he never thought that any particular invention by itself would be a 'war-winner'. His view was that *anything that could reduce the casualty bill, 'make a difference', get a decision and perhaps shorten the war* had to be used. The main arms had to fight in circumstances far from ideal or perfect and always changing, and they needed all possible assistance from inventions, whether or not conditions were 'ideal' for the invention in question, its operational specifications and techniques 'perfect' or the time precisely 'right'. J F C Fuller ceaselessly castigated Haig for this, but what would posterity have said if Haig had *not* used tanks to help the infantry because the design was faulty, factory production too meagre and training too imperfect (as they all were)? The head of the Tank Corps Hugh Elles commented more justly that Haig's view 'was always I think that he must use all his resources for what he considered decisive battles, whether those resources pulled their weight or did not pull their weight' so long as they added to 'the fighting capacity of the Army' (Elles to J E Edmonds, 4 Sept, 1934, PRO.CAB.45/200).

33 The account is from Trenchard's memoirs, quoted in M Occleshaw,

Armour Against Fate, p.55. Trenchard had made his name in the 1912 manoeuvres air-spotting for (a somewhat sceptical) Grierson's side against Haig. Haig and Trenchard struck up a friendship which lasted for the remainder of their lives and Haig's diary shows how greatly he believed in positive air power and relied upon Trenchard's views and opinions throughout the war. Sir Douglas gave Trenchard the rare accolade of 'magnificent' in the Final Despatch and it is my personal opinion that the latter was the second greatest British fighting commander in France, after Haig himself.

34 Rawlinson, commanding Fourth Army, was an infantryman – 'an expert in laying bets on and off any project for which he was responsible' (General Sir A Farrar-Hockley (*The Somme*, Pan, 1966, p.66), but his main advisers and his Chief of Staff – Birch, Budworth and Archie Montgomery were *all* artillerymen. If all these trained Gunners had perceived plans as seriously awry and open to correction by another course, surely a concerted stand should have been made. Cavan (XIV Corps) later showed he could stand up and speak out by himself, despite Fourth Army's grumbles about what 'the Chief' might say – and Haig agreed with Cavan.

35 Whatever it did not achieve, the Somme certainly took the pressure off Verdun, and it inflicted irreparable losses on the old professional German Army. As to the scale of that damage, on 18 November, 1916, Charteris had estimated German 'Somme' losses as 'at least 680,000' whereas on 5 December Haig put British casualties on the entire front for the five months at around 489,000 – post-war researches put them at 499,000 (Haig diary entries). Whether or not German postwar statements of losses are still open to doubt, Hindenburg's comment at Pless on 8 January, 1917, gave an expert German verdict on Verdun and the Somme: 'Things cannot be worse than they are now. The war must be brought to an end by the use of all means as soon as possible': *Official German Documents relating to the World War* (Carnegie Endowment, OUP, New York, 1923), vol. ii, p.1319.

36 It seems difficult to think that Haig should have set out some general objectives and then left it all to his subordinates – 'gone fishing', or stood as a benevolent but entirely passive onlooker at his subordinates' operations. That is what Buller notoriously did at Spion Kop – the classic example of what Monty called 'lack of grip'.

37 Professor Travers in *The Killing Ground* (Allen and Unwin, 1987), advanced the thesis that Haig was prisoner to the idea of a 'structured battle', to which Terraine commented in his review of the book: '"Structure", one gathers, is a Very Bad Thing. What Travers never explains is what an "unstructured" battle might be like, and in what important respects it would differ from a catastrophe.Neither does he

explain what else generals and staffs are for, if it is not to try to bring some degree of order out of chaos' (*British Army Review*, No 96, Dec 1990, pp.65–7).

38 Sir D Fraser, *And We Shall Shock Them* (Hodder and Stoughton, 1983), pp. 332–7 covers the story: his words here are from a shorter but nearly identical comment on 'Goodwood' in his review of Hamilton's biography of Monty, *The London Review of Books*, 22 Dec, 1983, italics in the original.

39 Duncan diary entry for June, 1917, p.362; *Collected Despatches*, Preface p.v.

40 Pocket diary NLS Acc.3155/2 O.

41 Haig to his wife, 'Tuesday morning, 26 Mar 18', NLS Acc.3155/150.

42 Sir David Fraser [ed], *In Good Company* (M Russell, 1990), p. 248, his father's diary, 17 April, 1918; E D Jackson and Sir John Kennedy in *The Scotsman*, 15 August, 1958, and 20 August, 1959, respectively; W C J Williams, *The Times*, 2 Feb, 1928; a Tommy's words to the Rev G S Duncan, diary 29 April, 1917, p. 350. Henry Williamson, taking issue with Leon Wolff's *In Flanders Fields*, commented '"Haig", said the common soldier, "was all right". How did Tommy Atkins know? What do most men respect? Cleverness? Sometimes. Character? Always'. *Time and Tide*, 21 March, 1959. See also C E Carrington: *Soldier from the Wars Returning* (Hutchinson, 1964), pp. 107–8.

43 Strategic surprise is difficult when the enemy overlooks your low-lying positions, as in 1916 and 1917. It is a mark of Haig's openness to new ideas that he gave long consideration in both years to getting behind the German defences by an amphibious operation using the new-born tanks on the Belgian coast.

44 Foch wrote to Clemenceau on 20 July, 1918: 'the year 1919 will be the decisive year of the war', *Les Armées françaises dans la Grande Guerre* (Impr Nat, Paris, 1923), tome vii, 1, Annexe No 178.

45 Haig feared *hubris* among the victors. Standing on the Hohenzollern Bridge in Cologne on 16 December, 1918, he warned journalists: 'For my part I sincerely hope that in our time of victory we may not lose our heads, as the Germans lost theirs after 1870, with the result that we are here'. (Quoted in C E Montague's diary in O Elton, *C E Montague, a Memoir* (Chatto, 1930, p.230); Montague later wrote: 'I think the speech was reported. But none of our foremen at home took any notice of it at all. They knew a trick worth two of Haig's. They were as moonstruck as any victorious Prussian'. (*Disenchantment* (Chatto, 1922), pp.181–82).

46 Lieutenant-General Braithwaite to Sir L E Kiggell in Guernsey, 7 Oct, 1918, letter in possession of the Kiggell family. Italics mine; some abbreviations have been extended for ease of reading.

Chapter 3

Ambition, Duty and Doctrine: Douglas Haig's Rise to High Command

Gerard J DeGroot

In 1905, Douglas Haig wrote to his sister about the difficulties of finding competent and trustworthy staff officers:

> The so called sharp people very often disappoint us or cheat or have some other drawback such as being disagreeable, bad-tempered, etc. All I require is people of average intelligence who are keen to do their work properly.[1]

In Haig's perfect Army, most officers were drones who could be trusted to perform their function adequately, but did not impose their egos, ambitions, intelligence or imagination on the conduct of operations. A select few, on the other hand, had peculiar gifts which singled them out for high command. There is no doubt that Haig always considered himself among the chosen. His rise was fuelled by a certainty that he possessed the ability and character to guide the Army. He once advised a nephew:

> Don't let the lives of mediocrities about you deflect you from your determination to belong to the few who can command or guide or benefit our great Empire. Believe me, the reservoir of such men is not boundless. As our Empire grows, so is there greater demand for them, and it behoves everyone to do his little and try and qualify for as high a position as possible. It is not ambition. This is *duty*.[2]

As a young boy Haig washed, put on his clothes and ate his porridge at strictly prescribed times. But though his upbringing was highly

37

ordered, it was not without love and warmth. Haig grew up doubly strengthened: motherly affection encouraged a formidable self-belief, while strict regimentation gave life a reassuring structure. By the time he entered Oxford in October 1880, he was a man with a mission who seemed considerably older and more serious than his peers. As he matured, fun and friendships became superfluous luxuries. A fellow cadet at Sandhurst remembered Haig as a taciturn young man fiercely determined to graduate at the top of his class.[3] He fulfilled this ambition and was rewarded with the praise of his instructors and the scorn of his peers. A similar approach was taken at the Staff College during the years 1896–97, but the results were less impressive, largely because the College rewarded independent minds more than pedants. At Camberley, his fellow students found him so humourless that, according to Sir George Barrow, 'no one would sit next to him at mess if there was a place vacant elsewhere.'[4] His only friend (the term hardly seems appropriate) was Arthur Blair, who by no coincidence was one of the least promising officers in the group. Throughout Haig's life, the only persons allowed to become remotely close to him were those who could not possibly pose a threat. He looked to them for validation, and they to him for the light which shone in their direction.

From the beginning, as a lieutenant in the 7th Hussars, Haig assumed a single-minded approach to his profession. He seldom attended concerts or plays and read neither novels nor newspapers, nor indeed any non-military literature.[5] The day to day routine of his life was only ever broken by the commencement of a new diet, based on the latest health fad. Something of a hypochondriac, Haig apparently worried that his health would not be the equal of his ambition. He regularly visited continental health spas, but unlike most of his contemporaries actually took the strict regimen of exercise and diet very seriously. While taking the waters, he partook in neither affairs nor aimless fraternizing, and relaxed only if the therapists so directed. Leaves were devoted not to enjoyment but to studying his profession. During long journeys by sea to various military posts, he would dutifully note in his diary the distances sailed, weather statistics and geographical points, but never the beauty of the scenery or observations on fellow passengers. He seems to have painstakingly ordered his life according to his own limited conception of what a commander was supposed to be like. Politics did not really interest him because he believed that soldiers were supposed to be the passive servants of the political authority and were not to question that authority. Besides, most politicians were fools.

If he ever possessed a creative or introspective side, it was effectively stifled by his approach to his profession. Haig's most striking feature was his boring ordinariness; one searches in vain for peculiarity or peccadillo. It is difficult to imagine him being anything other than a soldier, and at that a rather unexciting one. Unlike Kitchener, Wolseley, Roberts, Allenby and others, Haig never captured the imagination of his country. At a time when pictures of famous generals were passed among schoolboys like football cards are today, one suspects that Haig's was the least coveted and the most often traded away. His fame came not through the impression he made on his Army or his time, but rather via association – through his connection with the worst losses in British military history.

Perhaps Haig's personality should not be on trial. Norman Dixon's study of the psychological foundations of military incompetence reveals the danger of mixing history with psychoanalysis, especially when one's evidence is so scant and unreliable.[6] But personality factors are important and, if handled carefully, can provide illumination to Haig's command. An understanding of his character can go a long way toward revealing the nature of the British Army of his time, why he rose in it, and the way he eventually commanded.

The British Army of the late Victorian period mirrored the stratified society of which it was a product. It had for the previous half-century muddled through a succession of colonial wars – wars which, because they ended successfully, encouraged complacency and prescriptiveness. Perhaps the greatest fault of this Army was its recruitment patterns. Almost invariably only a certain type ever joined the officer corps and only an even more select type was promoted to high command. There was little possibility for variation on the Haig theme, as Lloyd George found when, in late 1917, he searched in vain for a replacement as Commander in Chief. Technically-minded middle class individuals who might have aided the Army's modernization either did not join or were not given much encouragement when they did. With individuality and imagination suppressed and cleverness deemed suspect, the institution remained safe and supreme. As Haig understood, the way to succeed was to conform to the institutional type.

Haig rose in the Army because he was able to project himself as a quintessential commander. His attainment of high command was a testimony to personal gifts and to an unquenchable and often hard-hearted ambition. His positive attributes were many. His mother provided the impressive pedigree which allowed entry into the cavalry, while his father's whisky fortune provided the money essential to keep him there. The regimentation and formality of his upbringing served him well – careful attention to dress and deportment meant that he learnt early how to look and act like a soldier. Physical attributes were an added bonus. A square jaw, piercing blue-grey eyes, strong neck and square shoulders suggested stability, honour and courage. Regular exercise and a careful diet kept him trim and healthy until late in life. His skill at polo was both a physical and a social asset. In a similar manner, racing and hunting interests kept him in the eyes of those who mattered. In a profession in which first impressions are enormously important, he looked a leader.

Haig was not perfect, but his faults were cunningly masked. Chief among the latter was his uncanny ability to tie his tongue into knots. He once congratulated the winners of an inter-regimental cross country race by remarking 'You have run well. I hope you will run as well in the presence of the enemy.'[7] His best speeches were short and faithful to his original script; when he extemporized disaster often resulted. Apparently aware of his limitations, Haig seems to have cultivated a quiet, soft-spoken image which suggested a man of few words but deep thoughts. Stolidity implied trust and dependability. Many felt that what he lacked in eloquence he made up in sincerity.

Upon arrival at a new post in India, Haig once wrote: 'You would be surprised at the amount of baggage I have to go about with – horses and clerks and office boxes and orderlies ... so l'arrivée is most impressive.' On another occasion, he commented that 'our staff is always considered well-dressed and clean. This has a good effect on all ranks.'[8] The careful cultivation of image reaped benefits. Charteris felt that his greatest asset was that 'nobody can conceive that any action of his is not prompted by the highest motive.'[9] Neville Lytton, a civilian who was otherwise disparaging of military types, wrote that he 'would never forget the impression that the Chief made' and that he 'would have been willing to die for him a hundred times over.' Adulation often spilled over into idolatry:

> His qualities were much more moral than intellectual; what intellectual qualities he has have been used almost entirely within his own profession, but he exhales such an atmosphere of honour, virtue, courage and sympathy that one feels uplifted like when one enters the Cathedral of Beauvais for the first time.[10]

Most people were quietly wooed in a manner similar to Lytton. By doing little, Haig made a massive impression.

Behind this screen of moral righteousness, Haig schemed and manoeuvred like almost any other ambitious soldier. In 1897, he used his sister's influence to secure a position on the Sudan expedition. The Adjutant-General, Sir Evelyn Woods needed someone to keep an eye on the expedition's commander, Herbert Kitchener, about whom

Wood had grave suspicions. Haig fitted the bill. Regular letters were sent to Wood detailing Kitchener's misdemeanours, however slight.

> You must not think I am finding points to criticise. (I'll tell you much more when I get back!) But as I owe my presence here to your kindness, it pleases me to write and tell you of any odd event which may not otherwise reach you ...'

In 1899, Haig landed a plum assignment in the cavalry force sent to South Africa after he lent its commander, Sir John French, £2500, a loan which allowed him to avoid the shame of bankruptcy.'² As long as a balance remained unpaid, and it took over ten years to be repaid, French continued to favour Haig with coveted appointments. When, in 1915, Haig decided that Sir John French was not fit for the role of Commander-in-Chief of the British Expeditionary Force, he did not hesitate to use his influence with George V to hasten French's removal, even though he was himself the logical successor. Haig was not the only senior commander to engage in scheming of this type. Intrigue had always been, and would remain, one of the main avenues to high command. But Haig's intrigue was effective because it was so well camouflaged.

Haig's ambition seems to have precluded romantic relations. Early in his career women seemed a danger, a distraction or a bore, therefore self-denial seemed appropriate. Wedded to his profession, he expected his men to be similarly attached. H. J. Harrison, a trooper and junior N.C.O. in the 7th Hussars, recalled how Haig wanted soldiers to be 'blindly devoted to their duties, with human sentiments totally eradicated'. The good soldier learned to 'ostracise from the mind everything soft or sentimental. He was solidly against a soldier being married and a man who approached him with an application to take unto himself a wife did so with fear and loathing.'¹³ In Haig's view, women were the source and inspiration for male weaknesses. It is impossible to find even the slightest hint of sexual scandal in his life. When, early in the Great War, he mistakenly found himself in a brothel, he reacted in a way which suggested that he hardly realized that such establishments existed.

In 1905, when Haig was 44, he found himself at a position in the Army where the right wife could be advantageous and where an unmarried man seemed slightly suspicious. True to form, he did not delay in correcting this deficiency. He met, became engaged to, and married the Honourable Dorothy Maud Vivian within the space of three weeks. Though the decision to marry was made quickly, the choice was a wise one. Formerly the lady-in-waiting to Queen Alexandra, Dorothy (or

'Doris') brought valuable social connections which Haig used to his advantage. She fitted the pattern of his other 'intimates': she was blindly devoted but, if her biography of him is any indication, did not really know him very well. When he was questioned about his whirlwind romance some years after his wedding, he characteristically replied that he had often spent less time deliberating much more important matters.

Haig's deepest devotion was to the cavalry, an attachment both pragmatic and sentimental. His social background and love of equine sports would, of course, have made him naturally suited to the arm. But he joined because it also offered the best chances for rapid professional advancement. The cavalry had always had a strange mix of personnel. Most officers fell into the category of fun-loving, slow-witted sons of country gentlemen who could satisfy the essential prerequisites of membership, chief among them a sizable income, a knowledge of wines and the ability to stay on a horse. For them, the arm offered maximum glamour in exchange for the bare minimum of personal sacrifice. But, for a small group of cavalry officers – Haig among them – the arm was a straight path to high command. Their chances for promotion were enhanced by the disproportionate prestige and power which the cavalry had always enjoyed within the Army. This was partly due to the élite, upper class status of cavalry officers in what was a status-conscious army, but also to the arm's heroic martial image. It had mystique – the famous cavalry spirit. Though by the time Haig joined the 7th Hussars this mystique bore little relation to the realities of modern warfare, it remained powerful, as the dominance of cavalrymen among the Army commanders in the Great War proves.[14]

But Haig did not simply ride his charger to the top of the Army. His determination to succeed was never fired solely by vain ambition. Driven though he undoubtedly was, his ambition was made even more formidable by sincere devotion to his profession. In other words, he was certain that he alone knew the right way forward for the Army. He did not hesitate to question openly the judgements of senior officers if he thought them faulty, a practice which would not always have helped his prospects for promotion. He was, as John Terraine argues, an educated soldier, though the scope of his education was limited.[15] While the content of his lessons was not always relevant to modern war, he did learn them well and with relish. The time which he gained from abstaining from an active social life was given over to the study of military topics. Between 1894 and 1896, for instance, while most wealthy officers spent leaves gambling at Monte Carlo or enjoying some mild hedonism in foreign cities, Haig spent his observing continental cavalry manoeuvres and translating foreign cavalry texts.

Frequent tours inspecting French or German cavalry units, and the reports which Haig submitted afterwards, were designed to improve the technique and thus the reputation of the British cavalry. Ever since the advent of accurate, long-range rifles, that reputation had suffered. Technology threatened the cavalry's very existence. The more progressive officers, like Lord Roberts, Ian Hamilton and Lord Kitchener recognized and accepted that the horseman was no match for modern weaponry and that 'knee to knee charges in future will be few and far between.'[16] These men sought to replace the traditional weapons of the cavalry, the lance and sword, with rifles. The horse, as a result of this change, would become simply a means of mobility rather than a tactical weapon in and of itself. They also promoted a second mounted force, the mounted infantry, which was designed to take advantage of the mobility of the horse but would do all of its fighting dismounted and if possible behind cover. To the traditional cavalryman, the very idea was blasphemous. Traditionalists correctly perceived the mounted infantry innovation as a threat to the cavalry's survival. Thus, Haig and the cavalry faithful fought a rearguard action aimed at saving the arm and its reputation.

This cavalry counter-reformation was successful in large part because of the prestige Haig gained through his success during active service. His first test came during the Sudan campaign of 1897–1898. Though he encountered no opportunity to demonstrate his talents as a leader of cavalry, he did show coolness under fire. He was not involved in the most momentous action involving cavalry, namely the disastrous charge by the 21st Lancers which resulted in the death of five officers, sixty-five men and 119 horses in less than two minutes. In a letter to Wood, Haig expressed regret at the effect the disaster might have:

> You will hear a lot of the charge made by the 21st Lancers ... The regiment ... was keen to do something and meant to charge something before the show was over. They got their charge, but at what cost? I trust for the sake of the British cavalry that more tactical knowledge exists in the ranks of the average regiment than we have seen displayed in this one.[17]

Haig felt that the disaster reflected not the decline of the arm, but the foolishness of a single commander. He was only partially right. A more open mind might have benefited from two very important lessons to arise from the incident. The first was the devastating effect which antiquated Dervish rifles had against the British charge. The way in which British cavalrymen were so easily shot from their saddles should have alerted Haig to the potential of modern firearms wielded by well-trained European infantry. The second, and equally important, lesson was that the 21st Lancers had extricated themselves from the predicament by dismounting and using their own rifles. Since accepting both of these lessons would have necessitated a complete reconsideration of his cavalry doctrine, Haig ignored them.

His only other experience of combat before 1914 came in the Boer War. Haig was in South Africa from the declaration of hostilities until some months after the treaty of Vereeniging. He began the war as a staff officer of a small cavalry force and ended it a Brigadier-General in command of a large area and a massive force of all arms. He served in every part of the country and was successful everywhere. While many careers were destroyed by the war, his stock soared.

The Boer War had three main effects upon Haig. The first was that it projected him into the front rank of Army officers, a man destined to make a mark on the new century. This was largely due to his success as a cavalry officer in what was a mobile war. The Boers were citizen-soldiers accustomed to living off the land. Their horsemanship and small, tough ponies were perfectly suited to the type of war they fought. They adapted classic guerrilla tactics to their environment and to the mobile nature of their force. A favourite tactic was to descend upon a British column from all directions, attack quickly and ruthlessly, and then retreat before the momentum shifted. These tactics demanded a mobile response from the British. For Haig, this meant traditional cavalry. In letters home, he called for massive reinforcements:

> The one thing required here is cavalry. I think the country ought to be alive now to the fact – which I have always pointed out – that we don't keep enough of the arm in peacetime. This mounted infantry craze is now I trust exploded. So far they have proved useless and are not likely to be of use until they learn to ride.[18]

Haig's prejudice against the mounted infantry was not entirely fair. They were not useless in this war. Theoretically, they should have been an effective response to Boer tactics, because in their ideal form they fought in a manner similar to the Boers. Mounted infantry were certainly more relevant to conditions in South Africa than traditional cavalry. But those units actually in South Africa did not conform to this ideal, in part because of the traditional cavalry's successful campaign to discredit it. Haig and his fellow traditionalists helped to ensure that the mounted infantry suffered from a lack of proper attention, funds and training. They were habitually given the poorest mounts. This meant that they could not possibly respond adequately to the challenges which faced them and that, consequently, the spoils of this mobile war were left for the conventional cavalry to harvest. Its occasional minor successes were blown out of proportion by a British press starved of good news. In truth, the cavalry did not perform well, as was demonstrated by the fact that Roberts had to dismiss twenty-one senior officers, including eleven of seventeen regimental commanders, during his year as a field commander in South Africa. Though Haig bitterly disagreed, critics of the cavalry blamed these failures on the 'reluctance to take a bold, logical grasp of the immense possibilities of the rifle.'[19]

The second effect that the Boer War had was that it confirmed Haig's traditional cavalry precepts. He did not seem bothered by the possibility that the lessons of a small war against a guerrilla force might not be wholly relevant to future campaigns in Europe. Instead, the actions in which he took part gave him the confidence to predict that cavalry had become a new element in tactics and that its role in warfare was secure. Haig was so eager to find validation for the continued relevance of cavalry doctrine that it is no surprise he found it in South Africa. The momentous event came on 15 February, 1900, on the veldt twenty miles from besieged Kimberley. The town had been surrounded for four months. One of the captives was Cecil Rhodes, who owned valuable diamond mines in the area. Rumours suggested that the garrison was ready to capitulate at any moment. The fate of the town was in the hands of the cavalry, or so it seemed to those in the saddle. The British arrived with a force of 8,000 cavalry, supported by 6,000 Mounted Infantry and fifty-six guns. Between them and the town were 800 Boers, fortified by two guns. The Boers were situated on two ridges through which the British had to drive. From the moment the British arrived, the battle was virtually decided. The Boers were good fighters, but not blind zealots; they recognized the hopelessness of their situation and saw no sense in fighting to the last man.

Haig, French and the rest of the British cavalry, on the other hand, were possessed by phantasmagoric notions of glorious combat. For a few minutes, life imitated myth. Captain C. Boyle, a galloper on French's staff, recounted the drama to *The Times*:

> The moment was one I can never forget. There was a pause during which we all looked at each other, I watched the General, wondering what he would do. It would have been simple enough to manoeuvre and fight, had we nothing to do but fight the enemy in front of us. But we had to get to Kimberley that night or fail. Suddenly the General decided to make a dash ... He sent for the Brigadiers, ordered three batteries up to play on the enemy, and the 16th and 19th Lancers to make a dash at once. ... a terrific fire opened up on them and as they disappeared into the dust one wondered how they could have fared. As the dust cleared the General decided to ride for it himself. ... We sat down and rode all we knew,

expecting the same fire on us. To our great surprise not a shot was fired. The moral effect of the cavalry charge across their front and the fear that we should work around their flank had been too much for the Boers and they had bolted. Still more remarkable was the little loss they had inflicted – a few dead horses and some wounded was all I saw on the plain. The whole thing was a marvellous example of what a cavalry dash can do.[20]

In truth, the charge of Kimberley was not a charge at all but rather the storming of a weakly defended position by an overwhelming force. Sabres and lances had not left their sheaths. It was not the charge, but the four day march which preceded it which saved Kimberley. Roberts had cleverly manoeuvred to the Boer weak spot. French then pierced it with an overwhelming force. The relief was a testimony to wise preparation rather than moral inspiration. But to the men involved, these technicalities did not matter. Kimberley was neatly converted into cavalry legend even before the dust settled. Every year on the anniversary of the event, until long after the Great War, heroes gathered in London to recall their moment of glory.

Haig drew inspiration from the glory, but was in truth more interested in what it would buy in practical terms. He did not waste the chance to use this dubious evidence of the cavalry's utility against those who had argued for reform of the arm. The day after the battle, he wrote to a fellow traditionalist:

> You will I think agree with me that the Cavalry – the despised Cavalry I should say – has saved the Empire. You must rub this fact into the wretched individuals who pretend to rule the Empire! And in any case, before they decide on reorganising the Army let them get the experience of those who have seen the effect of modern firearms and have learnt to realise that the old story is true, that moral[e] is everything.[21]

The combined result of the Boer War's first two effects upon Haig was that he used the reputation he had gained to put into practice what Kimberley had apparently proved. He became the foremost defender of traditional cavalry doctrine. Because he had always inspired respect, and because he now had the additional cachet of combat experience, he was successful in his quest, successful, in other words, at turning back the clock.

This annoyed progressives like Roberts, who once confessed: 'I consider it quite a misfortune that Haig should be of the old school in regard to the role of the Cavalry in the field. He is a clever, able fellow [but] he may do a great deal of mischief.'[22] The fact that the cavalry survived intact until the Great War and even experienced a revival early in the century was in large part due to the efforts of Haig and a few other doctrinaire officers. The Haldane Reforms of 1906-09, for which Haig was the government's principal military adviser, resulted in a slight shrinkage in the size of the Army, but the cavalry component was, significantly, unaffected. Haig and his allies designed exercises, organized training programs and studied techniques which sharpened the cavalry's performance in its traditional function, namely charging with lances and swords. They resisted attempts to replace the lance with the rifle because to use a rifle properly meant having to dismount, which in turn ruled out the charge. When Lord Roberts, in his role as Commander-in-Chief of the Army, successfully pushed through the abolition of the lance in 1905, Haig fought a determined campaign to have it reinstated. He succeeded in 1911, and also overturned many other reforms he perceived to be detrimental to the cavalry.

The third effect of the war was that it closed the book on Haig's development as a soldier. There were no subsequent actions to rival Kimberley's sublime drama. The twelve years between the Boer War and the Great War were spent consolidating his position within the Army. He moved up in rank, forged the necessary cliques, got married and strengthened his ties with politicians and royalty. But he did not fundamentally change. Aside from the difference in rank, the Haig who returned from war in 1902 was essentially the same Haig who went to war in 1914. While he and his co-religionists argued the merits of antique weapons and tactics, their minds were diverted from studying the implications of technological developments upon military science. This was unfortunate, for the Army, if not for Haig. He had many of the qualities of greatness. His unemotional, conservative nature was suited to crisis. His courage and devotion to his men and to his profession cannot be questioned. He was capable of clear thinking and decisive action. Nor was he unintelligent – as those who seek an easy explanation for the carnage of the Great War have often claimed. But a good commander was weakened by an irrational adherence to outdated doctrine.

In 1907, Haig predicted that the bullet of the small bore rifle would have 'little stopping power against the horse.'[23] The statement has been frequently misunderstood. It has often been used as evidence of Haig's stupidity and explanation for his costly tactics on the Somme. But he did not mean that bullets could not kill horses. What he meant was that the prospect of charging horsemen would inevitably cause infantrymen to lose their composure and fire erratically. Behind Haig's belief in the cavalry was a steadfast faith in the moral nature of war. His support for the arm was a desperate effort to defy war's depersonalization, to prove that moral factors outweighed weaponry, that man was more important than the machine. The cavalry *was* at one time an effective moral weapon. The famous cavalry spirit was not a chimera. But try as Haig might to deny the fact, war had become depersonalized and in the process moral factors had diminished in importance. The machine gun and barbed wire, two very impersonal developments, had rendered the charge suicidal and the cavalry spirit quaint nostalgia.

Perhaps even more important than Haig's continued belief in the moral nature of warfare was his faith in the type of battle for which the cavalry charge had been the inevitable denouement. Ironically, this type of combat had begun to disappear long before Haig entered the Army. He could describe in dramatic terms a battlefield scene which he himself had never actually experienced because it was part of cavalry scripture. Constant repetition had worn a groove in his mind, so much so that he was able to argue in 1907 that 'the role of the cavalry on the battlefield will always go on increasing.'[24] In his dream battles, two forces met on a battlefield and, after an initial clash of infantry and artillery, the strongest side would effect a breach in the other's line or turn the flank. The cavalry, armed with lance and sword, would then be released upon the disordered ranks, causing physical and moral annihilation. Mobile war of this type had not become obsolete, but had been placed temporarily on hold, due to the dominance of firepower over mobility in the early part of the century. This Haig failed to understand. As a result, in the Great War, while he did not send thousands of cavalrymen to their death in futile charges against German machine gunners, thousands of infantrymen did perish attempting to pave the way for the cavalry.

Another aspect of Haig's personality which deserves illumination in the light of the war is his administrative ability. This had been an asset throughout his career. The army of Haig's early career had hardly recovered from the embarrassment of the Crimea when it suffered the humiliation of South Africa. There was a slow realization that Britain could not remain aloof from continental affairs forever, and that an army which barely fulfilled its imperial function could not possibly be equal to the challenge of France or Germany. A group of officers recognized late in the Victorian period that the Army had to modernize in order to meet this challenge. Perhaps ironically, Haig was in the forefront of these officers who saw an urgent need for professionalization. He realized that the Army's administrative and educational organs were dilapidated and inefficient. His progressive attitude, when combined with his administrative skills and his ability to command respect, enabled him to carry out significant changes in Army administration at all levels. His efforts to modernize the Army reached fruition during his period as an adviser to the War Minister Richard Burdon Haldane from 1906 to 1909. The British Expeditionary Force, the Territorial Army and the mobilization plans which worked without a hitch in 1914 were the result of his effort, if not his inspiration.

This progressive attitude toward the reform of the Army may at first seem contradictory in relation to his more traditional tactical precepts. But for him there was no contradiction. For Haig, traditional tactical and strategic doctrines, and especially the spirit they implied, were the essence of the Army, based as they were on truths handed down from Wellington, Napoleon and Frederick the Great. These could not be questioned or changed. The administrative structure of the Army was simply the organ for the dissemination of these core beliefs. Haig polished the Army, but refused to remodel it. He developed modern techniques for the advancement of antiquated doctrine. His adminis-trative skills, like his rigidity and lack of imagination, probably stifled the possibility of serious reform of tactics and strategy. When a plan did not work well, his first reaction was to seek a logistical solution. Timetables were corrected, supply services improved, and the move-ment of men reorganized. But strategic aims remained the same.

By August 1914 Haig had risen to GOC-in-C Aldershot Command, the most prestigious command in the British Army short, perhaps, of Commander-in-Chief. The level of preparation within his division (and indeed within the British Expeditionary Force as a whole) was testi-mony to his considerable abilities as a commander and an administrator. That British mobilization went without hitch owes much to Haig's efforts during his tenure with Haldane and at Aldershot. But wars are not won through logistics alone. Ahead of Haig lay a war in which the factory and the machine would dominate, a war which would devour men in the way a blast furnace devours coal. The war would challenge and surprise everyone and test every individual's capacity for adaptation. It is unfortunate that, under these circum-stances, an otherwise promising commander should have his tactical perceptions clouded by a once glorious but now irrelevant cavalry myth.

Notes

1   Haig to Henrietta Jameson, 1 September, 1904, Haig MSS, Acc. 3155/6, National Library of Scotland.
2   Alfred Duff Cooper, *Haig*, (1936), pp. 91–2.
3   See unpublished autobiography of Sir James Edmonds, Edmonds MSS, III/2/10, Liddell Hart Centre for Military Archives, King's College, London (LCMH).
4   George Barrow to Lord Wavell, n.d., Allenby MSS, 6/III, LCMH.
5   See John Charteris, *Field Marshal Earl Haig*, (1929), pp. 68–9.
6   See Norman Dixon, *On the Psychology of Military Incompetence*, (1976).
7   Charteris, *Field Marshal Earl Haig*, p. 65.
8   Haig to Henrietta Jameson, 7 August, 1900; 26 November, 1903, Haig MSS, Acc. 3155/6.
9   John Charteris, *At GHQ*, (1931), p. 69.
10 Neville Lytton, *The Press and the General Staff*, (1920), p. 66.
11 Haig to Wood, 7 September, 1898, Haig MSS, Acc. 3155/6(g).
12 See Haig to Henrietta Jameson, 16 May, 1899, Haig MSS, Acc. 3155/6. Haig claimed the loan totalled £2500 while French apparently claimed it was for only £2000. See Richard Holmes, *The Little Field Marshal*, p. 51.
13 H. J. Harrison to Lady Haig, 17 April, 1937, Haig MSS, Acc. 3155/324(a).
14 During the Great War, both Commanders-in-Chief of the BEF, and five of ten Army commanders, were cavalrymen.
15 See John Terraine, *Douglas Haig: the Educated Soldier*, (1963).
16 Roberts to Kitchener, 24 September, 1903, Roberts MSS, 7101–23–122–6, National Army Museum.
17 Haig to Evelyn Wood, 7 September, 1898, Haig MSS, Acc. 3155/6(g).
18 Haig to Henrietta Jameson, 26 November, 1899, Haig MSS, Acc. 3155/6(c).
19 Erskine Childers to Roberts, 4 November, 1908, Roberts MSS, NAM 7101–23–222.
20 *The Times*, 6 April, 1900.
21 Haig to Lonsdale Hale, 2 March, 1900, Haig MSS, Acc. 3155/334(E). Throughout his career, Haig used the word 'moral' when, strictly speaking, he meant 'morale'.
22 Roberts to Kitchener, 28 January, 1904, Roberts MSS, NAM 7101–23–122–7.
23 Douglas Haig, *Cavalry Studies*, (1907), p. 9.
24 Ibid., p. 8.

Chapter 4

Haig and French

Ian F W Beckett

Watching a performance of the recent revival of the stage version of *Oh! What a Lovely War*, one is struck by the amount of background knowledge assumed of the audience. The intrigues culminating in the removal of Sir John French as commander-in-chief of the British Expeditionary Force (BEF), for example, are portrayed in a stylized ballroom scene, in which Sir Henry Rawlinson for one makes a brief appearance without explanation. It becomes fairly obvious, even to those with no prior knowledge, that Sir Douglas Haig must have presided over the debacles of the Somme and Passchendaele. The impression left by the appearance of French and Sir Henry Wilson in the opening scenes, however, is that they were some kind of comic duo, whose contribution to the war largely consisted of inflicting their lack of language skills on their allies.

It is probable that the audience of the original production by Joan Littlewood's Theatre Workshop in 1963 were far more familiar with the characters portrayed, given the flourishing popular interest in the Great War as the fiftieth anniversary approached. Leon Wolff's *In Flanders Fields* (1958) and Alan Clark's *The Donkeys* (1961) had made a considerable impact and John Terraine had also entered the lists with *Mons: The Retreat to Victory* (1960) and *Douglas Haig: The Educated Soldier*, which appeared in the same year as Littlewood's production. Within a year, of course, the BBC had launched *The Great War* series, attracting an audience averaging eight million for each of the twenty-six episodes.[1] It was clear at the revival, however, that there was little or no recognition of either particular events or personalities with the exception of Haig. By contrast, French has been all but eclipsed in popular memory.

In itself, this is an interesting reflection of the movement in the popular image of the war since French in the 1960s was still then a figure of controversy. Gerald French's several defences of his father's reputation had stretched from the 1930s to the publication of *The Kitchener-French Dispute: A Last Word* in 1960. Similarly, Sir Horace Smith-Dorrien's disputes with French, very much a sub-text in the 'battle of the memoirs' in the 1920s and 1930s, had not only been recalled by Terraine in his account of Mons, but Smith-Dorrien's own version of the 1914 campaign was to be aired in *The Man Who Disobeyed* by A. J. Smithers in 1970. Alan Clark's book, of course, had dealt with the campaigns of 1915 and it was French as much as Haig who stood condemned as a leading 'donkey'. Indeed, as Richard Holmes remarked in his biography of French, it was French whose very physical appearance suggested 'the archetypal First World War General, more familiar with the comfortable routine of a *château* than with the rigours of the trenches, cheerfully nailing British manhood to the cross of the Western Front'.[2] However, increasingly through the 1960s and 1970s, the Somme became the focus of popular attention, largely through the new emphasis on the 'Pals' battalions in the race to record the reminiscences of the dwindling band of veterans. Of course, the New Armies had first seen large scale offensive action under the overall direction of French at Loos in September 1915, the very battle which effectively sealed French's fate as commander-in-chief. It was on the Somme, however, under the direction of Haig, that the New Armies were truly blooded in popular memory although it can be noted that it was Passchendaele rather than the Somme that had more often summed up the apparent futility of the war to contemporaries prior to the 1960s. In the process of the creation of an obsession with the Somme, therefore, it was Haig rather than French who came to represent the 'donkeys'.

In the minds of earlier generations, however, Haig and French were closely linked and, understandably so, when their careers had been intertwined for a considerable period of time prior to the Great War. There is no comparison, of course, between the characters of the mercurial, womanizing French, who liked to think himself Anglo-Irish, and the dour, inarticulate and near misogynous Scot, Haig. Yet, there are certain similarities in their backgrounds. Both had little male influence in their upbringing, French being two when his father died and Haig being seventeen when his father, with whom he had had little contact, also died. French's mother went insane when he was ten and he was brought up by his elder sisters; Haig was heavily influenced by his mother and, after her death, when he was eighteen, by his elder sister, Henrietta. Both took slightly unusual routes into the army. French, whose father had been a naval officer, had begun as a naval cadet at Dartmouth at the age of fourteen but had then transferred from the navy to the militia and received his first commission in the 8th Hussars at the age of twenty-two. Haig progressed through Clifton and Brasenose College, Oxford – though not taking a degree through illness – and entered Sandhurst at the late age of twenty-three, being commissioned into the 7th Hussars at the age of twenty-four.

Not unexpectedly, French and Haig followed fairly conventional early career patterns once they were commissioned, although both made relatively rapid progress by the standards of the time. Quickly transferring to the 19th Hussars, French was a captain at the age of twenty-eight and regimental adjutant. After a spell as a yeomanry adjutant and promotion to major at thirty-one, French then saw active service in the Sudan during the Gordon Relief Expedition in 1884–85. Haig was regimental adjutant at twenty-seven and captain at thirty, being seconded to the Egyptian Army in 1898 and serving through the campaign to re-conquer the Sudan. Both men saw service in India, French being there as commanding officer of the 19th Hussars between 1891 and 1893 and Haig with his regiment from 1886 to 1892: indeed, they first met in India at a cavalry camp during an exercise in November 1891. Both men also found the patrons necessary for career progression in the late Victorian army. French attracted the notice of Sir Redvers Buller and Sir Evelyn Wood but also benefited from his contacts with the Inspector-General of Cavalry in India, Sir George Luck. Haig likewise came to the attention of Wood but also to the Inspector-General of Cavalry at home, Sir James Keith-Fraser: both were enlisted by Haig's sister, Henrietta, to reverse Buller's refusal to nominate Haig for the Staff College in 1893 after he had failed the mathematics paper. Haig then became Keith-Fraser's ADC. Ironically, Luck was then brought home to replace Keith-Fraser in 1894, French being rescued by Luck from the half-pay, to which one of his frequent sexual indiscretions – this time with a senior officer's wife – had condemned him, to work on a new edition of the manual, *Cavalry Drill*.[3] It was then Wood who got Haig to the Sudan in 1898, after which Haig became French's brigade-major with the First Cavalry Brigade at Aldershot. Haig went with French to South Africa in 1899, French to command the cavalry division and Haig as his principal staff officer. Consequently, both witnessed the remarkable success of the British cavalry in the small scale action at Elandslaagte in October 1899, before escaping together in the last train from Ladysmith before the Boers cut the track.

While Haig's loan of £2,000 to French in 1899 was a transaction liable to misinterpretation, it was the future of the cavalry which was the strongest bond between Haig and French. Both were equally unusual in taking their profession seriously. The magnificently malicious official historian of the Great War, Sir James Edmonds, always claimed that French only ever borrowed one book from the War Office Library – a copy of Sir Edward Hamley's *Operations of War* (1866) – had failed to understand it, and had never borrowed another. In fact, French was noted for his wide reading of military texts as a subaltern and knew his Hamley well enough to recall Hamley's emphasis on the importance of not being trapped in a fortress when the possibility of retreating into Mauberge presented itself in August 1914.[4] Having worked on *Cavalry Drill* and then made his reputation with the cavalry in South Africa, not only directing the action at Elandslaagte but also the operations for the relief of Kimberley in February 1900, French was considered to be a cavalry theorist of some prominence after the South African War.[5] In part, this was largely based upon relatively limited published pronouncements such as the preface.French wrote for the English translation of Friedrich von Bernhardi's *Cavalry in Future Wars* in 1906. At the same time, however, French's work as both GOC at Aldershot from 1902 to 1907 and Inspector-General of the Forces from 1907 to 1912 consolidated the reputation he had won in South Africa as a dynamic modernist. On the other hand, despite being considered as a possible Chief of the General Staff in 1903–1904 and then holding the post between 1912 and 1914, French did not attend the Staff College and his attitude towards staff training was at best ambivalent.

While there were only nine years in age between French and Haig, the significance of the Staff College for a soldier's career had grown immeasurably by the time Haig attempted the examination in 1893. Having failed to get to Camberley at that time, Haig was able to secure entry three years later. He had already made a mark with reports on cavalry training in India and had contributed directly to a new edition of the manual, *Cavalry Drill Book*, while with Keith-Fraser in 1896. Subsequently, Haig also contributed to *Cavalry Training* (1904) and, as Inspector-General of Cavalry in India between 1903 and 1906 and then successively Director of Military Training (DMT) and Director of Staff Duties (DSD) at the War Office between 1906 and 1909, he had a major influence on doctrinal matters. While working on what became *Field Service Regulations*, and with the assistance of Colonel Lonsdale Hale, Haig also wrote the book, *Cavalry Studies*, in 1907.[6] Subsequently, Haig was chief of staff in India from 1909 to 1912 before taking the Aldershot command. In 1914, therefore, French and Haig were two of only three serving soldiers to have held the army's only home corps command in peace-time: the other incumbent had been Smith-Dorrien between 1907 and 1912. Thus, Haig, too, acquired a reputation as a coming soldier. The irony was that both Haig and French were most progressive in terms of the most conservative and traditional arm of service.

The debate on the future of the *arme blanche* and the conflict between the advocates of a traditional cavalry role such as French and Haig on the one hand, and advocates of mounted infantry such as Lord Roberts and Erskine Childers on the other, is well known. Neither French nor Haig saw any reason to alter their views of the efficacy of sword and lance although, to be fair to them, the actual lessons of the South African War for cavalry were not as clear cut as sometimes supposed. Moreover, as Stephen Badsey has argued, the cavalry was trained adequately for both mounted and dismounted roles in 1914, even if the combination of tactical roles was overly ambitious and one that more traditionally minded cavalry officers such as Haig and French found difficult to grasp.[7] Certainly, their combined influence in the significant positions they held between 1902 and 1914 was of no little account in the general emphasis upon drawing moral rather than technical lessons from the experience of the South African and Russo-Japanese Wars and upon the value of the offensive over the defensive.[8]

The learning curve for both men in 1914 was a steep one. It is clear that French did grasp something of the nature of the tactical changes which occurred on the battlefields of France and Flanders. In his memoirs, *1914*, French wrote that, 'No previous experience, no conclusion I had been able to draw from campaigns in which I had taken part, or from a close study of the new conditions in which the war of today is waged had led me to anticipate a war of positions. All my thoughts, all my prospective plans, all my possible alternatives of action, were concentrated upon a war of movement and manpower.' Generally, French's memoirs are hardly reliable but, in this instance, he had written in very similar vein to Lieutenant-General Edward Hutton in December 1914 that 'modern weapons and conditions have completely revolutionized war. It is quite different from anything which you and I have known. A battle is a siege on one side and a fortress defence on the other, but on a gigantic scale.' French also quickly recognised the new importance of artillery as a result of his experience of the Aisne, reinforced by First Ypres.[9] This did not mean that French readily saw any solution to the deadlock evident by the end of 1914 but, to some extent, it is arguable that his approach was marginally more flexible than that of Haig.

Haig's views on the immutability of the battlefield – Tim Travers calls it a 'paradigm of normal war' – which he had formulated or, rather, absorbed, while at Staff College were unhelpful. Haig remained wedded to a highly deterministic concept of a battle unfolding in a structured sequence of events. Whatever the post-facto justification of the Somme or Passchendaele as necessary attrition, Haig's vision continued to embrace the ideal of a decisive breakthrough that was not actually technically obtainable before late 1917. Haig did recognize the significance of some technical changes such as the introduction of the tank, but others such as the importance of artillery he only dimly perceived. The pressures for tactical changes by late 1917 came from below rather than above while the more realistic limited operations of 1918 were largely forced upon him.[10]

Given not only their shared cavalry background but also the prevailing assumptions throughout the army in 1914, it is not surprising that French and Haig were more at ease with the relatively mobile warfare encountered prior to October 1914 and after August 1918. In strategic terms, both men also shared similar preferences although, again, French was arguably more imaginative than Haig. It has been suggested by Richard Holmes that French's candidature for the new post of Chief of the General Staff was pushed in 1903–1904 by Lord Esher and Sir John Fisher. French was then brought on to the Committee of Imperial Defence by Esher in 1905. Primarily, it is argued that this was because of French's relative willingness to consider the option of amphibious operations. Holmes considers, however, that French showed little consistency in his strategic ideas. Thus, while prepared to consider, at various times, operations in the Baltic as readily as in Belgium, French never fully made up his mind and, at the celebrated War Council on 5 August, 1914, happily proposed ignoring the mobilization plans and sending the BEF to Antwerp rather than Mauberge.[11]

Of course, the security of Belgium and the denial of its ports to the Germans had been the *casus belli* for British entry to the war. French's support for the transfer of the BEF from the Aisne to Flanders indicated the continuing importance of the coast and, though Antwerp, Zeebrugge and Ostend all fell to the Germans, the British salient secured around Ypres at great cost continued to hold its strategic significance. Subsequently, in December 1914 and January 1915, while fully committed to waging the main war on the Western Front, French wanted Territorial and New Army divisions unleashed on the Belgian coast in an attempt to seize Zeebrugge. In this French's strategic views were rather more consistent than Holmes allows, William Philpott arguing more recently that French was a significant influence on pre-war strategic planning with a broader outlook than many on the General Staff, which postulated a compromise between a 'maritime' and a 'continental' strategy. The Belgian option thus offered Britain a more independent role in keeping with Britain's national interest in safeguarding the Channel ports.[12]

An argument that French had more strategic imagination than Haig must be weighed against the actual practicality of French's ideas. Clearly, amphibious operations in the Baltic or against the German North Sea coast were not feasible in the face of an undefeated German fleet and coast defences. Moreover, it was not until after the Gallipoli experience and in preparation for the abortive landing on the Belgian coast in 1917 that techniques were sufficiently honed and specialist landing craft available to suggest a degree of success. At least it may be said that Haig, too, remained interested in the Belgian option. Interest in Zeebrugge was revived in the autumn of 1915 and early 1916. It resurfaced in the autumn of 1916, when the Admiralty grew increasingly concerned at the threat posed to Channel shipping by German surface vessels operating from Ostend and Zeebrugge. Indeed, cross-Channel troop transporting was temporarily suspended and this surface threat was far more potent than that posed underwater after the Germans launched unrestricted submarine warfare in February 1917.[13]

The attraction of Flanders and the launching of an independent British offensive towards the Belgian coast was considerable once Haig became Commander-in-Chief of the BEF, the Somme campaign having been dictated by the requirement to co-operate with the French when Britain was still the junior military partner. Nevertheless, Haig's own strategic vision was entirely limited to the Western Front in his commitment to the defeat of what he regarded as the main strength of the German army on the main front of the war. Consequently, like French, he resisted the diversion of forces elsewhere such as Italy or Palestine. On balance, the familiar defence of Haig's obsession with the Western Front is largely justified: in all probability, there was no real strategic alternative. Criticism, therefore, is far more justified when applied to Haig's conduct of operations, particularly his pursuit of the elusive breakthrough and the unnecessary prolongation of both the Somme and Passchendaele offensives when it was clear that no more could be achieved.

The question of the conduct of operations also raises the understanding of command on the part of both French and Haig. Both faced the new problems arising from the technical difficulties of overcoming deadlock and the managerial difficulties arising from the rapid expansion of the army. Both, too, were compelled to take account of troublesome allies since, as indicated above, Britain was initially the junior military partner of France and Russia. French's relations with Joffre and some individual French army commanders, such as

Lanrezac, mirrored Haig's problems with Nivelle and Pétain. As might be expected, French and Haig both clearly acted to maintain their operational independence within the alliance. After becoming an unofficial strategic adviser to Lloyd George, of course, French pushed for the establishment of an Allied Supreme War Council in the autumn of 1917, as well as favouring the 'Pétain option' of closing down large scale operations and awaiting the arrival of the Americans. Haig continued to resist the imposition of an Allied supreme commander until compelled, by the disintegration of his relationship with Pétain under the pressure of the German spring offensive, to accept Foch's appointment at Doullens on 26 March, 1918.

It is clear that there was a general understanding of the problem of command in the army as a whole, namely the need to find the correct balance between control and guidance, allowing subordinates sufficient initiative. Unfortunately, however, the rigidly hierarchical nature of the army and the intensely personalized relationships within the pre-war officer corps militated against finding such a balance. The problem was compounded by the absence, in terms of command as in most other military functions, of any agreed doctrine. Few officers had commanded higher formations other than during the annual autumn manoeuvres. By virtue of their tenure at Aldershot, French and Haig were more experienced than most. Yet, French had not commanded more than a division in the field previously nor Haig more than a column, equivalent to about half a division in size.[14] As indicated previously, French was ambivalent towards staff training: his choice of personal staff such as Algy Lawson inspired little confidence and did him more harm than good. By contrast, Haig was a trained staff officer but, ironically, equally surrounded himself largely with obsequious mediocrities, who would offer no challenge to his authority. Some of Haig's personal staff such as John Charteris also lacked staff training. General Headquarters (GHQ) was less isolated from the army when French was Commander-in-Chief than it became under Haig, but it was no more efficient.

French's command preferences were towards the traditional high visibility at the front and generally unsuited for the large scale of warfare encountered in France and Flanders. Haig certainly understood the delicate balance to be maintained by a commander-in-chief in establishing the strategic parameters and allowing subordinates to execute the operations. In practice, however, Haig was highly inconsistent. On some occasions, he could not stop interfering in operational matters as the planning processes for Neuve Chapelle, the Somme and Passchendaele demonstrated only too clearly. On others, Haig failed to assert his authority when he should have done, as in the considerable confusion concerning the planning for defence in the winter of 1917–1918.[15] In this, however, Haig was no more inconsistent than anyone else in the army and the pattern was repeated at army, corps, divisional and brigade level. In terms of personal leadership as opposed to command, French was superior to Haig in the response he could generate from ordinary soldiers. Yet, it can be argued that Haig's utter conviction in his fulfilling a divine mission and his ready acceptance of the necessity of casualties made him a far more robust commander than French, who was deeply affected by losses.[16]

Command involved dealing not only with allies but with politicians. French had come to the attention of Esher when testifying before the Elgin Commission on the South African War and, as already related, had then joined the Committee of Imperial Defence. French was a friend of Churchill but also Jack Seely, who became Secretary of State for War in 1912. The Liberal government as a whole was undoubtedly in French's debt after his willingness to stand by his duty during the Curragh incident in March 1914. Haig, too, was in credit with the Liberals, particularly Haldane, whose reforms he had greatly assisted while DMT and DSD, although Haig was careful to keep a foot in both camps at the time of the Curragh.[17] French, however, had never been on close terms with Lord Kitchener and Kitchener's appointment as Secretary of State for War in August 1914 brought about a marked deterioration in French's relationship with government. French later claimed a major part in the downfall of the Asquith coalition as a result of the publicity given his revelations of a shell shortage in France, but it was Kitchener who had been the real target.[18] Haig's relationship with politicians and his long struggle with Lloyd George is too well known to need repeating here, but it can be noted that, for all the weaknesses of his position by early 1918, Haig and his associates also came close to destroying the government during the Maurice affair in May 1918.[19] In the course of their commands, therefore, neither French nor Haig were unfamiliar with political intrigue involving politicians, press and the King. French had enjoyed a good relationship with Edward VII and Haig, whose wife had been lady-in-waiting to Queen Alexandra, subsequently also won the confidence of George V. Of course Haig also intrigued against French, notably over the issue of the placing of the reserves at the battle of Loos in September 1915[20] but, then, after his dismissal, French equally intrigued against Haig through his co-operation with Lloyd George.

The civil-military disputes of the Great War became the basic currency of much of the post-war 'battle of the memoirs'; episodes such as the Dardanelles expedition, the Somme, the Calais conference and the Nivelle offensive, Passchendaele, the creation of the Supreme War

Council and the Maurice affair becoming familiar signposts along the way. In this aspect of their careers – the presentation of their records for posterity – French and Haig were to take very different approaches, reflecting in many ways their divergent personalities. Unwisely, French sought to pursue his political vendetta with Kitchener and his military vendetta with Smith-Dorrien through the publication of the notoriously partial and inaccurate memoir, *1914*, prepared with the assistance of the journalist, Lovat Fraser.[21] Technically, French rendered himself open to prosecution as he was holding office as Lord Lieutenant of Ireland at the time of publication. By contrast, Haig worked more indirectly to establish his version of events and, with considerable disingenuousness, even declared himself 'very lazy on the question of the history of the war'.[22] In the event, while French played a significant part in destroying his own reputation, Haig's reputation was equally savaged by commentators like Basil Liddell Hart and J F C Fuller and, especially, by the publication of Lloyd George's six volumes of memoirs between 1933 and 1936.[23]

In many respects, the parameters of the debate surrounding the reputations of French and Haig have remained as they were established in the 1920s and 1930s. For reasons suggested earlier, French has had little attention devoted to him since the 1960s[24] but Haig remains just as capable of generating extraordinary passions in the 1990s as in the 1920s.[25] Indeed, popular contributions to the Haig 'industry' continue to plough the same furrows as previous authors, either oblivious to the advances of scholarship or consumed by bizarre conspiracy theories. Much more is now known about the British army during the Great War and it is likely that current work in operational history will continue to reveal important new aspects bearing upon the conduct of war on the Western Front.

The actual intention behind the original stage production and, particularly, the film version of *Oh! What a Lovely War* was apparently to focus not on French or Haig as characters, but on 'a personified attitude' which they represented. Consequently, the film was intended to be more anti-authority than anti-war.[26] Such a distinction may have been perceived more readily by audiences in the 1960s than the 1990s. The programme of the current production, however, has an all-too familiar emphasis upon 'irony' and futility. Whatever the original intent, therefore, the 'personified attitude' has become wholly indivisible from the perceived monolithic characters of French and Haig. Arguably, French and Haig bear rather more similarities than generally supposed, not least in being products of a particular military system that rendered both equally unsuited to meeting the new challenges of war after 1914. If there is an underlying truth in the 'irony' of *Oh! What a Lovely War* then it is that, while French and Haig were neither butchers nor bunglers, they were the best the system could produce at that time and place.

Notes

1 Alex Danchev, '"Bunking" and Debunking: The Controversies of the 1960s' in Brian Bond, ed., *The First World War and British Military History* (Oxford: Clarendon Press, 1991), p. 279.

2 Richard Holmes, *The Little Field-Marshal: Sir John French* (London: Cape, 1981), p. 1.

3 Ibid., pp. 44–9; Gerard De Groot, *Douglas Haig, 1861–1928* (London: Unwin Hyman, 1988), pp. 34–42.

4 Ian Beckett, 'The Pen and the Sword: Reflections on Military Thought in the British Army, 1854–1914', *Soldiers of the Queen* 68, 1992, pp. 3–7; Holmes, *Little Field-Marshal*, pp. 25–6, 219–20. On the matter of the loan, see ibid., pp. 51–2, and De Groot, *Haig*, p. 70.

5 Holmes, *Little Field-Marshal*, p. 164.

6 Gerard De Groot, 'Educated Soldier or Cavalry Officer?: Contradictions in the pre-1914 Career of Douglas Haig', *War and Society* 4, 1986, pp. 51–69. See also Holmes, *Little Field-Marshal*, pp. 151–65, and De Groot, *Haig*, pp. 94–112 for the respective contributions of French and Haig to the cavalry debate.

7 Stephen Badsey, 'Mounted Cavalry in the Second Boer War', *Sandhurst Journal of Military Studies* 2, 1991, pp. 11–28. For more critical views of the cavalry's performance in South Africa and its repercussions, see Brian Bond, 'Doctrine and Training in the British Cavalry, 1870–1914' in Michael Howard, ed., *The Theory and Practice of War* (London: Cassell, 1965), pp. 97–125; Edward Spiers, 'The British Cavalry, 1902–14', *Journal of the Society for Army Historical Research* 57, 1914, pp. 71–9. On cavalry in 1914, see Richard Holmes, 'The Last Hurrah: Cavalry on the Western Front, August to September 1914' in Hugh Cecil and Peter Liddle, eds., *Facing Armageddon: The First World War Experienced* (London: Leo Cooper, 1996), pp. 278–96.

8 Keith Neilson, '"That Dangerous and Difficult Enterprise": British Military Thinking and the Russo-Japanese War', *War and Society* 9, 1991, pp. 17–37.

9 Field-Marshal Viscount French, *1914* (London: 1919), p. 11; French to Hutton, quoted in Philip Towle, 'The Russo-Japanese War and British Military Thought', *Journal of the Royal United Services Institute for Defence Studies* 116, 1971, pp. 64–8; Holmes, *Little Field-Marshal*, p. 241, 217.

10 Tim Travers, *The Killing Ground: The British Army, the Western Front and the Emergence of Modern Warfare, 1900–18* (London: Allen &

Unwin, 1987), pp. 85–100; ibid., *How the War Was Won: Command and Technology in the Briish Army on the Western Front, 1917–18* (London: Routledge, 1992), pp. 32–49.

11   Holmes, *Little Field-Marshal*, pp. 126, 139–42, 196–8.

12   William Philpott, 'The Strategic Ideas of Sir John French', *Journal of Strategic Studies* 12, 1989, pp. 458–78; ibid., 'Kitchener and the 29th Division: A Study in Anglo-French Strategic Relations, 1914–15', *Journal of Strategic Studies* 16, 1993, pp. 375–407. On the evolution of the 'Belgian option', see Keith Wilson, 'The War Office, Churchill and the Belgian Option, August to December 1911' in Keith Wilson, ed., *Empire and Continent* London: Mansell, 1987), pp. 126–40.

13   For the continuing British interest in the Belgian coast, see William Philpott, *Anglo-French Relations and Strategy on the Western Front* (London: Macmillan, 1996); and, for the planned amphibious landings in 1917, see Andrew Wiest, *The Royal Navy and Passchendaele* (New York: Greenwood Press, 1995); ibid., 'The Planned Amphibious Assault' in Peter Liddle, ed., *Passchendaele in Perspective: the Third Battle of Ypres* (London: Leo Cooper, 1997), pp. 201–14; and Alf Peacock, 'The Proposed Landing on the Belgian Coast, 1917', *Gunfire* 11/12 (1988), pp. 2–50, 3–56.

14   On command generally, see John Bourne, 'British Generals in the First World War' in G. D. Sheffield, ed., *Leadership and Command: The Anglo-American Experience since 1861* (London: Brasseys, 1997), pp. 3–116; Robin Prior and Trevor Wilson, *Command on the Western Front* (Oxford: Blackwell, 1992), which concentrates on Rawlinson's experience; Tim Travers,'The Hidden Army: Structural Problems in the British Officer Corps, 1900–18', *Journal of Contemporary History* 17, 1982, pp. 523–44; and Ian Beckett, 'Hubert Gough, Neill Malcolm and Command on the Western Front' in Brian Bond, ed., *Look to Your Front* (Tunbridge Wells: Spellmount, 1999), pp. 1–12.

15   Travers, *Killing Ground*, pp. 85–126. See also ibid., 'A Particular Style of Command: Haig and GHQ, 1916–18', *Journal of Strategic Studies* 10, 1987, pp. 363–76.

16   Gerard De Groot, '"We Are Safe Whatever Happens": Douglas Haig, the Reverend George Duncan and the Conduct of the War, 1916–18' in N. Macdougall, ed., *Scotland and War, AD 79 to 1918* (Edinburgh: 1991), pp. 193–211; Holmes, *Little Field-Marshal*, pp. 276–8, 304–6, 314. See also Gerard De Groot, ed., 'The Reverend George S. Duncan at GHQ, 1916–18', *Military Miscellany I* (Stroud: Sutton Publishing for Army Records Society, 1996), pp. 266–436.

17   Holmes, *Little Field-Marshal*, pp. 193–4; Ian Beckett, ed., *The Army and the Curragh Incident, 1914* (London: Bodley Head for Army Records

Society, 1986), pp. 1–29; Ian Beckett, *Johnnie Gough, VC* (London: Tom Donovan, 1989), pp. 147–72.

18   Holmes, *Little Field-Marshal,* pp. 286–92; David French, 'The Military Background to the "Shell Crisis" of May 1915', *Journal of Strategic Studies* 2, 1979, pp. 195–205; Peter Fraser, 'British War Policy and the Crisis of Liberalism in May 1915', *Journal of Modern History* 54, 1982, pp. 1–26; John Turner, *British Politics and the Great War: Coalition and Conflict, 1915–18* (New Haven: Yale University Press, 1992), pp. 56–61.

19   The best guide to the civil-military disputes of Haig's command is David Woodward, *Lloyd George and the Generals* (Newark: University of Delaware Press, 1983). On the Maurice affair, see Nancy Maurice, ed., *The Maurice Case* London: Leo Cooper, 1972); David Woodward, 'Did Lloyd George Starve the British Army of Men Prior to the German Offensive of 21 March, 1918', *Historical Journal* 27, 1984, pp. 241–52; and John Gooch, *The Prospect of War: Studies in British Defence Policy, 1847–1942* (London: Frank Cass, 1981), pp. 146–63.

20   For an exhaustive investigation of the question of the reserves at Loos, see Peter Bryant, 'The Recall of Sir John French', *Stand To* 22/23/24, 1988, pp. 24–9, 32–8, 22–6.

21   Richard Holmes, 'Sir John French and Lord Kitchener' in Bond, *First World War and British Military History,* pp. 113–40.

22   Ian Beckett, *The Judgement of History: Sir Horace Smith-Dorrien, Lord French and 1914* (London: Tom Donovan, 1993), p. xvii. See also David French, 'Sir Douglas Haig's Reputation, 1918–28', *Historical Journal* 28, 1985, pp. 953–60.

23   Ian Beckett, 'Frocks and Brasshats' in Bond, *First World War and British Military History,* pp. 89–112.

24   The biography by Richard Holmes, already cited, is the most significant modern contribution to the understanding of French. George Cassar, *The Tragedy of Sir John French* (London: University of Delaware Press, 1985) draws remarkably similar conclusions to Holmes.

25   The best survey is Keith Simpson, 'The Reputation of Sir Douglas Haig' in Bond, *First World War and British Military History,* pp. 141–62.

26   Danchev, '"Bunking" and Debunking', pp. 284–5.

Chapter 5

Sir William Robertson and Sir Douglas Haig

David R Woodward

1915 ended on a grim note for Great Britain. The British attack at Loos had failed with heavy losses; the costly and mismanaged Dardanelles campaign was about to be liquidated; a new theatre had opened in Salonika with little thought to military ends and means; and the Turks rebuffed a British advance on Baghdad, with Major-General Sir Charles Townshend falling back to Kut. The depressing military situation led to a shake up of the British high command. Lord Kitchener, who acted as supreme war lord, was out of favour because of his secrecy, high-handedness and contradictory advice. The mercurial Sir John French, although a soldier of true grit, had not been up to the task of commanding the expanding British force in France and Flanders.

As French's replacement, the government initially considered Sir William Robertson, the BEF's chief of general staff. Sir John, in fact, designated him as his successor, and Kitchener informed Lord Esher on 4 December that the government was about to select him.[1] But Asquith concluded that Robertson could best serve his country by revitalizing the moribund Imperial General Staff. Kitchener was consequently pushed into the background and Robertson as CIGS became the government's strategic adviser. The greater prize, commander-in-chief of the BEF, went to Sir Douglas Haig, who had commanded troops since the war began. Both Haig and Robertson, however, were pleased at this outcome and had been working behind the scenes to promote each other's advancement. Having played a key role in Robertson's earlier appointment as the BEF's chief of general staff, Haig now wanted his formidable presence in London. 'The Government seems quite incapable of deciding on a sound military policy and sticking to it. A sound military adviser, a man of character, must be found to advise them',[2] was the way that Haig expressed his support.

The Haig-Robertson alignment became what was surely the most important and influential military partnership in British history. The belief that the war would be won or lost on the Western Front served as their common bond. Attending Staff College at Camberley in the 1890s, they had absorbed the strategic maxims of the day, which included concentrating forces in the theatre where the enemy had his main force. The Western Front throughout the war was that theatre. 'If we won there we won everywhere,' Robertson succinctly writes, 'and if we failed there we lost everywhere.'[3] Robertson and Haig expected that the reinforced BEF would provide the Allies with the margin of victory. Casualties were bound to be enormous, but Britain could not expect to win a favourable peace by fighting to the last Russian or Frenchman.

Suspicious of politicians and disdainful of the inevitable division and delays which are characteristic of a democracy at war, Robertson and Haig viewed the army as the cornerstone of the nation. They adhered to the prevailing military concept of loyalty or 'playing the game'. An extreme version of Robertson's view of the army's role is stated in a letter he wrote to Haig soon after he became CIGS.

'I was at a war committee meeting this morning, and have come away very depressed because of the lamentable display of inability to govern on the part of the Ministers. . . .

Fortunately purely military matters are not now interfered with, but I am very anxious as to everything else, & it is that which counts for much in this war of Exhaustion.

I am writing this with the object of saying that practically anything may happen to our boasted British Constitution before this war ends, and that the great asset is the army – whose value will be fixed largely by the extent to which we at the top stick together & stand firm.'[4]

Divided Robertson and Haig were vulnerable. United they represented a formidable barrier to civilian influence. Their resignation or removal would provoke a firestorm of press criticism and a public outcry.

Lloyd George has written that Robertson was 'terrified', 'overawed', and 'dominated'[5] by Haig, his senior in the army. Robertson, known for his forcefulness, showed great deference to Haig and probably felt inferior to him in status, especially after George V gave the Scotsman his baton shortly after the Battle of the Somme.[6] Yet Robertson neither feared nor was in awe of Haig. He had witnessed the schism between GHQ and the War Office when French and Kitchener had been at sixes and sevens. When the soldiers had spoken in different voices, the civilians had been unable to agree upon Britain's road to victory. Robertson's determination to maintain Britain's commitment to the western front and his misguided concept of military 'loyalty' meant that he served, not as an honest broker between the government and GHQ, but as the representative of Haig's point of view in London.

On a personal level, Haig and Robertson were not the monolith they appeared. Separated by temperament and class, they were never close. Rather than the affectionate 'Wully', Haig at times referred to Robertson as 'The Iron Ration' or 'Old Wully', the latter nickname apparently suggesting that Robertson lacked drive or energy. Robertson was born of illegitimate parents in a small village in Lincolnshire; Haig came from perhaps the oldest family on the Scottish border. Robertson's formal education ended when he was thirteen, and he worked as a domestic servant before enlisting in the army. Haig attended Oxford, graduated from Sandhurst and moved in the highest social circles. Referring to his social inferior, Haig once noted: 'I am sure that it is good for the government and the country to have such a man in authority at the War Office at this time . . . How much easier, though, it is to work with a gentleman.'[7] Haig was aloof (really shy), a gracious host, and kept his emotions under tight control. 'Don't fuss' was his frigid response to anyone who became emotional or excited in his presence. Robertson, on the other hand, wore his feelings on his sleeve and could be difficult. When upset his countenance took on the appearance of an approaching storm. 'I frequently trembled lest the food were not of the proper English kind,' one of his subordinates has written, 'the carriage not properly warmed, or the bottle of whisky not forthcoming . . . No, he was not always easy to deal with.'[8]

Robertson and Haig were quick to dismiss articulate men such as Lloyd George and Winston Churchill as 'debaters'. Having devoted their careers to the serious study and practice of warfare, 'facts' and 'logical reasoning' were what mattered, not the 'opinions', 'instinct', or 'imagination' of the 'amateurs'. One can, however, discern one important distinction in their mental make-up's. Although equally committed to offensive warfare on the Western Front, Robertson was much more cautious about what was feasible.

While serving with the BEF, Robertson and his alter ego, Sir Frederick Maurice, his Director of Military Operations in France as well as in the War Office, sought a solution to the riddle of 'fortress' warfare. They concluded that a single battle was unlikely to result in a decisive victory over an enemy force in the millions, supplied by rail, and armed with the lethal weapons of the machine age. Without the technical means, especially the ability to maintain the momentum of the advance, a break-in would be difficult to convert to a break-through. With mechanized warfare in its embryonic phase, cavalry offered the best hope of rapid movement, but horse soldiers did not belong on the same battlefield with barbed wire and machine guns. Robertson's and Maurice's solution was to concentrate on a sector of the front where the Germans must hold their ground or surrender territory of strategic value. With the enemy 'nailed' to his defences, the BEF could pursue a limited offensive that emphasized methodical preparation and concentration of heavy artillery. Instead of the one-step break-thorough supported by cavalry that appealed so much to Haig, Robertson wanted a slow and gradual advance to make attrition work in Britain's favour.[9] Robertson told the government after the Battle of the Somme that it would be 1918 before the enemy's reserves were exhausted and decisive victory possible. Robertson's view of what was possible in trench warfare in 1916–1917, correct though it proved to be, had a serious disadvantage. The sacrifice of men in indecisive battles of 'attrition' did not seem commensurate with the results. Haig's offensives in 1916–1917, on the other hand, were directed toward a break-through and an overwhelming victory, a result which would have made the inevitable heavy casualties more palatable to the civilians.

When Robertson sought his government's approval for a push on the Somme, he knew little of Haig's actual plans. After visits to the front, he told Charles à Court Repington, a leading British war correspondent, that Haig was 'a shrewd Scot who would not do anything rash.'[10] When heavy fighting at Verdun forced the French to reduce their original commitment to the joint Anglo-French offensive, Robertson told the War Committee that Haig 'had no idea of any attempt to break through the German lines.' He only planned 'to "dègager" [rescue] the French.'[11] This was not correct. General Sir Henry Rawlinson, the commander of the Fourth Army, advocated the sort of limited offensive that Robertson favoured.[12] But Haig's tinkering created confusion at the operational level. His ambitious first-day objectives almost doubled the German defences to be covered by artillery. Some of his divisional commanders prepared for deep and rapid penetration while others developed a step-by-step advance.

The initial results of the first day of the Somme shook Robertson's confidence in Haig's leadership. The shocking casualties (almost 60,000 on the first day) were wildly out of line with his attritional strategy which focused on killing Germans rather than conquering territory. Behind Haig's back, Robertson wrote Rawlinson and Lieutenant-General L. E. Kiggell, the Chief of General Staff at GHQ.

Instructing Kiggell not 'to show this letter to **anyone**,' he suggested that the BEF should 'plod on carefully, slowly, and deliberately until we get through, and we can only do this by powerful artillery action as a preliminary and for this we want concentration and not dispersion of artillery fire.' To prevent the Germans from 'having the better manpower policy,' he told Rawlinson to use 'common-sense, careful methods, and not to be too hide-bound by the books we used to study before the war.'[13]

Robertson apparently expected Haig to switch off to the Second Army in the Ypres sector in the north if his offensive miscarried.[14] As the battle continued with little progress, Robertson's frustration grew, in part because of the paucity of information he received from GHQ. 'I have seen several Cabinet Ministers and the first question has always been how you are getting on and what you propose to do next,' he wrote to Haig. 'As regards the first I have said that you are getting on very well, but that it would be a slow business. As regards the second I have been able to say that I do not know what you propose to do next, that being the truth.'[15] Robertson's requests for information and for weekly progress updates angered Haig, who believed that he was unrealistically being held accountable for the results of each week's fighting.

The BEF's casualties for July exceeded all expectations and were unsustainable. 'The powers that be,' Robertson informed Haig on 29 July, 'are beginning to get a little uneasy in regard to the situation. . . . It is thought that the primary object – relief of pressure on Verdun – has to some extent been achieved.' This letter infuriated Haig ('Not exactly the letter of a C.I.G.S.!'),[16] but he reluctantly fell in line with Robertson's position of conducting a 'wearing-out' battle rather than seeking decisive results.[17]

With the BEF reducing its casualties in August by emphasizing artillery and limiting its objectives, Robertson sought to mend his fences with Haig. A false rumour circulated within the army that Robertson was after Haig's job.[18] Armed with a letter of support for Haig from the War Committee, Robertson assured him that his recent correspondence in no way suggested a lack of confidence. 'Your position is quite all right – you need have no fear. It always has been. My desire was to keep it so – hence my request for an appreciation.' Robertson also pointedly told Lord Esher, who was in close contact with GHQ, that Haig 'has done mighty well. I could not have done what he has. I knew he was the only man to command the Army. I might have had the command myself, but I knew he was the better man, and that my place is where I am now.'[19]

Lloyd George's emergence as Prime Minister in December prompted

Robertson to draw even closer to Haig. Believing that the Welshman was committed to a war to the finish and would provide forceful leadership, Robertson had favoured him during the political crisis that deposed Asquith. But Robertson knew that Lloyd George was much more inclined than Asquith to interfere with the soldiers' conduct of the war. 'Our new Prime Minister is well on the move,' Robertson was soon reporting to Haig. 'Though he is off Salonika, he is **on** Egypt, and wants to get to Jerusalem! For this he is hankering after 2 Divisions from France for the winter. He is also after lending some of your big guns to Italy for the winter. I have done my best with him, and in company with you I've no doubt we can keep him straight.'[20] Although Robertson remained the new government's military adviser, he was now often excluded from important strategic discussions. Using Captain Maurice Hankey, the secretary of the War Cabinet, as a substitute for the CIGS, Lloyd George hoped to thwart plans in place for a resumption of the Somme offensive with the British taking 'a larger, and the French armies a correspondingly smaller, share of the main offensive in the spring than had hitherto been the custom.'[21] Although Haig had no better luck than Robertson in convincing the new prime minister of the primacy of the Western Front, he expected Robertson to keep the government in line.

Unable to convince Britain's allies to transfer the main effort from the western to the Italian front, Lloyd George next embraced the offensive plans of the new French commander-in-chief, Robert Georges Nivelle, who opposed attritional warfare and was second to none in his expectations for a break-through. Yet Haig was unhappy. Nivelle's plan once again relegated the BEF to a supporting role and forced Haig to reduce his reserves by occupying French trenches. Moreover, if Nivelle's attack did not live up to its grandiose expectations, a rupture of the enemy front in twenty-four to forty-eight hours, his mainly British offensive in Flanders planned for later in the year might be either compromised or sacrificed. When Nivelle and Haig disagreed over the pace of British preparations, the War Cabinet over Robertson's protests took the extraordinary step of ordering Haig to conform with Nivelle's time-table.

Robertson, who wanted Haig to resolve his differences with Nivelle soldier to soldier, became alarmed when the Field-Marshal requested an Anglo-French conference to address the French railway crisis which he insisted was delaying his offensive. Haig's request for a conference gave Lloyd George an opportunity to ambush the High Command. At the Calais Conference, 26–27 February, 1917, the French, encouraged by Lloyd George, produced an astonishing document that reduced Haig to a cipher and turned over this troops, including their arms and food, to an arrogant and untested foreign commander. Although his command was in jeopardy, Haig remained strangely passive. After issuing a strong protest, he remained aloof from the heated negotiations that ensued. Robertson, no stranger to confrontation with civilians, fought to protect the BEF's integrity. In retrospect Robertson believed that he and Haig should have reacted differently. He blamed Haig for giving the civilians the opportunity to make mischief while serving ostensibly as mediators. But he even more regretted that he had persuaded Haig to join him in signing the revised agreement which allowed Nivelle to retain strategical (though not tactical) control of the BEF during the forthcoming campaign.[22] Their signatures gave the government the upper hand. On the other hand, their resignations might have seriously undermined the war effort by crippling or destroying Lloyd George's ministry and driving a wedge between Paris and London.

Nivelle's offensive could not live up to its inflated expectations, with disastrous results for French morale. With Russia already paralysed by revolution, the decline of the French army created anxiety in London over its European allies. Jan Christiaan Smuts spoke for the majority of the War Cabinet when he asserted on 1 May: 'to relinquish the offensive in the third year of the War would be fatal, and would be the beginning of the end.'[23] Two days later Lloyd George informed Robertson and Haig that he would support their plans. But whose plans? Robertson's or Haig's? Robertson had just discussed methods with Haig:

'I cannot help thinking that Nivelle has attached too much importance to what is called "breaking the enemy's front." The best plan seems to be to go back to one of the old principles, that of defeating the enemy's army. In other words instead of aiming at breaking through the enemy's front, aim at breaking down the enemy's army, and that means inflicting heavier losses upon him than one suffers oneself. If this old principle is kept in view and the object of breaking the enemy's army is achieved the front will look after itself, and the casualty bill will be less.'[24]

Haig was unimpressed. His response was to place Sir Hubert Gough, 'a devotee of the "hurroosh" – the rapid advance',[25] in charge of the operations in Flanders.

Believing that artillery was the key to success, Robertson endorsed a campaign in the Ypres salient despite the topographical obstacles it posed to an attacking force. Because he believed that the Germans had to stand and fight or give up territory of strategical value,[26] there might be no repeat of the German withdrawal on the eve of Nivelle's attack.

70

Believing in British artillery superiority, Robertson told Haig: 'we can blast him out of the country and preserve our infantry as he is apparently intent on preserving his'.[27]

The continued decline of the French, however, made Robertson apprehensive over the consequences of taking on the German army without considerable French assistance. 'When Autumn came around, Britain would then be without an Army!'[28] he bluntly told Haig. The BEF's commander was undeterred. He believed that the German army was nearing exhaustion, a point of view rejected by the War Office. When Haig submitted his plans to the government in mid-June, Robertson refused to include his questionable assessment of Germany's staying power. 'I cannot possibly agree with some of the statements in the appendix,'[29] he telegraphed. Haig's belief that he could defeat the Germans in 1917 remained unshaken. As a recent commentator notes, the 'conviction that he could defeat the German army in the west grew in inverse proportion to the apparent decline in French morale.'[30] Despite their differences, Robertson closed ranks with Haig. Their direction of the war was once again under attack in London. After telling the ministers that their military advisers had often been wrong, Lloyd George created a committee to review Britain's next move. 'There is trouble in the land just now,' Robertson reported to Haig. 'The War Cabinet, under the influence of L.G., has started, quite amongst themselves plus Smuts, to review the whole policy and strategy of the war, and to "get at facts."'[31] Robertson wanted Haig to avoid Nivelle's hype. 'Don't argue that you can finish the war this year,' he urged, 'or that the German is already beaten. Argue that your plan is the best plan – as it is – that no other would be **safe** let alone decisive, and then leave them to reject your advice and mine. They dare not do that.'[32]

Robertson's unbending support of Haig prevented the civilians from exploring – Robertson would have used the word 'exploiting' – their differences. Haig emphasized artillery and gave lip service to Robertson's step-by-step advance, but the ambiguity and flaws in his tactical planning went unexamined. Approval of the offensive, however, was not given unconditionally. Determined to prevent a repetition of the Somme, the ministers insisted that an unsuccessful offensive would be quickly terminated and an alternative plan pursued. Concerned about the looming manpower crisis, Robertson initially was prepared to accept this limitation. On 21 July, he wrote Haig that unless his attack was 'more or less a disastrous failure', he had informed the ministers that it would not be possible 'to pronounce a verdict' for 'several weeks'.[33] That Robertson had held out for a time frame of several weeks instead of a few days was cold comfort to GHQ.

When Robertson arrived in France on the next day, he was confronted by Haig and his staff. Kiggell gave him a paper 'concurred in & approved by C in C' which made clear that the BEF's leadership had no intention of aborting its offensive for Lloyd George's favourite front, Italy. 'The chance of anything positive being achieved in Italy is – to anyone acquainted with the A.B.C. of war – infinitesimal,' Kiggell had written. 'Be firmer and play the man, and, if need be, resign,' was Haig's stern advice. Robertson was soon assuring Haig that 'he would never omit to impress upon the War Cabinet. . . the necessity of supporting wholeheartedly a plan which has once been approved.'[34] Heavy rain hampered the progress of the advance in August and diminished the effectiveness of artillery, but Haig, maintaining that German casualties exceeded his by as much as one hundred percent, persisted in his attacks. GHQ as usual was vague about the course of the battle. 'It is rather difficult for me to say much as I have nothing to rely upon but the Communiqué and the slight additions you occasionally send to me,'[35] Robertson complained to Kiggell. A word from Robertson would have given the government the confidence to halt the offensive. But Robertson kept his doubts to himself throughout August despite – or more because of – Lloyd George's efforts to divert British divisions and guns from the west to support an Italian offensive (the Eleventh Battle of the Isonzo) which briefly showed promise.

In September, with all of Britain's allies flagging, Robertson and the Prime Minister discussed German peace feelers with Haig at his headquarters. Robertson described how the military situation looked from London: 'Russia is practically finished for the purposes of the war – a view he held himself. The Italians are not fighting, and the French are not fighting. How, then does the war look? We cannot singlehanded [sic.] defeat the German army.'[36] Haig, insisting that the Germans were nearing the end of their tether, remained upbeat.

It was apparently on this visit to the front in September that Robertson consulted Haig's Army commanders. When questioned about the feasibility of continuing his offensive Haig told Robertson that he should speak to the Army commanders. Robertson's diplomatic response was to insist that Haig be present. With their Commander-in-Chief looking on, the Army commanders kept whatever misgivings they had to themselves. 'Haig and his Army commanders being better judges of the enemy's condition than I could claim to be,' Robertson later writes, 'I was not prepared to carry my doubts to the extent of opposing him, and of thereby obstructing the application of that little extra pressure upon the enemy which experience has so often shown may convert an inconclusive battle into a decisive victory.'[37] Robertson clearly regretted his acquiescence. The continuation of the offensive into November left the BEF in a depleted and exhausted state.

Robertson's role in the Flanders offensive undermined both his position in London and his relationship with Haig. His scepticism about the strategical breakthrough was taken as criticism by the BEF's leadership, as was his rejection of GHQ's views on the deterioration of the German army. German morale, Robertson cautioned Haig, could 'best be estimated . . . by what takes place in battle, and, so far as I am in a position to judge, it would seem to be a denial of the well-known efficiency of our troops to say that the enemy troops do not continue, as a whole, to fight well, although there may be and are exceptions to this.'[38] The Battle of Cambrai soon demonstrated the truth of this statement. A British success became a defeat when the Germans counter-attacked. Coming on the heels of the barren Flanders offensive, this setback provoked a reaction bordering on panic in London.

In mid-December Robertson crossed the Channel on an awkward mission: the purging of key members of Haig's staff. Robertson hoped to surround Haig with more competent officers. He may also have wanted to diminish criticism of Haig by sacrificing officers such as Kiggell and Brigadier-General John Charteris, the controversial Chief of Military Intelligence. In his pocket he carried a letter from the Secretary of State for War to be used as a direct order if Haig resisted the changes.[39] It must have been a most uncomfortable meeting in more ways than one. Both men had reason to believe that the purge of the army might eventually reach them.

The new strategic map which favoured the Central Powers forced the high command to turn its attention to defence. With Russia out of the war and with German troops massing in the west, Robertson wanted a general reserve of French and British divisions. The command of such a force became a ticklish issue. Although Haig opposed a *generalissimo* in any form and balked at delegating some of his divisions to a general reserve, Robertson was prepared to accept Joffre as Allied commander if he were appointed his chief of staff. Determined to resist Robertson's influence, Lloyd George had other ideas. He wanted to use the new Supreme War Council, which had its own body of military advisers at Versailles, to bypass his general staff and redirect the British war effort. He thus proposed a body (the Executive War Board), composed of the Allied military advisers at Versailles, and chaired by General Ferdinand Foch, to control the proposed Allied general reserve.[40]

Haig at first joined Robertson in opposing this new Allied body which would include their bugbear Sir Henry Wilson, who had been Lloyd George's choice for the British permanent representative at

Versailles. Once the Allied leaders had acted, however, Haig sought to remain aloof from the public controversy which ensued. Two months earlier he had emphasized the importance of Robertson's remaining CIGS.[41] He now seemed indifferent to his protector's fate. When consulted, he accepted Lloyd George's proposal to have Robertson and Sir Henry Wilson exchange positions, Wilson coming to the War Office as CIGS and Robertson replacing him at Versailles as the British permanent military representative. When Robertson resisted, Haig bluntly told him that it was 'his **duty** to go to Versailles or anywhere else if the Government wished it.'[42] Robertson's continued rejection of Lloyd George's formula for the command of the general reserve led to his removal as CIGS. The Prime Minister greeted Haig's position with relief. 'We discussed the whole question for hours,' Lloyd George recalls in his memoirs, 'Haig put up no fight for Robertson.'[43] When Lloyd George suggested that a command might be found for Robertson in France, Haig demurred. The Field Marshal did, however, make it clear that his public silence during the controversy could not be used by the government to suggest that he agreed with the new Versailles machinery. He was prepared to work under the new arrangement, but that was not the same as saying that it was 'workable'.[44]

Robertson reacted bitterly to Haig's refusal to walk the plank with him. As he told Repington, 'he had found that he had many more friends than he knew, but fewer on whom he could count than he expected. Everybody had told him to stand firm, but few, except Gwynne and I, had stood by him when he did so.'[45] It seems that Haig compartmentalized his and Robertson's duties. As CIGS Robertson had a political role to fight the army's battles in London and resign if necessary. Haig hoped to avoid any direct part in this civil-military strife. He saw his duty as staying at his post as long as the government saw fit to retain him. Haig also believed that Robertson, who had been unable to prevent the transfer of some of his divisions to Italy after Caporetto or prevent a forward policy in Palestine, had outlived his usefulness. 'He has not resolutely adhered to the policy of "concentration on the Western Front,"' he wrote his wife. 'He has said that this is his policy, but has allowed all kinds of resources to be diverted to distant theatres at the bidding of his political masters.'[46] Nor did Haig believe that Robertson had represented his interests in the decision to have the BEF take over more of the French front.[47] This was unfair. If anything, Robertson had gone too far in his support of Haig. He had destroyed his position and along with it his alliance with Haig because he refused to embrace the strategical flexibility which the civilians believed was required to deal with the fluid political, economic, and military situation which existed during the winter of 1917–1918.

Haig prospered after Robertson's demise. His relations with Robertson's successor, Sir Henry Wilson, were much better than he could have anticipated. Foch's appointment as *generalissimo* gave him surprising independence from Lloyd George because it shielded his command from political interference. The successful Hundred Days' campaign served as a riposte to critics of his leadership during the Somme and Flanders offensives. As Haig led his forces to victory, Robertson served out the war in relative obscurity, first in the Eastern Command, and then as Commander-in-Chief, Home Forces. His pride may have kept him from a measure of vindication. When the British Fifth Army had been destroyed by the first of the great 1918 German attacks, some newspapers attacked Lloyd George and demanded Robertson's recall. To silence his critics, Lloyd George explored sending Robertson to France to serve as Haig's second in command. Robertson, however, wrote to Haig: 'My job is C.I.G.S. or nothing.'[48]

After the war Haig was created an Earl and granted £100,000. A national subscription was raised to purchase Bemersyde, the ancestral home of the Haigs. Robertson got a baronetcy and £10,000.

At a post-Armistice dinner given to the army commanders by Lord Milner at the Senior Service Club, Haig made a speech in which he praised Wilson and failed to mention Robertson's role as CIGS. 'I'll never go farting with 'aig again,'[49] was Robertson's parting response to this slight as he left the dinner.

Notes

1 Diary entry of 4 December, 1915, Esher MSS, 2/15; and Asquith to Stamfordham, 6 December, 1915, RA Geo. V Q. 838/52.

2 Robert Blake, ed., *The Private Papers of Douglas Haig* (London, 1952), 109.

3 Sir William Robertson, *Soldiers and Statesmen 1914–1918*. 2 vols. (New York, 1926), vol. 2, 294.

4 Robertson sent an identical letter to General Sir A. J. Murray. Robertson to Haig, 8 March, 1916, Robertson MSS, I/22/30.

5 David Lloyd George, *War Memoirs of David Lloyd George*. 2 vols. (London, 1938), vol. 1, 468; vol. 2, 1410.

6 Robertson had argued against promoting Haig while the battle was still under way. See Robertson to Lord Stamfordham, 10 August, 1916, David R. Woodward, ed., *The Military Correspondence of Field-Marshal Sir William Robertson: Chief of the Imperial General Staff December 1915 – February 1918* (London 1989), 81.

7 Gerard J. De Groot, *Douglas Haig, 1861–1928* (London, 1988), 214.

8 Sir Edward Spears, *Prelude to Victory* (London, 1939), 35.

9 David R. Woodward, *Field Marshal Sir William Robertson Chief of the Imperial General Staff in the Great War* (Westport, CT and London, 1998), 11–1 4.

10 Charles à Court Repington, *The First World War*. 2 vols. (London, 1921), vol. 1, 196.

11 War Committee, 30 May, 1916, CAB 42/14/12.

12 Diary entries of 5 April and 27 June, 1916, Haig MSS, Nos. 105 and 106.

13 Robertson to Kiggell, 5 July, 1916, and Robertson to Rawlinson, 26 July, 1916, Woodward, ed., *Military Correspondence of Robertson*, 64–65, 72–73.

14 On the eve of the offensive, Maurice had written to Sir Arthur Lynden-Bell, who headed the general staff in Egypt, that 'Haig is quite clear in his mind that he does not mean to knock his head against a brick wall, and if he finds he is only making a bulge and is meeting with heavy opposition he means to stop and consolidate and try somewhere else.' Maurice to Lynden-Bell, 29 June, 1916, Lynden-Bell MSS, vol. 1.

15 Robertson to Haig, 5 July, 1917, Woodward, ed., *Military Correspondence of Robertson*, 66.

16 Robertson to Haig, 29 July, 1917, Haig MSS, No. 107. For another example of GHQ's reaction to this letter, see diary entry of 2 August, 1916, Clive MSS, CAB 45/201.

17 Kiggell to Rawlinson and Gough, 2 August, 1916, Haig MSS, No. 107.

18 For this army gossip, see Tim Travers, *The Killing Ground: The British Army, the Western Front and the Emergence of Modern Warfare 1900–1918* (London, 1987), 19.

19 Robertson to Haig, 8 August, 1916, Woodward, ed., *Military Correspondence of Robertson*, 79–80; entry of 23 September, 1916, Esher MSS, 2/17.

20 Robertson to Haig, 12 December, 1916, Woodward, ed., *Military Correspondence of Robertson*, 129.

21 Robertson, *Soldiers and Statesmen*, vol. 2, 192.

22 Robertson to Haig, 3 March, 1917, Woodward, ed., *Military Correspondence of Robertson*, 156.

23 War Cabinet (128 A), 1 May, 1917, CAB 23/13.

24 Robertson to Haig, 20 April, 1917, Woodward, ed., *Military Correspondence of Robertson*, 179.

25 Robin Prior and Trevor Wilson, *Passchendaele: The Untold Story* (New Haven and London, 1996), 51.

26 After talking with Robertson, Hankey told Lloyd George: 'If the enemy retires he gives us what we want [Belgian ports]. If he stands, he exposes himself to colossal losses from our heavy artillery. Either way we stand to gain.' Memorandum by Hankey, 18 April, 1917, Hankey MSS, CAB 63/20.

27 Robertson to Haig, 14 April, 1917, Woodward, ed., *Military Correspondence of Robertson*, 173.

28 Blake, ed., Papers of Haig, 236.

29 Ibid.

30 David French, *The Strategy of the Lloyd George Coalition 1916–1918* (Oxford, 1995), 111.

31 Blake, ed., Papers of Haig, 239.

32 Ibid.

33 Robertson, *Soldiers and Statesmen*, vol. 2, 249.

34 Kiggell, 'Note', 22 July, 1917, WO 158/22; Blake, ed., Papers of Haig, 246; and Robertson to Haig, 28 July, 1917, WO 158/24.

35 Robertson to Kiggell, 2 August, 1917, Woodward, ed., *Military Correspondence of Robertson*, 211.

36 Hankey's minutes of this meeting are found in CAB 1/25/16. Two pages are in Hankey's handwriting, dated 26 September, and there are typed minutes, dated 29 September, 1917, apparently prepared after Hankey returned to London.

37 Robertson gives no date for this meeting. Robertson, *Soldiers and Statesmen*, vol. 2, 262.

38 Robertson to Haig, 18 October, 1917, WO 158/24.

39 Woodward, *Sir William Robertson*, 177.

40 For the involved controversy over the command of the general reserve, see David R. Woodward, *Lloyd George and the Generals* (Newark: University of Delaware Press; London and Toronto: Associated University Presses, 1983), 253–81.

41 Blake, ed., *Papers of Haig*, 271.

42 Ibid., 284.

43 Lloyd George, *War Memoirs*, vol. 2, 1689.

44 J. M. McEwen, ed., *The Riddell Diaries 1908–1923* (London, 1986), 218; and Davidson to Hankey, 18 February, 1918, Bonar Law MSS, 84/7/3.

46 Blake, ed., *Papers of Haig*, 283.

45 Repington, *First World War*, vol. 2, 246.

47 Ibid., 256.

48 Robertson to Haig, 19 April, 1918, Haig MSS, No. 126.

49 'Talk with Maurice Hankey at United Service Club,' 8 December, 1932, Liddell Hart MSS, 11/1932/43.

Chapter 6

HAIG AND THE ARMY COMMANDERS

Peter Simkins

On the morning of 11 November, 1918, Field-Marshal Sir Douglas Haig and his five Army commanders assembled in Cambrai for a conference. Haig recorded in his diary:

> 'After the Conference we were all taken on the Cinema! General Plumer, whom I told to "go off and be cinemaed" went off most obediently and stood before the camera, trying to look his best while Byng and others near them were chaffing the old man and trying to make him laugh'.[1]

In the resulting film footage, Haig and his senior subordinates can be seen chatting in a relaxed manner as they pose for the cinematographer. The impression created is that of a confident group of professional colleagues who are at ease with each other and who appear, both collectively and individually, to have a feeling of quiet satisfaction at a job well done.[2] However, had relations always been so cordial? Did Haig and his Army commanders resemble, in any sense, Nelson and his 'Band of Brothers'? How had their personal and professional relationships affected, or been influenced by, the conduct of operations between December 1915 and November 1918?

Of the five Army commanders filmed alongside Haig on 11 November, 1918, only General Sir Herbert Plumer had been in post when Haig became Commander-in-Chief, Plumer having been appointed to command the Second Army in May, 1915. He had remained at its head ever since, save for a brief period between November, 1917, and March, 1918, when he commanded the British forces in Italy.[3] The next longest-serving was General Sir Henry

Rawlinson, who had temporarily commanded the First Army in December, 1915, and January, 1916, before being given the newly-formed Fourth Army. Rawlinson had been told of his appointment by Haig on 24 January, 1916, his staff had formed on 5 February and the Fourth Army officially came into existence on 1 March, 1916.[4] As in the case of Plumer, Rawlinson's tenure of the Fourth Army command was not continuous. He actually took over the Second Army from Plumer in November, 1917, the formation being renamed the Fourth Army on 14 December, 1917, but reverting to its old title when Plumer returned from Italy in March, 1918. In February, 1918, Rawlinson was called upon to serve as the British Military Representative on the Executive War Board of the Supreme War Council at Versailles, a post he held only until 28 March, when he succeeded General Sir Hubert Gough in command of the Fifth Army during the German offensive in Picardy. Fifth Army was, in turn, redesignated as the Fourth Army on 2 April, 1918, and thereafter Rawlinson's period in command was unbroken.[5]

General Sir Henry Horne had assumed command of the First Army on 30 September, 1916, replacing General Sir Charles Monro, who had been appointed Commander-in-Chief in India.[6] General the Hon. Sir Julian Byng took over the Third Army from General Sir Edmund Allenby on 9 June, 1917, when the latter left the Western Front to command the Egyptian Expeditionary Force in Palestine.[7] General Sir William Birdwood's command of the reconstituted Fifth Army was relatively short, dating only from 23 May, 1918.[8] Apart from Plumer, therefore, the Army commanders of November, 1918, all owed their appointments very largely to Haig.

As indicated above, three other senior officers held Army commands for significant periods under Haig. Monro, who had previously commanded the Third Army between July and October, 1915, went on a special mission to Gallipoli before coming back to France early in 1916 to head the First Army, which he commanded from 4 February to 13 September, shortly before his departure for India.[9] Allenby had commanded the Third Army from 23 October, 1915, to June, 1917, while Hubert Gough led the Reserve Army from its formation on 23 May, 1916, and its official constitution on 3 July, retaining command when it became the Fifth Army at the end of October, 1916. Gough's tenure terminated abruptly on 28 March, 1918, when he became the scapegoat for Fifth Army's reverses in the face of the German *Michael* offensive and he was replaced by Rawlinson.[10]

Although only four years younger than Plumer, Haig frequently referred to him as 'the old man'.[11] While not intellectually brilliant, Plumer was blessed with sound common sense and an even temper, and was invariably kind, helpful and encouraging to subordinates as well as sensitive to the needs of his troops. He was, nevertheless, also a strict disciplinarian who disliked unpunctuality and over-familiarity and could, when necessary, deliver a stinging reprimand to transgressors.[12] General Sir Tom Bridges, who served under Plumer in 1917 as commander of the 19th (Western) Division, recalled that he was 'as loyal to subordinates as he was to those above him', observing that Plumer, rather than Haig, would probably have been the army's choice as Commander-in-Chief in succession to Sir John French.[13] This may have soured Haig's relations with Plumer early in 1916 and, following the loss of The Bluff on 14–15 February, Haig clearly considered 'degumming' him. On 17 February Haig asked Sir William Robertson, the CIGS., to 'try and give Plumer some other job so as to let him down lightly'.[14] The next day, after visiting Second Army, Haig noted that Plumer had been 'quite ready to go if I thought it desirable' but added that Plumer 'behaved in such a straightforward way and is such a thorough gentleman that I said I would think over the matter and let him know tomorrow'. Later in the day, Haig wrote to Plumer saying that he wanted him to continue in his command, provided that he strengthened his defences as quickly as possible. If, after a reasonable time, there was insufficient improvement in the 'general arrangements and conditions' of the Second Army, Haig would then ask Plumer to resign. Haig felt that Plumer was too kind to some of his subordinates and, in reporting his decision to Robertson, stated that he had told Plumer 'to take hold of his Corps Commanders more, and to make them in their turn grip their Generals of Division and so on down the scale'.[15] Another crisis followed the loss of the St.Eloi craters by the 2nd Canadian Division in April. Ironically, on this occasion, when Plumer wished to demonstrate his 'grip' by recommending the removal of Major-General Richard Turner VC, the divisional commander, Haig – taking the broader view to avoid a 'serious feud' between the Canadians and British – rejected Plumer's advice and decided to retain Turner.[16]

A key moment in the relationship came with the selection, in June, 1916, of Brigadier-General C.H.'Tim' Harington – then with the Canadian Corps – as Plumer's new chief of staff. Both Edmonds and Geoffrey Powell, Plumer's latest biographer, attribute this posting to Haig himself.[17] If so, it was an inspired choice, as Harington became the catalyst for a marked improvement in the performance and reputation of the Second Army. Brigadier-General John Charteris, Haig's head of Intelligence, subsequently wrote of Plumer and Harington: 'They are a wonderful combination, much the most popular, as a team, of any of the Army Commanders ... The troops love them'.[18]

Meticulous planning and preparation laid the foundations for the Second Army's ensuing successes, the vital factors – in Harington's words – being 'Trust, Training and Thoroughness'.[19] All the same, it took time for Haig to be convinced of Second Army's virtues. Plumer's proposals during the preliminary planning stages for the Third Battle of Ypres were – though endorsed to some extent by Rawlinson – regarded by Haig as too limited and cautious.[20] This influenced Haig's decision, at the end of April, 1917, to hand the principal role in the forthcoming Ypres offensive to the 'thruster', Hubert Gough, and not to Plumer or Rawlinson. Even Gough later admitted it was a mistake not to entrust the offensive to Plumer, who knew the ground, while John Terraine has called it 'Haig's greatest and most fatal error'.[21] As preparations for Plumer's set-piece assault on Messines Ridge neared completion, however, Haig was evidently coming to appreciate the qualities of Second Army. On 22 May, 1917, he recorded that he found Plumer 'a most pleasant fellow to work with and Harington . . . and all his staff work very kindly with G.H.Q. All are most ready to take advice'.[22] The latter quality, and the ability to tolerate close super-vision, proved essential as Haig subjected Plumer's corps commanders to a searching cross-examination about their plans before the assault and also extended the limits of the proposed advance to include the Oosttaverne Line – an alteration which, in the event, caused many additional casualties.[23] When it was clear that the initial assault had been an outstanding success, Haig commented that the 'old man deserves the highest praise' and, the same evening, he told Charteris that Plumer was now 'his most reliable Army Commander'.[24]

Plumer's reliability prompted Haig, in the last week of August, 1917, to begin to transfer to him the main weight of responsibility for the Third Battle of Ypres, and particularly the capture of the Gheluvelt plateau, following the failure of Gough's Fifth Army to make the desired progress in the opening phases of the battle.[25] Before the Menin Road Ridge attack on 20 September, Haig again cross-examined the corps and divisions involved about their plans and was once more reas-sured: 'Every detail had been gone into most thoroughly and the troops most carefully trained . . . Altogether I felt it was most exhilarating to go round such a very knowledgeable and confident body of leaders'.[26] Second Army's successes in late September perhaps caused Plumer and Harington to become a touch over-confident, first expressing a few fleeting reservations about Haig's ideas regarding the timing and scope of the possible exploitation phase after the Broodseinde attack in early October, and then appearing to abandon their own principles and allow themselves to rush the preparations for Poelcappelle.[27] Plumer's occasional dissent on individual aspects of the campaign did not, however, constitute fundamental disagreement and, as Prior and Wilson have emphasized, there is no real documentary evidence for the official historian's assertion that, on 7 October, Plumer and Gough advised Haig to close down the offensive.[28] Despite Lloyd George's statements to the contrary, Plumer was as shocked and sorry to have to leave the Western Front for Italy in November, 1917, as Haig was reluctant to see him go, Plumer's loyalty to Haig and Robertson being underlined the following February when he turned down the opportunity of becoming CIGS.[29] On Plumer's return in March, 1918, Haig quickly told him that it was 'a great satisfaction to me to have you again at the head of an Army here'.[30] Plumer reciprocated by helpfully releasing divisions from Second Army to bolster other threatened sectors during the German offensives in March and April, a grateful Haig remarking that:'It is most satisfactory to have a Commander of Plumer's temperament at a time of crisis like the present'.[31] Not surprisingly, therefore, Haig fought vigorously in October, 1918 – at the risk of a serious dispute with Foch – to reclaim Plumer and Second Army for the BEF following their temporary attachment to the *Groupe d'Armeés des Flandres* (G.A.F.), Haig even having shown himself prepared to acquiesce in Plumer's uncharacteristic readiness to ignore orders and break free from the constraints of the flank guard role assigned to him by the G.A.F.[32]

Whereas Haig learned to respect and trust Plumer, his relations with Allenby had a different outcome. Haig and Allenby were contemporaries at the Staff College, where the popular Allenby was elected Master of the Drag Hounds in preference to the aloof, single-minded Haig. Although Haig almost certainly viewed Allenby, a fellow-cavalryman, as a potential rival for promotion, Allenby – according to his most recent biographer – thought that Haig was, in fact, 'infernally jealous' of him.[33] Allenby had wide non-military interests and could converse easily on such diverse subjects as Shakespeare and natural history. Charles Grant, who became GSO1 at Third Army Headquarters at the end of 1916, remarked that Allenby was 'delightful to serve, expected a straightforward answer, and trusted all his subordinates to do their work, supporting them in every way . . .' J.F.C. Fuller, a GSO2 under Allenby for some six months, recalled that 'fools irritated him' but also that his staff 'was the happiest I ever served on, everybody fitted in'.[34] Another staff officer, Spencer Hollond, wrote that once Allenby had decided upon a particular course of action, 'nothing would make him change his mind'. However, Allenby confided to Hollond that shyness had almost ruined his life.[35] To hide this, he adopted the manner of a martinet, becoming to many a frightening and unpredictable creature whose outward toughness, iron discipline, sudden outbursts of rage and unbending intolerance of petty misdemeanours earned him the nickname of 'The Bull'. Gough felt that his truculence disguised a general who was out of his depth. A former A.D.C. observed that Allenby's violent temper 'detracted very largely from the pleasure and encouragement which his frequent visits to the front line trenches in France would otherwise have given to the Battn. Commanders and troops'.[36]

The fact that Allenby was an appointee of Sir John French may have counted against him in Haig's eyes but while relations were, in the main, coolly professional – and certainly never warm – both Haig and Allenby believed in the importance of cultivating the offensive spirit in the B.E.F. and in the value of aggressive trench raids as a means of raising and maintaining morale. For most of his time as an Army commander, Allenby was conspicuously loyal to Haig and would not permit his own subordinates to criticize G.H.Q.[37] Haig similarly showed that he was prepared to back Allenby, supporting him, for example, when he sought the removal, in August, 1916, of Lieutenant-General Sir John Keir of VI Corps – an officer whose willingness to stand up to, and formally complain about, Allenby's bullying caused him to become known as 'The Toreador'.[38]

Charles Grant claims that Allenby felt bitter that the principal role in the Somme offensive was transferred to Rawlinson's new Fourth Army when the German attack at Verdun obliged Third Army to side-step to the left to release the French Tenth Army from the Arras sector. An indifferent performance at Gommecourt on 1 July, 1916 – which precipitated the sacking of Stuart-Wortley, the commander of the 46th Division – did not improve the Third Army's reputation but, contrary to Allenby's fears, he was given the central part in the Arras offensive in 1917.[39] Preparations cannot have been smoothed by the mutual inability of Allenby and Haig to express their ideas lucidly whenever they met. As Charteris noted, they may actually have understood each other in a curious tongue-tied way but, because their respective staffs only understood their own immediate superior, 'a good deal of explanation has to be gone into afterwards and cleared up'.[40] Allenby's tendency to dig in his heels on some issues manifested itself in the dispute over the length of the preliminary bombardment for the Arras offensive. To achieve a measure of surprise, Allenby and his MGRA., Major-General A.E.A.Holland, favoured a hurricane bombardment of only forty-eight hours, whereas Haig and his artillery adviser, Major-General J.F.N.'Curly' Birch, argued for a longer, four-day bombardment. To be fair to Haig and Birch, artillery techniques and training at that time were still not quite up to the task Allenby and Holland proposed to set, and the corps and divisional commanders concerned, as well as senior officers such as Rawlinson, took GHQ's side on the issue. Allenby did manage to resist GHQ's attempts to remove Snow, the commander of VII Corps, who was alleged to be 'tired', and he also gave vent to his fury while fighting off a GHQ suggestion that he should hand over Snow's corps to Gough's Fifth Army on the right for better co-ordination.[41] In fact, Allenby's initial successes at Arras drew praise from all quarters. 'I have had many congratulations, including those of the Commander-in-Chief', he told his wife on 11 April.[42]

The goodwill soon evaporated. Although it was decided on 12 April that the moment for 'great risks' had passed and that the advance should henceforth be more methodical and deliberate, Allenby's handling of the battle drove three of his divisional commanders to take the uncommon and perilous step of registering a formal protest against isolated, narrow-front operations which exposed the attackers to concentrated flanking fire. Reading between the lines of the later correspondence between Edmonds and A.B.Acheson of the Cabinet Office, it would seem that this damaging protest may have been made directly to Haig over Allenby's head and that the account which appeared in the official history (written by Falls) was a 'toned-down' version of the truth. Certainly, Edmonds confesses that he helped 'to falsify this bit of history'.[43] By early May, 1917, Allenby himself had growing doubts about the Third Army's capacity to make even small efforts with limited objectives; he was irritated by Gough's influence over the planning of the later stages of the offensive, not least in pushing Haig into a disastrous compromise over the timing of zero hour for the assault on 3 May; and he made his feelings known in a memorandum to G.H.Q. on 1 May and also at a conference of Army commanders on 7 May. It was not a good time for a previously obedient and reliable subordinate to offer criticisms to Haig, who was all too aware of enemies at home and of the current plight of the French Army. Happily for Haig, Murray's failures at Gaza presented an ideal opportunity, with Sir William Robertson's help, for Allenby to be 'degummed'. Within a month, Allenby had been posted to Palestine and replaced by Byng. Not knowing what future honours awaited him, Allenby, before leaving France, called on Byng and 'broke down very badly' in front of him. Edmonds subsequently emphasized that feelings against Allenby were, by then, very strong, and indicated that, as a consequence of Allenby's mishandling of operations at Arras 'and much else', Haig had asked for his removal from France.[44]

Rawlinson – who like Plumer and Monro, was an infantryman – could also, when necessary, prove obstinate and undoubtedly incurred his share of displeasure from Haig, but he nevertheless survived a difficult 1916 and a frustrating 1917 to become arguably the BEF's most successful Army commander in the final months of the war. This may have been partly due to an equable temperament and to a comparatively subtle and malleable attitude to his dealings with Haig. 'Rawly had a way of floating over and away from his troubles', Edward Spears recalled. Charteris lumped Rawlinson and Henry Wilson together as 'born intriguers'. Sir Frederick Maurice admitted that, to some, he had the reputation of being 'hard and cold, of putting his own advancement first' but Maurice contends that Rawlinson 'deliberately adopted this method as one which seemed to him calculated to get the most work out of others . . . .'[45] Tim Travers concludes that Rawlinson was afraid of Haig, had qualms about approaching him, 'and could never sit down in a frank atmosphere of "give and take" to thrash out differences and problems'.[46]

Yet a detailed examination of Rawlinson's own diaries does not wholly support the idea that Rawlinson was frightened of Haig. It is true, for example, that, on certain occasions before and during the 1916 Somme offensive, Rawlinson foresaw trouble, and recorded criticism, from Haig on particular tactical issues or perceived shortcomings in his own performance. In April he predicted 'a tussle' with Haig over his proposals for 'bite and hold' tactics at the start of the offensive; in August he noted that Haig 'seemed rather put out' at Fourth Army's continuing failure to capture Guillemont; and in November he anticipated a cool reception for a letter he had sent to GHQ. regarding the implications, for training and future operations, of the losses of experienced officers and NCOs : 'I daresay D.H. won't like it', he wrote, 'but it is my duty to point it out to him. I think he now realizes that he cannot continue the offensive all through the winter without prejudicing our chances of another big success in the spring'. However, there is also ample evidence of regular, friendly and fruitful contacts. On 20 July, 1916, Rawlinson noted a visit from Haig, who had been 'very helpful and nice'; after another visit, on 4 August, he recorded that Haig had come to Fourth Army Headquarters in mid-afternoon, 'and we talked over the situation. He was very helpful as usual'; and, on 29 September, 'D.H. came at 4 p.m. and stayed nearly an hour discussing plans . . . '[47] In addition, he made scathing references to Churchill, Lloyd George, F.E.Smith and others who were reported to be critical of Haig: 'It is a monstrous thing that such disloyal people should be found and jealousy [is] no doubt at the bottom of it'.[48] One might agree that Rawlinson's diaries for 1916 cumulatively present a picture of an officer who is consciously dependent upon Haig for his own survival as a senior commander, who occasionally appears nervous about Haig's possible reactions and who is also a trifle too eager to record the

Commander-in-Chief's praise for him. Equally, one should acknowledge that, in his diaries at least, Rawlinson – while noting differences of opinion – rarely, if ever, criticizes Haig with any real venom and certainly does not appear to have lived in daily fear of him. Possibly the best clue to Rawlinson's own attitude to command and command relationships lies in the entry of 20 July, 1916: 'There are many worries and troubles in fighting a battle like this but I sleep like a top so am always fresh again the next day'.[49]

It is now widely accepted that, prior to 1 July, 1916, the basic divergence of concepts for the Somme offensive between Haig, who envisaged a breakthrough, and Rawlinson, who favoured 'bite and hold' operations, was never properly resolved, the final plan for the initial attack being full of false assumptions and contradictions, with catastrophic consequences. Part of the blame obviously rests with Haig for his inability to see that the available means were insufficient to achieve the desired ends. Haig's authority as Commander-in-Chief, and the nature of Rawlinson's own individual relationship with him, deterred Rawlinson from voicing outright objections to his superior's views. Indeed, as Prior and Wilson put it, Rawlinson 'proved sadly amenable to launching, without protest, an unlimited campaign in accordance with the ideas of the high command'.[50] He was, however, more successful – after some opposition – in overcoming the reservations of Haig and GHQ regarding the proposed night assembly and dawn assault between Longueval and Bazentin le Petit Wood on 14 July, an attack which captured a 6,000-yard stretch of the German second position in only a few hours.[51] This might have encouraged Rawlinson, when planning future operations, to try to extract concessions from Haig and to resist unwelcome amendments. Unfortunately for Rawlinson, Haig became increasingly critical of the conduct of Fourth Army's operations from mid-July. On 9 August Kiggell conveyed a message that the Fourth Army's failures at Guillemont had convinced Haig that 'the method of the attack adopted requires careful and full reconsideration'. Two weeks later, Haig left Rawlinson in no doubt that he was dissatisfied with the latter's repeated attacks with inadequate forces on narrow frontages, and he also delivered a terse reminder of the duties of an Army commander, making it clear that he was not impressed by the want of close supervision by Rawlinson of his subordinates.[52] Given these rebukes, it is perhaps small wonder that when his step-by-step plan for the mid-September attack, with tanks, at Flers-Courcelette, was thought to lack the requisite boldness, Rawlinson meekly succumbed and embraced Haig's suggestions.[53] For all the apparent disfavour into which he had slipped at times in 1916, Rawlinson was 'highly honoured' when he received strong indications from Haig that he would have a leading role in the 1917 Flanders offensive, possibly commanding the northern part of the operations.[54] He was thus very 'dispirited and disappointed' when, in May 1917, he learned that Gough had been entrusted with the northern part of the attack and that his own role would be reduced to commanding operations in the coastal sector, which would include an amphibious landing near Ostend.[55] Once more, over-caution in his planning proposals appears to have militated against him in Haig's judgement.

The projected landing on the Belgian coast was ultimately cancelled, making 1917 a barren year for Rawlinson but, after his return to operational command in the spring of 1918, he conducted the defence of Amiens with some skill, considering his slender resources. At the Second Battle of Villers Bretonneux on 24 April, Haig too did exactly what was needed from a Commander-in-Chief – visiting Fourth Army and III Corps headquarters to assess the situation and applying pressure to the French to co-operate in the defence but *not* meddling unnecessarily in the tactical handling of the battle.[56] By the summer the overall improvement in tactics and techniques, the greater array of firepower and expertise available, the transition to semi-open warfare, the accelerating devolution of tactical command downwards to corps and divisional level and the more general awareness, throughout the BEF, of what was operationally feasible, all combined to reduce the role of Rawlinson and his fellow Army commanders – making each of them 'less and less the creator of great operations' and more like 'a manager drawing forth and co-ordinating the endeavours of others'.[57] Haig still showed a tendency to interfere, as in the final planning stages before the attack at Amiens in August when, not for the first time, he thought Rawlinson was being too cautious and so insisted on extending the objectives.[58] However, in contrast to previous years, Haig was now more frequently receptive to advice from below and, on 14 August, with German resistance stiffening, he accepted the urgings of Rawlinson and Lieutenant-General Sir Arthur Currie, the Canadian Corps commander, to shift the weight of the offensive north to the Third Army's sector.[59] Though Rawlinson never quite lost his curious air of detachment from the recurrent crises of command, Fourth Army's successes in the 'Hundred Days' helped, finally, to place his relationship with Haig on an even keel. When, soon after the Armistice, Rawlinson congratulated Haig, the reply was genuinely appreciative. 'My dear Harry', wrote Haig, ' . . . I must congratulate you, too, on all that you have achieved since the very beginning of the war; and at the same time thank you for the whole-hearted support you have at all times given me'.[60]

Hubert Gough, whose command style might at last have found its true outlet in the semi-open warfare of the 'Hundred Days', was denied the chance of proving himself in the final offensive of the war. His fall from grace in 1918 was all the more marked because, less than two years earlier, he had enjoyed several distinct advantages over the other Army commanders in his relations with Haig. For example, if Haig (as one of his biographers has claimed) respected but did not particularly like Rawlinson, he does seem to have had a real affinity with Gough , who was nine years Haig's junior and the youngest of the Army commanders by nearly five years.[61] Gough shared with Haig a love of horses, a deep-seated belief in the value of cavalry and a high sense of professionalism. F.S.Oliver wrote that Gough brought 'something in the nature of religious fervour into his profession', a quality with which Haig would readily have empathized.[62] The reserved, introspective Haig, who was never at ease with strangers, appears to have discovered in the spirited, direct and witty Gough a younger officer whom he could admire and encourage as a protégé and, following the death in 1915 of Johnnie Gough – Haig's chief of staff in the opening months of the war – Hubert replaced his younger brother, to some extent, as Haig's confidant and sounding-board.[63] These factors undoubtedly aided Hubert's rapid rise to senior command, his hot temper and natural impetuosity not yet – in the first half of the war – being seen as obstacles to his progress. Indeed, given Gough's reputation for drive, quick decision and offensive-mindedness, it is easy to understand why Haig viewed him as an obvious candidate to command the Reserve Army in its anticipated exploitation role on the Somme although, as late as 22 June, 1916, it was still envisaged that he would be largely under Rawlinson's orders.[64]

Gough's impulsiveness was soon evident during the Somme offensive when, in the third week of July, 1916, he had to be dissuaded from launching the 1st Australian Division against Pozières at barely twenty-four hours' notice. Even Haig thought it necessary to remind Gough 'to go into all difficulties carefully, as 1st Australian Division had not been engaged in France before and possibly overlooked the difficulties of this kind of fighting'.[65] Gough's propensity for repeated shallow attacks on narrow frontages – often delivered seemingly regardless of the prevailing tactical and climatic conditions – did not endear him to the Australian and Canadian formations carrying them out in the late summer and autumn of 1916, but his ability to present Haig with the occasional outstanding success, such as the capture of Thiepval, preserved his standing with the Commander-in-Chief. Anxious for yet another success on the eve of the inter-Allied conference at Chantilly in mid-November, Haig allowed Gough a fair amount of latitude in his planning for the attack astride the Ancre. On this as on other occasions,

Haig placed the responsibility for deciding whether the attack should proceed on the shoulders of the Army commander concerned, so ensuring that, in the event of a success, Haig would get the credit at Chantilly but, if the attack failed, Gough would take the blame. On 12 November, the day before the assault, Kiggell informed Gough that Haig did not, in any way, wish to bring on a battle in unfavourable conditions, while Haig himself noted that 'the necessity for a success must not blind eyes to the difficulties of ground and weather. Nothing is so costly as a failure'. The taking of Beaumont Hamel on 13 November handed Haig the prize he wanted and made him more inclined to let Gough continue the Ancre operations longer than was sensible. In Kiggell's words: '. . . as things turned out the later stages of the fight were hardly justified, but Gough was so keen and confident the C-in-C decided to permit them'.[66]

Despite the fact that Gough was seen by some, in March, 1917, as a potential replacement for Haig, he remained loyal to the Commander-in-Chief who allowed Gough to expand Fifth Army's part in the Arras offensive beyond what had originally been conceived and, at First Bullecourt on 10–11 April, yet again indulged Gough's tendency to launch precipitate and ill-considered attacks. Allenby, in particular, was annoyed by the apparent favouritism shown to Gough at conferences of Army commanders, and the failures at First and Second Bullecourt did not deter Haig from giving Fifth Army the leading role in the later offensive at Ypres.[67] The respective contributions made by Haig and Gough to the planning of the Third Battle of Ypres have been subjected to such intense scrutiny of late that there is no necessity for a further detailed survey here. Many historians now agree that, as before the Somme in 1916, there were dangerous ambiguities in the orders and messages emanating from Haig and GHQ concerning the goals of the campaign, and a simultaneous failure on the part of the Army commander principally involved either to heed advice or to seek clarification.[68] Haig, on the one hand, hoped for a breakthrough but also recognized the need for a systematic step-by-step advance; Gough, on the other, 'was not subtle enough to understand the dual nature of the offensive', nor sufficiently brave and canny to 'understand or confront an aloof and overbearing Haig'. Gough was also in the wrong for not accepting what *were* clear instructions about the importance of securing the whole of the Gheluvelt plateau. However, in the final analysis, the responsibility for issuing and enforcing precise and unambiguous orders lay with Haig and GHQ, as did the task of making sure that possible differences and misunderstandings were ironed out.[69]

All these command failures and problems notwithstanding, there were definite signs of Haig's growing disenchantment with Gough by early September, 1917. Between 7 and 12 September he repeatedly questioned the advisability of wasteful minor attacks being organized by Fifth Army, with the result that Gough eventually called a halt to them. On 10 September Haig recorded Kiggell's fears that 'some of Gough's subordinates do not always tell Gough their true opinion as regards their ability to carry out an operation', and on 18 September he complained that the 'Fifth Army staff work is not as satisfactory as last year'. Kiggell left Haig in no doubt that divisions positively disliked the prospect of serving in Fifth Army, ascribing this to the ruinous influence of Gough's chief of staff, Neill Malcolm – a loyal and competent, but also a severe and unsympathetic, officer described by Haig himself as a 'fussy little man'.[70]

Curiously, Haig at first thought it best 'not to mention to Gough the state of feeling amongst the troops' lest it 'might make Gough lose confidence in himself' but, after Passchendaele, Malcolm was removed from Gough's staff and given command of the 66th Division.[71] This did nothing to quieten the swelling chorus of criticism of Gough in Whitehall. Even before the German March offensive in 1918, the Secretary of State for War, Lord Derby, gave Haig a clear indication that, if the Commander-in-Chief had any personal misgivings about Gough, he now had 'a loophole which would make your task easier if you desire to make a change'.[72] Thus although, from 21 March onwards, Gough conducted a skilful fighting retreat in extremely disadvantageous circumstances and against great odds, there was possibly little that Haig could have done – whatever the rights and wrongs of his own strategic dispositions on the eve of the offensive – to have prevented Gough being made a scapegoat for the crisis in Picardy. To Haig's credit, he did make some attempt to plead Gough's case and to find him an alternative job in France, but, on 4 April, he was told unequivocally that Lloyd George wanted Gough to 'return home'.[73] It is also worth remarking that there were limits to Haig's support for Gough. As he informed Gough's friend and former staff officer, Edward Beddington, in 1919: ' . . . after considerable thought I decided that the public at home . . . demanded a scapegoat, and that the only possible ones were Hubert or me'. He added candidly, 'I was conceited enough to think that the Army could not spare me'.[74]

Loyalty to the Commander-in-Chief was a shared characteristic of most, if not all, of Haig's Army commanders, however strained their personal relationships might sometimes have become. For example, while Haig reconized the value of Monro's work as Commandant of the Hythe School of Musketry between 1903 and 1907, he would have preferred to have seen Rawlinson appointed to the First Army in January, 1916, but his advice was rejected by Kitchener. This was hardly conducive to a trouble-free relationship but Monro's compliant attitude was summed up by his own statement later in 1916:'I was brought up never to question the decisions of my superiors and never to refuse any appointment offered me however much I dislike it'.[75] First Army's record was undistinguished under Monro. The poor performance of Henry Wilson's IV Corps at Vimy Ridge in May, 1916, was followed by the failure of the subsidiary attack at Fromelles on 19–20 July, another occasion on which Haig gave the Army commander involved full discretion to cancel or postpone the operation if conditions or resources were deemed to be unsatisfactory.[76] Judging from the relevant entries in Haig's diary in August, 1916, he did not fight too hard to retain Monro's services, once the latter had been selected to go to India, and seems to have been more concerned about attempts by the 'Home authorities' to limit his own powers of appointment.[77]

Birdwood, Byng, Cavan, Haking, Horne and Henry Wilson were all viewed as possible replacements for Monro – Horne's appointment to the command of First Army being agreed by 20 August, 1916. Horne, the only gunner among Haig's Army commanders, had served as C.R.A. in I Corps in 1914 and his letters to his wife in 1916 suggest that his return to France from Egypt and his subsequent elevation to an Army command owed a great deal to Haig's influence.[78] A Scot and a devout Christian like Haig, Horne has been described by Sir Hastings Anderson – his chief of staff from February, 1917 – as stern, reticent and impatient of slackness, indiscipline and 'eyewash', and as an officer who was 'somewhat lonely in his high position'. Anderson also stressed that he was calm and confident in the exercise of his duties; that his decisions were generally 'sound, crisp and reasoned'; and that he was usually happy to leave the detailed execution of orders to his staff. From 9 April, 1917, to 11 November, 1918, Horne 'never once sent for me between 11 o'clock at night and 7 o'clock in the morning', Anderson recalled.[79] Byng – when still commander of the Canadian Corps – acknowledged that Horne had been 'more than helpful and backed me up in everything' at Vimy Ridge in April, 1917. That particular success of the First Army not only enhanced Horne's overall reputation but also, one suspects, confirmed Haig's opinion of him as a safe pair of hands. Even so, as in the planning of the Canal du Nord assault in September, 1918, Haig was prepared, when the need arose, to accept the tactical advice of Horne's subordinates – especially Arthur Currie – rather than that of Horne himself. As Shane Schreiber has recently commented: 'Haig's refusal to overrule Currie on Horne's behalf supports the position that Haig trusted Currie's judgement in operational matters more than some of his own Army commanders'.

Perhaps this lay behind Horne's acid post-war remark that the Canadian Corps was 'apt to take all the credit it can for everything and to consider that the B.E.F. consists of the Canadian Corps and some other troops'.[80]

As noted above, Byng's suitability for an Army command had already been considered in August, 1916, and his abilities as a tactician and trainer were underlined by the storming of Vimy Ridge by the Canadian Corps the following April, making him an obvious choice to succeed Allenby in command of Third Army. Byng was not universally popular. Gough called him an 'extraordinary intriguer' and once wrote: 'I hate that way of Byng of always trying to get the better of others while pretending the most friendly feelings. I have known several instances of this and would not trust him one yard as a friend'. The majority of his brother officers, however, would probably have concurred with Brudenell White's assessment of him as an 'unambitious man without any desire for personal fame – a very rare thing in generals . . . '[81] After Cambrai, Haig accepted the full responsibility for insisting that Byng should prolong the costly attacks on the Bourlon position beyond 22 November, and he also took Byng's side in the controversy which arose in the wake of the German counter-stroke of 30 November, 1917. Byng's apparent readiness to exonerate the senior commanders and to blame the poor performance of machine-gunners and the lack of training of junior officers, NCOs and men for the failure to block the German counter-attack, was criticized in the press and Parliament – discouraging Byng himself from making any future comments of substance on the conduct of the war. Since neither Byng nor his chief of staff, Louis Vaughan, were called as witnesses by the Cambrai court of inquiry in January, 1918, it is difficult to escape the impression that there was little intention to probe command problems at the very top, even if Byng was willing and ruthless enough to see three corps commanders – Pulteney (III Corps), Woollcombe (IV Corps) and Snow (VII Corps) – replaced in the aftermath of the battle.[82] Byng also avoided widespread censure for the delay in evacuating the Flesquières Salient during the German March offensive in 1918, the Third Army's dogged resistance from 26 March – particularly in repulsing the *Mars* attack at Arras on 28 March – having restored his credit. His personal loyalty to Haig was undiminished and, soon after Gough's dismissal, he wrote: 'Whatever else happens, we must keep D.H. where he is'.[83] The Third Army – the largest of the five by the 'Hundred Days' – went on to play a vital part in the final offensive between August and November, 1918, although Haig predictably considered Byng's plans for the attack at Albert on 21 August too cautious and also showed his disapproval of Byng's desire to allow his inexperienced conscripts a pause to regroup after only one day of the battle.[84]

Of all those appointed to Army commands under Haig, the elevation of Birdwood is the most curious, as Haig seems to have long disliked him as an Indian Army officer and as a 'tool' of Kitchener. In September, 1916, Haig remarked that Birdwood was 'not much use for directing operations. His taste lies in making speeches to the Australian rank and file'. As late as February, 1918, Haig was comparing the efficiency of the Australian Corps unfavourably with that of the Canadians and put this down to Birdwood, 'who, instead of facing the problem, has gone in for the easier way of saying everything is perfect and making himself as popular as possible'.[85] Even Brudenell White, his own chief of staff in I Anzac Corps and the Australian Corps, stated that Birdwood hardly, if ever, drew up the plans of an operation and, when he went out for the day, 'never brought back with him a reliable summary of what he had seen'.[86] Birdwood himself was clearly not an unqualified admirer of Haig, describing the latter in 1916 as devoid of 'any great human sympathies, and ... inclined to regard men more as part of a machine than human beings'.[87] Yet, when it came to the point – as at Pozières and Bullecourt – Birdwood was largely unwilling to stand up to his superiors and was much less effective than Currie in this regard. Gough, for one, wrote that Birdwood was 'always easy to work with'.[88] He became more assertive in September, 1917 – demanding a rest for the Australian Corps after Broodseinde and Poelcappelle – and the key contribution made by the Australian divisions in the defensive battles of March and April, 1918, as well as his own seniority and reputation for compliance, and Haig's desire to promote Monash, probably all helped to win Birdwood his Army command. The reconstituted Fifth Army did not, however, play a leading part in the 'Hundred Days', while an analysis of Haig's diary entries for August to November, 1918, suggests that, apart from the full conferences of Army commanders, he had only two or three formal meetings with Birdwood during that period.[89]

In recent years, several scholars – particularly Tim Travers – have paid a great deal of attention to the command failings of Haig and GHQ. Travers argues that Haig's rigid and aloof character, coupled with his personal views on the role and authority of the Commander-in-Chief – as derived from his time at the Staff College – did much to isolate GHQ in 1916 and 1917 and give it 'an unnecessarily authoritarian aspect'. According to Travers, Haig believed that the Commander-in-Chief must be 'determined and display singleness of purpose'; that there should be unanimity at GHQ; and that the authority of the Commander-in-Chief would be impaired by permitting subordinates to advance their own ideas. In general, the Commander-in-Chief should lay down the broad strategic objectives but leave the detailed conduct of the battle to subordinates. The Army commanders – known at GHQ as the 'Wicked Barons' – were therefore left largely alone. However, as Travers explains, while Haig was, in principle, committed 'to setting strategy and leaving the tactics to his army and commanders', he often interfered or intervened in matters of 'grand tactics' – such as the depth of objectives or the length of a bombardment. All this led to confusion and compromise on some occasions and to a command vacuum and paralysis at the top on others.[90]

The planning failures and contradictions before the Somme and Passchendaele, and in the preparations for the Fifth Army's defence in March, 1918, tend to support the thesis presented by Travers, as do the instances already noted regarding Haig's questioning of, or interference in, the plans of subordinates on the Somme and at Arras, Messines and Third Ypres. Nevertheless, the apparent inconsistencies in Haig's command style should not be exaggerated. As a case in point, Haig's own strictures to Rawlinson on 24 August, 1916, are highly revealing. Haig confirmed his belief that in 'actual *execution* of plans, when control by higher commanders is impossible, subordinates on the spot must act on their own initiative, and they must be trained to do so'. Conversely, he also stated that 'close supervision by higher Commanders is not only possible but is their duty, to such extent as they find necessary to ensure that everything is done that can be done to ensure success'. He added: 'This close supervision is especially necessary in the case of a comparatively new army. It is not "interference" but a legitimate and necessary exercise of the functions of a Commander on whom the ultimate responsibility for success or failure lies'.[91] In other words, Haig did not view a 'hands-off' approach on some occasions and close supervision on others as inconsistent or incompatible. Precisely because he did carry the 'ultimate responsibility for success or failure', it should hardly come as a surprise to scholars that Haig sometimes felt it necessary or desirable to intervene at a tactical level, however unfortunate the end product of such interference may have proved.

A further strand of the Travers thesis is that there were 'serious gaps in communication' between Haig and his Army commanders, partly because most senior officers were 'simply afraid of Haig and were not prepared to question him', and partly because there was no effective forum for regular and frank discussion of alternative strategic policies and tactics. To quote Gough:'There were not enough discussions, between the HQ Staff and the Army Commanders concerned – when we could sit round a table with all the maps before us, and really thrash out the problems'.[92]

The machinery for such discussions did, of course, exist in the form of the weekly conferences with his Army commanders which Haig instituted soon after becoming Commander-in-Chief. These took place at GHQ or at the different Army headquarters in rotation, normally from 10 or 11 a.m. to lunchtime and lasting about two to two-and-a-half hours. The conferences would often start with a briefing by the chief of Intelligence at GHQ; each of the Army commanders would then report on the situation on their front; and, finally, Haig might present an outline of future plans or take the opportunity to expound on a topic of current importance – such as the use of Lewis guns in an advance, machine-gun training for divisional cavalry and cyclists, or the tactical handling of tanks.[93] The conferences became less regular as the months passed. The diaries of Haig, Rawlinson and Horne indicate, for example, that between mid-March and the end of May, 1917, there were five conferences involving three or more of the Army commanders while, similarly, there were only seven such meetings during the 'Hundred Days' in 1918. It has been noted earlier that Allenby found these conferences frustrating and there is other evidence to reinforce the view that they did not provide an open forum for genuine discussion. Haig himself records that, on 14 January, 1916, Plumer told him what he proposed to say at the next day's conference, listened to Haig's criticisms and then agreed to amend his statement. Travers also cites an occasion in 1918 when Birdwood was persuaded by the other Army commanders to suggest alterations to an official pamphlet on divisions in defence and was told by Haig:'I won't have anyone criticizing my orders'.[94] Here too, however, the case against Haig may have been overstated. Much of the evidence about the isolation and authoritarianism of GHQ came from Gough in the post-war period, when he had an axe to grind, or from Henry Wilson and Aylmer Haldane – hardly evenhanded observers – and was often related to Edmonds or Liddell Hart, both avid collectors of gossip. Moreover, there is at least some counterevidence about the value of the conferences. On 6 May, 1916, Rawlinson noted that there was 'a considerable discussion on training at the Army Comrs. conference and [I] gave my views freely', while Haig's record of the meeting of 21 September, 1918, also strongly suggests that there was a useful and wide-ranging exchange on the current situation, with each Army commander being encouraged to voice his opinions. Haig even comments wryly that, before he intervened, 'Byng and Rawlinson were each inclined to try and get the better of the other!'[95]

It is equally important to emphasize that Haig's personal contacts with his Army commanders were by no means confined to these conferences. Like all of his Army commanders, Haig spent many afternoons every month visiting subordinate commanders and formations. For example, during the Somme offensive in 1916, he met Rawlinson on at least thirty-eight separate occasions other than Army commanders' conferences, the vast majority of these contacts resulting from visits by Haig to Rawlinson's headquarters and not from visits by Rawlinson to G.H.Q. Four of Haig's visits were on consecutive days (8–11 July) and he also saw Rawlinson five times between 13 and 21 July. The frequency of Haig's meetings with individual Army commanders tended – not surprisingly – to increase when that particular commander was most heavily involved in planning or conducting what Haig saw as the most important operations. Thus, between 31 July and the end of November, 1917 – the period of Third Ypres and Cambrai – he met Gough on some twenty-two occasions, Plumer on seventeen, Rawlinson on thirteen, Byng on twelve and Horne only seven times. Ten of Byng's twelve meetings with Haig at that time were in October and November, immediately prior to, and during, Cambrai. Again, in the period 8 August-11 November, 1918, Haig met Rawlinson *individually* at least fourteen times, Byng thirteen and Horne six, whereas – outside of the larger conferences – he appears to have seen Plumer and Birdwood, individually or together, on a *combined* total of only five occasions.[96] The frequency of his contacts with Gough during Third Ypres certainly expose the somewhat bogus nature of Gough's post-war claim that Haig and GHQ left him largely alone – though it is true that, during the German March offensive, Haig did not visit Gough until 23 March and then, rather pointedly, did not invite him to the crucial conference of Army commanders on 26 March, two days before his dismissal.[97] Haig's numerous visits to Rawlinson in July and August, 1916, and his similar patterns of contact with other commanders during other battles, may also perhaps reflect the more human side of a Commander-in-Chief who, given his crushing responsibilities, was, above all, seeking reassurance that everything possible was being done to ensure success. Such frequent contacts could be construed as interference on Haig's part but by no stretch of the imagination should they be taken to signify *isolation*.

The fact is that, while problems and disagreements still occurred in the second half of 1918, the general improvement, from top to bottom, in the BEF was accompanied by a reduction of tension in command relationships at the highest level. As Robin Prior and Trevor Wilson have perceptively observed, the role of Haig and the Army commanders diminished and became less relevant as the forces under their direction 'grew in expertise and complexity'. Indeed, Haig, like his senior sub-ordinates, 'proved far more effective as a commander once the sphere of his activities began to diminish to an extent that brought them within the limits of his capabilities'.[98] It is also evident that Haig did come to appreciate the collective qualities of his Army commanders. On 14 June, 1917, Rawlinson was told by Haig that, whereas 'last year he had only one Army Comr.(me) now he had five who knew their busi-ness', and in September, 1918, Haig told Henry Wilson that the BEF possessed 'a surprisingly large number of *very capable* generals' to whose 'sound military knowledge' and 'steady adherence to the principles of our FSR Part I' the current successes must be 'chiefly attributed'.[99] It can be argued, therefore, that there was a detectable 'learning curve' in the command relationships of Haig's BEF just as there was in its tactics and techniques.

Notes

1 Haig Diary, 11 November, 1918, Public Record Office (PRO) WO 256/37.

2 Imperial War Museum (IWM) Film and Video Archive, 'Haig and his Army Commanders on 11th November, 1918', IWM Film No.132.

3 General Sir Charles Harington, *Plumer of Messines*, Murray, London, 1935, pp. 134-5, 146-8; Geoffrey Powell, *Plumer, The Soldier's General: A Biography of Field-Marshal Viscount Plumer of Messines*, Leo Cooper, London, 1990, pp. 124-5, 227-254.

4 Brigadier-General Sir James Edmonds, *Military Operations: France and Belgium, 1916. Vol.I*, Macmillan, London, 1932, pp. 19, 30 (hereafter *OH*); Robin Prior and Trevor Wilson, *Command on the Western Front: The Military Career of Sir Henry Rawlinson, 1914–1918*, Blackwell, Oxford, 1992, p.137; Rawlinson Diary, 5 February, and 1 March, 1916, Rawlinson papers, Churchill College, Cambridge (hereafter CC) 1/5.

5 *OH, 1918, I*, Macmillan, London, 1935, pp.25, 115 and *OH, 1918, II*, Macmillan, London, 1937, pp.27–8, 109; Prior and Wilson, *Command on the Western Front*, pp.273–280; Major-General Sir Frederick Maurice, *The Life of General Lord Rawlinson of Trent: From his Journals and Letters*, Cassell, London, 1928, pp.202, 206–216; Rawlinson Diary, 9 November, 1917, and 26 and 28 March, 1918, Rawlinson papers, CC 1/9.

6 Captain Wilfrid Miles, *Military Operations: France and Belgium, 1916, Vol.II*, Macmillan, London, 1938, p.428; Lieutenant-General Sir Hastings Anderson, 'Lord Horne as an Army Commander', *Journal of the Royal Artillery Institution*, Vol.LVI, No.4, 1930, p.408; Horne Diary, 30 September, 1916, Horne papers, IWM 62/54/9.

7 *OH, 1917, II*, HMSO, London, 1948, p.107; Jeffery Williams, *Byng of Vimy: General and Governor-General*, Leo Cooper, London, 1983, pp.168–9.

8 *OH, 1918, III*, Macmillan, London, 1939, p.138.

9 *OH, 1916, I*, Macmillan, London, 1932, p.30 and *OH, 1916, II*, p.543; General Sir George Barrow, *The Life of General Sir Charles Carmichael Monro*, Hutchinson, London, 1931, pp.106–114. Lieutenant-General Sir Richard Haking temporarily commanded the First Army from 13 to 30 September, 1916.

10 Sir Archibald Wavell, *Allenby: A Study in Greatness*, Harrap, London, 1940, pp.160, 184–5; Lawrence James, *Imperial Warrior: The Life and Times of Field-Marshal Viscount Allenby, 1861–1936*, Weidenfeld and Nicolson, London, 1993, pp.78, 106–7; Anthony Farrar-Hockley, *Goughie: The Life of General Sir Hubert Gough*, Hart-Davis,

MacGibbon, London, 1975, pp.182, 192, 308–312; *OH, 1916, I*, p.193; *OH, 1916, II*, pp.11, 460; *OH, 1918, II*, pp.27–8, 109.

11 See, for instance, Haig Diary, 7 June, 1917, PRO WO 256/19.

12 Harington, *Plumer of Messines*, pp.xiv-xv, 164–5, 191; Brigadier-General John Charteris, *At G.H.Q.*, Cassell, London, 1931, p.226.

13 General Sir Tom Bridges, *Alarms and Excursions*, Longmans, Green, London, 1938, pp.138, 163.

14 Haig to Robertson, 17 February, 1916, Robertson papers, Liddell Hart Centre for Military Archives, King's College London (hereafter LHCMA/KCL) I/22/23a; *OH, 1916, I*, pp.162–172.

15 Haig Diary, 18 February, 1916, PRO WO 256/8; Haig to Robertson, 18 February, 1916, Robertson papers, LHCMA/KCL I/22/24a.

16 Haig Diary, 21 and 23 April, 1916, PRO WO 256/9; *OH, 1916, I*, pp.177–191.

17 Powell, *Plumer: The Soldier's General*, p.153; see also Edmonds to Lieutenant-General Sir Aylmer Haldane, 17 March, 1931, Haldane papers, National Library of Scotland (NLS).

18 Charteris, *At G.H.Q.*, p.226.

19 Harington, op.cit., p.74.

20 *OH, 1917, II*, pp.9–20, also Appendix V, pp.206–7; 'Army Instructions for Main Offensive on Second Army Front', PRO WO 158/38; Kiggell to Plumer, 27 January, 1917, Kiggell papers, LHCMA/KCL 4/1–129; Second Army to G.H.Q., 30 January, 1917, PRO WO 158/38; Robin Prior and Trevor Wilson, *Passchendaele: The Untold Story*, Yale University Press, 1996, pp.45–8, 57–8; Andrew A Wiest, 'Haig, Gough and Passchendaele', in G.D.Sheffield (ed.), *Leadership and Command: The Anglo-American Military Experience since 1861*, Brassey's, London, 1997, pp.77–92.

21 Gough to Edmonds, 18 March, 1944, quoted in *OH, 1917, II*, p.127; see also Prior and Wilson, *Passchendaele*, pp.49–51; Powell, *Plumer*, pp.166–169; John Terraine, *Douglas Haig: The Educated Soldier*, Hutchinson, London, 1963, p.337.

22 Haig Diary, 22 May, 1917, PRO WO 256/18.

23 *OH, 1917, II*, p.418; Powell, op.cit., pp.184–6; Prior and Wilson, *Passchendaele*, p.65; Terraine, *Haig*, pp.315–317.

24 Haig Diary, 7 June, 1917, PRO WO 256/19; Charteris, op.cit., p.228.

25 Haig Diary, 25 August, 1917, PRO WO 256/21; Haig to Gough (OAD 609), 28 August, 1917, Fifth Army Operations File, August-October, 1917, PRO WO 158/250; 'Notes of a Conference held at Cassel on Thursday, 30th August, 1917', ibid., PRO WO 158/250; *OH, 1917, II*, pp.206–207; Prior and Wilson, *Passchendaele*, pp.108–110.

26 Haig Diary, 17 September, 1917, PRO WO 256/22. A copy of Haig's check-list, 'Questions to Corps', is attached to the diary.

27 *OH, 1917, II,* pp.296–9; 323–7; Prior and Wilson, *Passchendaele,* pp.133–8, 159–164; Powell, op.cit., pp.221–5.

28 *OH, 1917, II,* p.325; Prior and Wilson, *Passchendaele,* p.160.

29 David Lloyd George, *War Memoirs, Vol. V,* Ivor Nicholson and Watson, London, 1936, pp.2332, 2820–1; Harington, *Plumer,* pp.133–4; see also *Tim Harington Looks Back,* Murray, London, 1940, pp.167–8, although Harington's memory of dates is faulty in the latter account; Note made by Lord Stamfordham (Private Secretary to King George V) of a meeting with Lloyd George, 22 January, 1918, Royal Archives (RA) GV F1259/4; *OH, 1918, I,* p.88; Powell, op.cit., pp.247–253; Haig Diary, 15 February, 1918, PRO WO 256/27; Stephen Roskill, *Hankey: Man of Secrets, Vol.I, 1877–1918,* Collins, London, 1970, pp.493–6; Lieutenant-Colonel W.Robertson to Edmonds, 31 August, 1945, Edmonds papers, LHCMA/KCL VI/9. Lieutenant-Colonel Robertson was GSO1 (Operations) at Second Army headquarters in 1917–1918.

30 Haig to Plumer, 18 March, 1918, quoted in Harington, *Plumer of Messines,* p.147.

31 Haig Diary, 23 March, 1918, PRO WO 256/28.

32 Haig Diary, 24 and 28 October, 1918, PRO WO 256/37; *OH, 1918, V,* HMSO, London, 1947, pp.283–292, 426–453; Powell, op.cit., pp.276–8.

33 Quoted in James, *Imperial Warrior,* p.23; see also Gerard J.De Groot, *Douglas Haig, 1861–1928,* Unwin Hyman, London, 1988, p.48.

34 See, for example, the evidence of Lieutenant-Colonel E.A.Bradford (GSO1, Training, Third Army, in 1917) to Wavell, 27 January, 1937, Allenby papers, LHCMA/KCL 6/7/13, and Surgeon-General J.M. Irwin (Director of Medical Services, Third Army) to Wavell, 25 June, 1937, Allenby papers, LHCMA/KCL 6/7/36. Also Lieutenant-General Sir Charles Grant (GSO1 (O), Third Army), TS notes (5pp.) sent to Wavell with covering letter, 21 November, 1936, Allenby papers, LHCMA/KCL 6/7/25–6; J.F.C.Fuller to Wavell, 10 December, 1936, Allenby papers, LHCMA/KCL 6/7/23.

35 General Spencer E.Hollond (GSO1 (O), Third Army, 1916), TS notes (4pp.) sent to Wavell with covering letter, 4 December, 1937[?], Allenby papers, LHCMA/KCL 6/7/30–31.

36 James, op.cit., pp.45–6, 79–82; R.H.Andrew (ADC to Allenby, 1917) to Wavell, 17 October, 1938, Allenby papers, LHCMA/KCL 6/7/8.

37 James, op.cit., pp.77–80, 85–6, 91; Terraine, *Haig,* p.308; Robert Blake (ed.), *The Private Papers of Douglas Haig, 1914–1918,* Eyre and Spottiswoode, London, 1952, pp.158–9; Jonathan Walker, *The Blood Tub: General Gough and the Battle of Bullecourt, 1917,* Spellmount, Staplehurst, 1998, p.67; Lieutenant-Colonel H.W.Snow (AAG, Third Army), TS notes (5pp.) sent with covering letter to Wavell, 29 April, 1937, Allenby papers, LHCMA/KCL 6/7/55–6.

38 James, op.cit., p.84; Walker, *The Blood Tub*, p.67; Tim Travers, *The Killing Ground: The British Army, the Western Front and the Emergence of Modern Warfare, 1900–1918*, Allen and Unwin, London, 1987, p.106.

39 Rawlinson Diary, 23 and 24 February, 1916, Rawlinson papers, CC 1/5; Grant to Wavell, 21 November, 1936, Allenby papers, LHCMA/KCL 6/7/25–6; Spencer Hollond to Wavell, 16 October, 1938, Allenby papers, LHCMA/KCL 6/7/33.

40 Spencer Hollond to Wavell, 16 October, 1938, Allenby papers, LHCMA/KCL 6/7/33; Charteris. op.cit., pp.210–211.

41 Captain Cyril Falls, *Military Operations: France and Belgium, 1917, Vol.I*, Macmillan, London, 1940, pp.177–181, 541–2; Allenby to Major-General Sir Edward Spears, 31 October, 1934, Spears papers, LHCMA/KCL 2/3/1; R.H. Andrew, TS notes (16pp.) sent with covering letter to Wavell, 13 October, 1938, Allenby papers, LHCMA/KCL 6/7/7; Cyril Falls, notes on draft chapter by Wavell with covering letter, 13 October, 1938, Allenby papers, LHCMA/KCL 6/7/21–2; Rawlinson Diary, 26 January, 1917, Rawlinson papers, CC 1/7; Spencer Hollond to Wavell, 4 December, 1937[?], Allenby papers, LHCMA/KCL 6/7/30–1 ; Grant to Wavell, 21 November, 1936, Allenby papers, LHCMA/KCL 6/7/25–6.

42 Allenby to Lady Allenby, 11 April, 1917, Allenby papers, LHCMA/KCL 1/8/3.

43 James, op.cit., pp.102–3; *OH, 1917, I*, pp.279–80, 378–9; Haig Diary, 12, 13 and 14 April, 1917, PRO WO 256/17; Edmonds to Acheson, 19 July, 1950, and Acheson to Edmonds, 18 and 27 July, 1950, in correspondence relating to the 'Preparation of One-Volume History by Brigadier.-General. Sir J.Edmonds', PRO CAB 103/113, Items 101–2, 111. The divisional commanders in question were Robertson (17th Division), de Lisle (29th Division) and Wilkinson (50th Division).

44 James, op.cit., pp.103–7; Minutes of Conference at Noyelle Vion, 30 April, 1917, PRO WO 158/311; Memorandum to G.H.Q., 1 May, 1917, War Diary, Headquarters of Third Army, Appendix A30, PRO WO 95/361; Minutes of Conference at Doullens, 7 May, 1917, PRO WO 158/311; Haig Diary, 12 May and 15 June, 1917, PRO WO 256/18; Minutes of Conference at Doullens, 5 June, 1917, PRO WO 158/311; General Sir William Robertson to Haig, 15 April, 1917, Haig papers, NLS Acc.3155, No.112; Lieutenant-Colonel H.W. Snow to Wavell, 29 April, 1937, Allenby papers, LHCMA/KCL 6/7/55–6; Edmonds to Acheson, 19 July, 1950, PRO CAB 103/113, Item 102.

45 Major-General Sir Edward Spears, quoted in David R.Woodward, *The Military Correspondence of Field-Marshal Sir William Robertson, Chief of the Imperial General Staff, December 1915-February 1918*, Bodley Head for the Army Records Society, London, 1989, see 'Biographical

Notes', p.343; Charteris, op.cit., p.87; Maurice, *Life of General Lord Rawlinson*, p.xiii.

46 Travers, *The Killing Ground*, pp.105,166. De Groot, in *Douglas Haig*, pp.181–2, also suggests that Rawlinson was afraid and in awe of Haig, candour between the two becoming even less likely after Haig had saved Rawlinson from being sacked for command mistakes at Neuve Chapelle in March, 1915.

47 Rawlinson Diary, 4 April, 20 July, 4 August, 22 August, 29 September and 7 November, 1916, Rawlinson papers, CC 1/5 and 1/7.

48 Ibid, 10 August and 15 October, 1916, CC 1/5 and 1/7.

49 Ibid, 20 July, 1916, CC 1/5.

50 Travers, *The Killing Ground*, pp.127–146; Prior and Wilson, *Command on the Western Front*, pp.137–170, 395.

51 Rawlinson Diary, 8, 9, 11, 12 and 14 July, 1916, Rawlinson papers, CC 1/5;Haig Diary, 10, 11 and 12 July, 1916, PRO WO 256/11; 'Note of discussion as to attack of Longueval Plateau and the Commander-in-Chief's decision thereon', 11 July, 1916 (OAD 60), Fourth Army papers, IWM, Vol.1; ''Review of Discussion over Rawlinson's 14 July Night Attack', Advanced G.H.Q., 13 July, 1916, PRO WO 158/234; Travers, op.cit., pp.171–2; Prior and Wilson, *Command on the Western Front*, pp.192–5; *OH, 1916, II*, pp.62–88.

52 Note of an interview at Querrieu, at 11.00 a.m., 9th August, 1916, between Rawlinson, Kiggell, Montgomery and Davidson', Fourth Army papers, IWM. Vol. 2; Rawlinson Diary, 9 and 22 August, 1916, Rawlinson papers, CC 1/5; G.H.Q. to Fourth Army (OAD 123), 24 August, 1916, Fourth Army papers, IWM Vol.5.

53 Rawlinson Diary, 28, 29 and 30 August, 1916, Rawlinson papers, CC 1/5; Rawlinson to Advanced G.H.Q., 28 August, 1916, PRO WO 158/235 (with notes by Haig added in pencil on 29 August); Haig to Kiggell, 'Notes on September Offensive', 29 August, 1916, PRO WO 158/235; Kiggell, 'September Offensive. Discussion with Reserve and Fourth Army Commanders on 1 September, 1916', PRO WO 158/235; 'Report of Conversation between Commander-in-Chief and Rawlinson at Querrieu at 3.50 p.m.', 14 September, 1916, PRO WO 158/236; Haig Diary, 10, 11 and 12 September, 1916, PRO WO 256/13; Travers, op.cit., pp.178–180.

54 Rawlinson Diary, 29 January, 1917, Rawlinson papers, CC 1/7; Kiggell to Gough, 27 January, 1917, Kiggell papers, LHCMA/KCL 4/1–129; Kiggell to Plumer, 27 January, 1917, Kiggell papers, LHCMA/KCL, 4/1–129.

55 Rawlinson Diary, 7 May, 1917, Rawlinson papers, CC 1/7. In *Command on the Western Front*, Prior and Wilson render the word 'dispirited' as 'disgusted'.However one interprets Rawlinson's handwriting, it is quite

clear that he was unhappy at Haig's change of mind. See also Rawlinson to Kiggell, 8 May, 1917, and Kiggell to Rawlinson, 9 May, 1917, Kiggell papers, LHCMA/KCL 4/1–129; Andrew A.Wiest, *Passchendaele and the Royal Navy*, Greenwood, Westport, 1995, *passim*; William Philpott, 'The Great Landing : Haig's Plan to Invade Belgium from the Sea in 1917', *Imperial War Museum Review*, No.10, 1995, pp.84–9.

56 *OH, 1918, II*, pp.395–6. See also C.E.W.Bean, *Official History of Australia in the War of 1914–18, Vol.V : The Australian Imperial Force during the Main German Offensive, 1918*, Angus and Robertson, Sydney, 1939, pp.569, 571, 630.

57 Prior and Wilson, *Command on the Western Front*, p.300.

58 Haig Diary, 5 August, 1918, PRO WO 256/34.

59 Haig Diary, 14 August, 1918, PRO WO 256/34; Rawlinson Diary, 14 August, 1918, Rawlinson papers, CC 1/11.

60 Quoted in Maurice, *Life of General Lord Rawlinson*, p.250.

61 See De Groot, *Douglas Haig*, p.215, for the comment on Haig's relations with Rawlinson. Hubert Gough was born on 12 August, 1870, the next youngest Army commander in the First World War being Birdwood, who was born on 13 September, 1865. Gough was over thirteen years younger than Plumer (born 13 March, 1857).

62 Farrar-Hockley, *Goughie*, pp.164–5; Walker, *The Blood Tub*, pp.1–2, 7–10; Stephen Gwynn (ed.), *The Anvil of War: Letters between F.S.Oliver and his Brother*, Macmillan, London, 1936, p.144.

63 Farrar-Hockley, op.cit., pp.164–5; Walker, op.cit., pp.2, 7, 9–10; Ian F.W. Beckett, *Johnnie Gough VC : A Biography of Brigadier-General Sir John Edmond Gough, V.C., K.C.B.*, Tom Donovan, London, 1989, pp.148–9, 208.

64 See, for example, Rawlinson Diary, 1, 10, 17, 18, 19, 22 and 27 June, 1916, Rawlinson papers, CC 1/5.

65 Haig Diary, 20 July, 1916, PRO WO 256/11; Farrar-Hockley, op.cit., pp.188–9; Peter Charlton, *Pozières 1916 : Australians on the Somme*, Leo Cooper/Secker and Warburg, London, 1986, pp.124–5; *OH, 1916, II*, pp.114–6; Bean, *Vol.III : The Australian Imperial Force in France, 1916*, Angus and Robertson, Sydney, 1929, p.468. According to Charlton's analysis, it was the combined resistance of Major-General H.B. 'Hooky' Walker (commander of the 1st Australian Division), Birdwood (then commanding I Anzac Corps) and Major-General Brudenell White (Birdwood's chief of staff) that persuaded Gough to postpone the Australian attack on Pozières.

66 *OH, 1916, II*, pp.458–462, 476; Haig Diary, 12 November, 1916, PRO WO 256/14; Kiggell to Edmonds, 4 June, 1938, PRO CAB 45/135. See also Peter Simkins, 'Somme Footnote: The Battle of the Ancre and the

Struggle for Frankfort Trench, November 1916', *Imperial War Museum Review*, No.9, 1994, pp.84–101.

67   David R.Woodward, *Lloyd George and the Generals*, Associated University Presses, East Brunswick, New Jersey, 1983, p.151; De Groot, op.cit., p.307; Lord Esher, Journal, 9 March, 1917, see M.V. Brett and Viscount Esher (eds.), *Journals and Letters of Reginald Viscount Esher, Vol IV*, Nicholson and Watson, London, 1938, p. 95; General Sir Hubert Gough, *The Fifth Army*, Hodder and Stoughton, London, 1931, p.174; E.M.Andrews, 'Bean and Bullecourt: Weaknesses and Strengths of the Official History of Australia in the First World War', *Revue Internationale d'Histoire Militaire*, No.72, 1990, pp.25–30, 46–7; Walker, op.cit., p.69; Gough to Falls, 25 November, 1937, PRO CAB 45/116; R.H.Andrew to Wavell, 13 August, 1937, Allenby papers, LHCMA/KCL 6/7/7 and Grant to Wavell, 21 November, 1936, Allenby papers LHCMA/KCL 6/7/25–6.

68   See Travers, *The Killing Ground*, pp.203–217; Prior and Wilson, *Passchendaele*, pp.73–77; Wiest, 'Haig, Gough and Passchendaele', pp.81, 83, 90; Ian F.W.Beckett, 'Operational Command : The Plans and Conduct of Battle', in Peter H Liddle (ed.), *Passchendaele in Perspective: The Third Battle of Ypres*, Leo Cooper, London, 1997, pp.107–113.

69   Wiest, 'Haig, Gough and Passchendaele', p.90; Travers, *The Killing Ground*, pp.215–7; see also Travers, 'A Particular Style of Command: Haig and G.H.Q., 1916–1 8', *Journal of Strategic Studies*, Vol.10, No.3, 1987, pp.363–376, and particularly p.371.

70   Haig Diary, 7, 9, 10, 11 and 12 September, 5 October and 8 November, 1917, PRO WO 256/22, WO 256/23 and WO 256/24; also Farrar-Hockley, op.cit., pp.226–7; Beckett, 'Operational Command', p.110; Walker, *The Blood Tub*, p.71; B.H.Liddell Hart, Note of a conversation with Gough and Lloyd George, 27 January, 1936, Liddell Hart papers, LHCMA/KCL LH11/1936/31.

71   Haig Diary, 8 November, 1917, PRO WO 256/24; Farrar-Hockley, op.cit., pp.228, 239–240.

72   This 'loophole' was offered by Lord Derby to Haig on 5 March, 1918. Derby had earlier warned Haig, in November and December, 1917, about Gough's growing unpopularity in the BEF – particularly among Canadian units – as well as at home in Britain. Changes to Gough's staff appear to have assuaged the criticisms for a while. See Lord Derby to Haig, 11 November and 12 December, 1917, and 26 January and 5 March, 1918, Derby Papers, Liverpool Central Library (LCL), 920 DER (17) 27/2.

73   Haig Diary, 3 and 4 April, 1918, PRO WO 256/29; De Groot, op.cit., p.376; Farrar-Hockley, op.cit., pp.312–3; Lord Derby to Haig, 4 April, 1918, Derby Papers, LCL 920 DER (17) 27/2.

74 Edward Beddington, 'My Life', Beddington papers, LHCMA/KCL, pp.173–4.

75 Barrow, *Life of Monro*, pp.33–36, 114; De Groot, op.cit., p.219; Blake, *Private Papers of Douglas Haig*, p.71.

76 *OH, 1916, I*, pp.210–224; *OH, 1916, II*, pp.124–5, 134.

77 Haig Diary, 2, 3, 11 and 13 August, 1916, PRO WO 256/12.

78 Haig Diary, 11, 13 and 20 August, 1916, PRO WO 256/12; Horne, letters to his wife, 26 March, 11 April, 28, 29 and 30 August, and 26, 29 and 30 September, 1916, Horne papers, IWM 62/54/9.

79 Anderson, 'Lord Horne as an Army Commander', pp.408–9, 417–8.

80 Byng to his wife, 15 April, 1917, quoted in Williams, *Byng of Vimy*, p.165; Horne to Arthur Currie, 27 March, 1919, Horne papers, IWM 73/60/2; Tim Travers, 'Comment' in R.J.Q.Adams (ed.), *The Great War, 1914–1918: Essays on the Military, Political and Social History of the First World War*, Macmillan, London, 1990, p.186; Shane B.Schreiber, *Shock Army of the British Empire: The Canadian Corps in the Last 100 Days of the Great War*, Praeger, Westport, 1997, pp.4, 98–9.

81 Farrar-Hockley, op.cit., p.51; Major-General C.B.B.White, quoted in Denis Winter, *Haig's Command: A Reassessment*, Viking, London, 1991, p.267.

82 Captain Wilfrid Miles, *Military Operations: France and Belgium, 1917, Vol. III*, HMSO, London, 1948, pp.293–304; William Moore, *A Wood Called Bourlon: The Cover-up after Cambrai, 1917*, Leo Cooper, London, 1988, pp.165-200; Tim Travers, *How the War was Won: Command and Technology in the British Army on the Western Front, 1917–1918*, Routledge, London, 1992, pp.30–1 ; Williams, op.cit., pp.206–212; Lieutenant-General Sir Louis Vaughan,'Byng of Vimy: An Appreciation', *Army Quarterly*, Vol.LXXI, October, 1935, pp.11–16; Byng to G.H.Q., 'Secret', 18 December, 1917, PRO WO 158/54; Lieutenant-General Sir A.Hamilton-Gordon to CGS, 'Secret', 2 February, 1918, enclosing Cambrai court of inquiry 'Sequence of Events' and 'Causes of German Success', 29 January, 1918, PRO WO 158/53.

83 Byng to R.D.Blumenfeld (Editor of the *Daily Express*), 10 April, 1918, House of Lords Record Office HLRO B7.28.

84 Haig Diary, 19 and 21 August, 1918, PRO WO 256/35.

85 Haig Diary, 2 September, 1916, PRO WO 256/13; Blake, op.cit., p.290.

86 Bean Diary, Australian War Memorial (AWM) 38 3DRL/606–113, pp.10–11; Walker, op.cit., p.30; P.A.Pedersen, *Monash as Military Commander*, Melbourne University Press, 1985, p.298. Rawlinson also felt that 'Birdie is not much good at making plans', Rawlinson Diary, 24 May, 1918, Rawlinson papers, CCI/11.

87 Birdwood to Sir Ronald Munro Ferguson (Governor-General of Australia), 4 July, 1916, Birdwood papers, AWM, quoted in Pedersen,

Monash, p.155. In later life, Birdwood told the present Earl Haig of his warm affection and regard for the latter's father: Note from Earl Haig to the author, 22 January, 1999.

88 Gough, *Fifth Army*, p.145; E.M.Andrews, 'Bean and Bullecourt', pp.33–4.

89 Haig Diary, 1 August to 11 November, 1918, PRO WO 256/34, 256/35, 256/36 and 256/37. See also the entry on Birdwood in *The Oxford Companion to Australian Military History*, Oxford University Press, Melbourne, 1995, pp.97–8.

90 Travers, 'A Particular Style of Command', pp.363–376. See also *The Killing Ground*, pp.101–118.

91 G.H.Q. to Fourth Army (OAD 123), 24 August, 1916, Fourth Army papers, IWM , Vol.5.

92 Travers, 'A Particular Style of Command', p.373; Gough to Edmonds, 27 May, 1945, PRO CAB 45/140.

93 Brigadier-General John Charteris, *Field-Marshal Earl Haig*, Cassell, London, 1929, p.204; see also Haig Diary, 4, 15 and 25 March, 1916, and 30 August, 1918, PRO WO 256/9 and 256/35; and Rawlinson Diary, 9 December, 1916, and 14 June, 1917, Rawlinson papers, CC 1/7.

94 Haig Diary, 14 January, 1916, PRO WO 256/7; Travers, 'A Particular Style of Command', p.366.

95 Rawlinson Diary, 6 May, 1916, Rawlinson papers, CC 1/5; Haig Diary, 21 September, 1918, PRO WO 256/36.

96 These conclusions are based upon a detailed examination of the Haig, Horne and Rawlinson diaries for the periods in question.

97 Liddell Hart, talk with Lloyd George and Gough, 27 January, 1936, Liddell Hart papers, LHCMA/KCL LH 11/1936/31.

98 Prior and Wilson, *Command on the Western Front*, p.305.

99 Rawlinson Diary, 14 June, 1917, Rawlinson papers, CC 1/7; Haig to Wilson, 20 September, 1918, copy attached to Haig Diary, PRO WO 256/36.

Chapter 7

Haig and the Government, 1916 – 1918

Keith Grieves

Asquith resigned as Prime Minister on 5 December, 1916, and throughout the following day the War Office kept General Sir Douglas Haig, Commander-in-Chief, British armies in France, informed of political developments which led to the formation of Lloyd George's coalition government. Haig reflected sympathetically on Asquith's downfall but informed his wife, 'However, I expect more action and less talk is needed now'.[1] Earlier in December Haig received a visit from the newly appointed Master General of the Ordnance. His diary entry stated that he 'advised him to do his utmost to help Lloyd George as S[ecretary] of S[tate] for War, because he was really in earnest to win the war. Furse is rather apt to be "agin" the Government always, so I thought a word of friendly advice on my part would be helpful'. Haig contemplated Lloyd George's rise to the premiership with equanimity and believed that politicians would continue to defer to military advisers for the strategic direction of the war.[2]

During the political crisis of early December 1916 Haig gained no sense that the new government would seriously question his expectation that all material and manpower resources should be concentrated on the main front for decisive victory. On 23 November, 1916, he attended the War Committee and re-iterated the unified military perspective, long since accepted by Asquith, that 'since the principle that the Western Front is the decisive theatre of war had been officially accepted, we should faithfully give effect to everything which that principle implied'.[3] One week earlier, the paramountcy of the Western Theatre was endorsed at the Chantilly Conference, which accepted that resources sought for other theatres in 1917 would be reduced to reinforce the Anglo-French spring offensive on the main front. Haig demanded that Italian troops and guns should be sent to France and asserted that the despatch of two British divisions to Salonika could not be justified on military grounds. He had no reason to believe that his view in these matters would be questioned.

If there were occasional reasons for anxiety, these were more than offset by reassurances that energetic action was about to be taken to secure National Organization on the home front. In addition to relief at the prospect of firm political leadership, involving the enlargement of business expertise for supply ministries in Whitehall and the onset of industrial compulsion, Haig's one year old appointment as Commander-in-Chief was confirmed at the demand of senior Conservatives who joined the government on 7 December and through the promotion of Lord Derby to Secretary of State for War. This self-appointed soldier's friend was intent on ensuring that ministerial action at the War Office would always conform to the Western Front Strategy.

Furthermore, in these sanguine moments, Lloyd George's support for the 'knock out' blow was on public record and he had done more than most politicians to organize resources for artillery battles on the Western Front in 1917: firstly, as Minister of Munitions, in ending the shell crisis and rectifying gun ammunition output by the construction of national filling factories; secondly, in August 1916, as Secretary of State for War, by sending Eric Geddes to General Headquarters (GHQ), British armies in France to survey and improve communications behind the front line in the British zone. His appointment as Director General of Transportation was deftly managed by Lloyd George but always regarded by Haig as a fine exemplification of the benefits which GHQ obtained from readily welcoming temporary soldiers who had specific logistical expertise. Initially disputatious, Lloyd George and Haig eventually settled their differences on circumstances surrounding Geddes's appointment. Lloyd George concluded that Haig had 'showed himself a big man' in reconciling himself to the benefits of an expert civilian at GHQ.[4]

In contrast to Haig's centrality to strategic decision-making, Lloyd George frequently encountered the constraints of ministerial power during his period at the War Office and made little progress in 'the battle of civilian control'.[5] He extended the benefits of civil investigation from military railways to the army clothing department but found General Sir William Robertson, Chief of Imperial General Staff, resistant to any suggestion that plans for military operations should be more openly discussed in conferences of soldiers and statesmen. Lloyd George grasped a central Asquithian dynamic of civil-military relations in 1916 when he noted of his role that 'the soldier's view is that it is his duty to find the men, but that after they have been thrown into the cauldron, he has no further responsibility.'[6] On the question of whether great victories had really been secured during the Somme offensive, by 'using up our splendid men and our hoarded munitions', Lloyd George's plea for imagination, ingenuity and inventiveness in staff planning was unavailing.[7] These expressions of uneasiness by the people's tribune were not endorsed at meetings of the War Committee.

Haig had the support of Lord Esher and Lord Northcliffe in his assertion that the deployment and management of the British armies in France, and its conduct of war, lay beyond the purview of ministers who had no expertise with which to criticize generalship. In September 1916 Lord Esher's ill defined mission in France became more explicitly resistant of political interference in Haig's command. His advice was predicated on the existence of *another* public opinion, known to this courtly liaison officer, who were loyal to Haig and disliked 'a clever political adventurer seeking the limelight'.[8] In particular, anyone who sought 'the cheers of the soldiers' must be suspect.[9] In an era when public opinion could be variously defined, and rarely trusted to express its unguided thoughts, Lord Northcliffe, proprietor of *The Times* and The *Daily Mail*, drew authoritarian succour from ugly rumours in Paris, the views of friends in the Red Cross and privileged personal access to GHQ to demand general satisfaction that in the British army, 'From Havre to Pozières the organization is as well nigh perfect as it can be'.[10]

As the watchdog of the nation, Lord Northcliffe warned Lloyd George that 'some of your colleagues are dissatisfied with the losses. An indiscreet remark by one of your associates is being passed freely from mouth to mouth here. The troops at the front do not consider the losses dear in view of the fact that a breach in the German fortification has been made'. Beyond the supply of men, Lord Northcliffe asserted and publicized the notion that 'Ministerial meddling means military muddling'.[11] In the *Daily Mail* a 'Hands off the Army' campaign was mounted to preserve well-defined and apparently age-old spheres of military and civilian responsibility.[12] But the logical corollary of radical intervention in the economy, to improve the supply of munitions, was the scrutiny of material and manpower deployment in the theatres of war as the regulatory processes of the state, as producer and consumer of national resources, became more dominant.

The finite human and economic resources available in emergent total war conditions, in which Britain had rapidly assumed the role of a European land power, required regular political assessments of military plans which, hitherto, had gone unchallenged. Poor progress in this direction in the autumn months of 1916 reflected the focus on untrammelled continental war and the unwillingness of politicians systematically to manage material, manpower and morale. Instead, the army drew strength from patriotic goodwill bestowed in 'right minded' households. From this perspective the development of war weariness would always be difficult to comprehend and the increasing complexity of sustaining the economic infrastructure and social fabric of community life, alongside an insatiable attritional war, ill understood. In 1917–18 the gradual diminution of the 'large army first' principle, to strengthen neglected and crisis-ridden sections of the war economy, arose from a transformative political process which modified GHQ's presumption that 'wearing out' battles of long duration on the Western Front would lead to certain victory.

Lloyd George's intentions were diffuse and nebulous in aim and practical effect before he became Prime Minister, but on 24 December, 1916, Robertson informed Haig, 'There is a very dangerous tendency becoming apparent for the War Cabinet to direct military operations'.[13] This note of apprehension was premature. The War Cabinet was not an instrument of co-ordinated, civilianized strategic policy-making until December 1917. Instead, for many months, Lloyd George privately vented his frustration and quietly acknowledged his inability to determine the location and duration of Britain's contribution to the Western Front strategy in 1917. Lloyd George intended to become the trustee of lives at the front. In private conversation on 15 January, 1917, he noted, 'I will never let him [Haig] rest. I will raise the subject again and again until I *nag* him out of it – until he knows that as soon as the casualty lists get large he will get nothing but black looks and scowls and awkward questions'.[14] The weakness of Lloyd George's executive authority over the generals was painfully revealed in this statement. Gradually, the issue of manpower drove the politicization of the higher direction of the war in 1917 and greatly exacerbated the argument between continental and peripheral strategic options.

A new phase of inter-connected civil-military relations became apparent when three French journalists interviewed Haig on 1 February, 1917. Haig thought that the occasion went very well.[15] He drew attention to the shortage of gun ammunition, the new mileage of railways behind the British line and urged the necessity for concentrated effort on the Western Front.[16] He made it clear that a permanent peace would only ensue from the defeat of German armies on the battlefield. Lloyd George regarded the version which appeared in *The Times* as wholly unhelpful to the stiffening of home morale and controversial in its self-confident expectation that all available resources should be in France before the spring offensive. Brigadier-General Charteris, Chief of Intelligence at GHQ, censored the interview manuscript for military purposes but its political implications were not subjected to the same scrutiny.[17] Haig assumed that the journalists understood that he could not be quoted as a source of opinion. Charteris complacently concluded, 'I suppose these things appear larger to politicians at home than they do to us out here'. He referred to a 'trifling incident' but not for 'birds with ruffled plummage'.[18]

At GHQ this episode was simplified to the problem of dealing with sensitive, egotistical politicians who were intent on employing any incident to challenge Haig's authority. The issues were more deep seated, yet always interpreted at different levels of meaning and often in highly personal ways. For example, for Haig the significance of the Calais conference of 27–28 February, 1917 lay in the threat to his authority, and therefore to the prestige of the army, from the subordination of his command to General Nivelle's plans for a spring offensive. Without warning, this change in the system of command was sought by Lloyd George. Haig both offered and threatened to resign in the knowledge that the King, who was asked to remain watchful, supported him and that two members of the War Cabinet, Lord Curzon and Lord Milner, were uneasy about this experimental approach to Allied unity of command.[19] Haig wondered, 'Will History ever forgive the members of the War Cabinet for declining in January 1917 to have any confidence in the power of the British Army to play its part with credit on the Western Front?[20]

The Anglo-French negotiations contained deviousness on a magisterial scale but for Lloyd George its meaning was quite different as he attempted to curb British casualty rates on the Western Front.[21] Since September 1916 Lloyd George had regularly sought information on French fighting methods and concluded, from anecdotal evidence, that British troops should take responsibility for holding portions of the French line because 'If we lend them the men, they will take twice as much ground with half the loss'.[22] In his imitable 'Man for the job' approach, Lloyd George drew the disastrous conclusion that General Nivelle 'proved to be a Man at Verdun' and had the best record of success. According to Colonel Hankey, Secretary to the War Cabinet, Lloyd George met Haig's objections with the comment, 'Well, Field-Marshal, I know the private soldier very well. He speaks very freely to me, and there are people he criticizes a good deal more strongly than General Nivelle!'[23]

Lord Esher could not understand the 'mentality of the Prime Minister'.[24] However, the underlying issue was the Government's failure to adjudicate on conflicting demands for manpower early in 1917 and the survival of an unrestrained priority for military enlistment, which led to 329,000 new recruits in the first quarter of the year, within a total for 1917 of 820,000 men.[25] The War Office and GHQ continued to emphasize an insufficiency of new drafts which ensured that the 'man question' remained an issue of abiding concern in civil-military relations. In private letters to Haig, Robertson explained that the War Cabinet had not secured 'proper organization' in the country and 'are afraid to do more than has hitherto been done'.[26] Apart from unrealized War Cabinet threats to curtail drafts after April 1917 the unpleasant, 'first class row' at Calais illustrated the limited range of options open to the government as another year of battles on the Western Front beckoned politicians to acquiesce to the attritional imperatives of continental warfare.[27]

Haig remained steady and self-possessed in the unchanging knowledge, recorded in the opening month of the Somme offensive, that 'we must fully spend all we have, energy, life, money, everything in fact, without counting the cost. Our objectives cannot be obtained without the greatest sacrifice from each one of us'.[28] The belief that casualties were a necessary redemptive sacrifice on behalf of the nation, the unyielding view at GHQ that the British army had not failed and sharp condemnation of 'heretical amateur strategy' were fuelled by Lloyd George's attempts to reshape supreme command on the Western Front in February 1917.[29] Moreover, Haig successfully transformed his role as 'Chief of Staff' to Nivelle into a temporary arrangement. Lloyd George's inability to remove Haig and the subsequent failure of Nivelle's offensive, and his replacement on 15 May, 1917, ensured that civil-military relations in Britain were severely embittered without any advance in political control.[30]

As war weariness became more widespread in Britain after May 1917, Lloyd George realized that his 'unmitigated' defeat at Calais disadvantaged him in relation to Haig's urgent intention to inflict heavy losses on German divisions in Flanders.[31] On 1 May, 1917, Haig summarized the progress of the British offensive, which had commenced on 9 April, and presented plans to the War Cabinet for continuing to attack 'the enemy on a front where he cannot refuse to fight'. After outlining the guiding principles of 'wearing down' offensive action and expressing concern that British divisions were, in total, already 60,000 men below war establishment, Haig argued, 'The enemy has already been weakened appreciably but a long time is required to wear down such great numbers of troops composed of fine fighting material, and he is still fighting with such energy and determination, that the situation is not yet ripe for a decisive blow. Our action must therefore continue for the present to be of a wearing down character until his power of resistance has been further reduced'.[32]

Lord Milner noted the 'great *Messines* success, coming so soon after Vimy'.[33] Fortified by some acknowledgement of British advances, and by the parlous condition of the French armies after the Nivelle offensive, Haig sought confirmation in May, 1917, for an offensive 'to obtain valuable results on land and sea' or 'considerably improve our defensive positions in the Ypres salient'.[34] In the context of the race for food endurance, an emergency merchant shipbuilding programme to offset tonnage sunk by U-boats, air raids on London, the formation of radical discharged ex-servicemen's organizations and labour unrest caused by the extension of dilution in the engineering industry, Haig claimed, 'If our resources are concentrated in France to the fullest possible extent, the British armies are capable, and can be relied on, to effect great results this summer – results which will make final victory more assured and which may even bring it within reach this year'.[35]

Despite all the evidence which suggested that the need for economizing resources was the most appropriate guiding principle for governmental action, involving 'the best use of everything, not only of men but supplies, material, horses, petrol & c',[36] the War Cabinet moved to the dangerous conclusion that military advantages which might accrue from the Third Battle of Ypres would outweigh the political damage which would stem from its failure. No progress was apparent in enabling GHQ to understand why pessimism pervaded the deliberations of the War Cabinet at the prospect of a further offensive on the Western Front.[37] Lloyd George freely stated ' "grave misgivings of the advice" he had received from his Military Advisers'[38] but the Cabinet Committee on War Policy, in its exploratory survey of strategic options in June 1917, continued the practice of deferring to military expertise. On 19 June, 1917, the War Cabinet questioned Haig at length, to his irritation, and on 28 June Charteris noted that the Chief had encountered 'great difficulties' in London.[39] Soldiers and statesmen had yet to meet for truly discursive examination of the proposals.

The War Cabinet gave its formal approval for the Flanders offensive on 20 July, 1917, long after the decision had ceased to have any meaning in relation to the course of events on the Western Front.[40] Haig drew attention to 'very changed conditions of the German Army since the commencement of the Somme battle last July' by citing the shortage of German telephone equipment, the use of iron (rather than brass) cartridge cases and the generally reduced physique of men in German field units.[41] These remarks from intelligence summaries rarely proffered any limitation on the extent of gains envisaged in the field. Consequently, Cabinet approval included the remarkable provision that a 'step by step system of advance was adhered to' so that casualties would not mount as infantry moved ahead of artillery support.[42] Haig remained unflinching in his expectation that the government should restrict its energies to identifying the number of men available and, according to Kitchener's original instruction, 'placed at your disposal in order to carry out your mission'.[43] For example, in thanking Robertson for pursuing the 'man question' Haig noted, 'The country when it discovers what the Gov[ernmen]t has failed to do in this vital matter, will never forgive them'.[44]

On receiving unwanted advice on the depth to which advances might be planned, Haig insisted that 'he should have the confidence of his Government in his ability to judge' matters on the spot.[45] Put more broadly, the failure of the War Cabinet whole-heartedly to endorse the view that the war could only be won in Flanders persistently over-shadowed civil-military relations in the lengthening quest for the Passchendaele Ridge.[46] The War Cabinet had no control over the duration of the offensive. Furthermore, it had no criteria with which to judge success, or otherwise, as references to clearing the Belgian coast and a cavalry breakthrough were subsumed by the language of attritional warfare. In pursuit of 'Boche killing', Lieutenant-General Sir Launcelot Kiggell, Chief of the General Staff, proposed a nebulous modification of wearing out attacks 'to jump well within our power', in correspondence with General Sir Hubert Gough, commander of Fifth Army. Further, he reminded Gough, 'our politicians are not really whole-hearted in their belief in our power to win decisively and it is urgently important to convince them. Nothing will do that so surely as to let them see that at each bound we gain the line aimed at and main-tain it intact against counter-attack, and with moderate losses'.[47]

During the Passchendaele offensive another 'battle' took place in London over the control of manpower and future planning on the Western Front. In particular, deliberations in the months of September to November 1917 provided the genesis of a more unified, decisive War Cabinet which freed itself from the advocates of excessive continen-talism. Although purposeful and resolute, Haig felt keenly the damaging withdrawal of support from individual Cabinet ministers for the military, and hitherto dominant, perspective on the route to decisive victory and, thereby, the preservation of the existing social order.[48] He noted, 'I have been in the field now for 3 years & know what I am writing about'.[49] But his facts, or their categorization, into the poor state of German troops, the high standard of efficiency of British troops and the power of artillery to dominate enemy guns, were doubted and his conclusion that the morale of the Germany army was in permanent decline became illusory at Cambrai. Indeed, few German troops bolted at the sight of the tanks. Consequently, the 'desirability of pressing the Enemy all we can *before* winter in order not to give him time to train + refit during winter' became controvertible for politicians with widely varying backgrounds.[50]

Lord Milner was for so long the 'strongest member of the War

Cabinet and the best informed', in Haig's words, which meant that he was very supportive of the presuppositions of GHQ.[51] However, on 17 October he informed Lord Curzon, who was becoming ever more ambivalent in his adherence to the soldier's view, 'I am sorry to say that the doubts ... about the probability of success in the policy of Hammer, Hammer, Hammer on the Western Front, are becoming increasingly strong in my own mind'.[52] Similarly, the (fragile) unanimity of high military opinion found Andrew Bonar Law less responsive in September 1917 than had previously been the case. He told Lloyd George, 'I had lost absolutely all hope of anything coming of Haig's offensive and though he [Robertson] did not say so in so many words, I understood that he took the same view'.[53]

On 13 September Haig learned that Winston Churchill, Minister of Munitions, thought that the defeat of German forces on the Western Front was unlikely.[54] Six days later the Rev. George Duncan, Chaplain at GHQ, noted that 'The Chief has had a bad time with politicians of late' and recorded Lieutenant-Colonel Fletcher's plea, as ADC to Haig, ' "Why cannot they leave him alone?" [55] On this occasion the issue was the despatch of British guns from France to the Italian front. The War Cabinet's request was firmly stated and Haig was left in no doubt as to his course of action. Apart from Asquith, who favoured a 'vigorous offensive' on the Western Front and was 'head and shoulders above any other politician who had visited my H[ea]d Q[uarte]rs', [56] Haig enjoyed the visits of Sir Edward Carson to the front. He was the only member of the War Cabinet who adhered to the view that 'military experts must be given full power, not only to advise, but to carry out their plans'.[57]

Alongside Carson and Lord Curzon, Lord Robert Cecil dissociated himself from the despatch of guns to Italy. As a direct result of this decision he advised, 'so long as the Western Offensive continues, I cannot think that it is right to do anything which in the opinion of the Commander-in-Chief will interfere with its success'. However, few ministers supported the anachronistic recommendation of 'accepting responsibility for actions over which they have an incomplete control'.[58] The duration, intensity and ambiguous strategic significance of the Passchendaele campaign had rendered the fatalistic ministerial position of 'incomplete control' untenable. Accusations of interference enjoyed far less popularity as the decisions of military service tribunals encouraged the government to question the affordability of autonomous military decision-making which, encouraged by Lord Derby, existed beyond parliamentary scrutiny.

In the last three months of 1917 politicians took heed of the linkage between the rise of disaffected sectional interests, as a more pronounced form of war weariness, and the most disquieting feature of memoranda emanating from GHQ, namely, the optimistic rhetoric of 'wearing down' and 'decisive blow'. Instead, the arithmetical calculation of wastage rates based on casualty lists of 26,000 men per week led George Barnes to conclude, 'we cannot go on for long at that rate and I think Haig ought to be so informed'.[59] Consequently, Lloyd George announced his intention to challenge the principles of civil-military relations which were embedded in three years of acquiescing to the requirements of the generals in the field. At a meeting in Paris on 4 November, 1917, which Haig attended, Frances Stevenson recorded that Lloyd George 'made it quite plain that the time had come when he was going to assert himself, & if necessary let the public know the truth about the soldiers & their strategy'.[60]

At that meeting Lloyd George indicated his firm intention to obtain an inter-allied Supreme War Council (and transnational general staff) which, Haig knew, would subvert the concentration of resources on the Western Front. On 10 October, 1917, alternative military advisers, Field-Marshal Lord French and General Sir Henry Wilson, were asked to write independent papers on the present situation and future plans. Lord French placed emphasis on awaiting the arrival of American troops and Wilson recommended the overhaul of executive machinery for conducting the war.[61] Lloyd George relished this advice which was delivered by the end of the month. He became ever more intent to identify interchangeable resources for France and Italy and sustain British forces in Egypt as a focus for peripheral strategic options.

It was a measure of the distrust which existed between the chief protagonists in civil-military relations that Haig assumed that the Allied War Council was primarily designed to vindicate Lloyd George's 'conduct of war in the eyes of the public and try and put the people against the soldiers'.[62] On 12 November, 1917, the dispute between the government and its senior military advisers finally became public. Lloyd George aired his criticism in Paris of the cost of 'great victories' on the Western Front, which would have been outrageous interference in military affairs in 1915.[63] Ominously, for GHQ, Lloyd George signalled that the assumptions of 1916 and 1917 would have little influence in 1918.[64] The initiatives in the inter-allied control at Versailles were partly designed to modify national particularism, which was very evident at GHQ, and circumvent intransigent military opinion as an urgent response to the scarcity of railway equipment, coal and shipping as well as the need for a general reserve behind the front line in France and Flanders.

As statesmen became more confident in their relations with soldiers it is important to emphasise that the profound shift in their relations stemmed from political problems arising from the management of material, manpower and morale in the light of uncertain outcomes from the Western Front during 1917, rather than unforgiving personality clashes. Of course some senior Conservative ministers, such as Lord Derby, resisted the upsurge of doubt about the performance of GHQ to maintain an unchanging perspective on the proper separation of military and civilian activity which the War Cabinet had long since eschewed. It was also significant that at this stage in the war Lloyd George was resigned to Haig's survival in post and drew the conclusion that they could co-exist provided substantial modifications were made to GHQ's expectations for 1918, in the form of only allowing heavy counter-strikes on the Western Front.[65]

Furthermore, in the aftermath of the German counter-attack at Cambrai on 30 November, 1917, Lord Northcliffe's support for an autonomous GHQ, so important in 1916, ebbed away. He noted that the British people were at the end of their patience. He had 'heard much criticism from soldiers going on leave', specifically of Brigadier-General Charteris, who was removed because the diminution of German morale was much overdone at GHQ.[66] On this occasion Haig's support for Charteris was unavailing. He observed that his Chief of Intelligence had been made a ' "whipping boy" for the charge of undue optimism brought against myself'.[67] The departure of such an important member of his staff, against his will, was emblematic of the War Cabinet's determination to reduce the flow of speculative pronouncements on the imminent collapse of Germany. In December 1917 Lord Esher noted Lloyd George's determination to stop fresh offensives without the critical commentary which usually accompanied his descriptions of political activity which impinged on the Western Front.[68] He disengaged after years of informal representation of GHQ's interests in Paris.

On 10 December, 1917, the War Cabinet, sitting as a Committee on Manpower, finally initiated the most complete review of the labour supply and allocation of Lloyd George's premiership. It proceeded to reduce the army's demand for 600,000 men for 1918 to 150,000 men.[69] The 'frocks' had not wilfully subordinated the 'brasshats' but recognized the vital importance of maintaining shipbuilding, munitions production, aeroplane manufacture and manning warships for escort duties.[70] C.P. Scott, editor of the *Manchester Guardian* and staunchly supportive in this phase of reformulating the machinery of war, noted that, at last, Lloyd George was 'endeavouring to assert the authority of the civil power in determining policy and to curb the unlimited demands for men and to turn the Generals' flank by establishing the inter-Allied Council and making the Paris speech'.[71] Even Charteris appreciated that the 'inner meaning' of these developments was the manpower problem, whose solution was mistakenly assisted by Haig's opinion at the War Cabinet on 17 January, 1918, that he did not anticipate a German attack.[72] He hastened to rectify the meaning which was attached to this statement in a forum where he now vied with many competing claims for labour, munitions and shipping. Even Liberal ministers convened meetings to discuss evolving plans for military operations and assert the importance of the Supreme War Council.[73] The 'great results' expected in 1917 were barely tangible and Lord Northcliffe joined vociferous doubters who wondered what happened to men and materials when they fell under the management of GHQ. He felt that staff officers close to Haig needed to be told about conditions on the home front so that the structure and organization of the British armies in France could more accurately reflect the society from whence they came, 'The War is more than three-and-a-half years long. Every institution at home is being scoured for men. I went to my Paper Mill at Gravesend on Monday last, and found that practically the whole of the manpower had gone, the work being conducted by invalids, women and boys. I do not grumble. These Mills are only typical, but in common with others, I ask myself, what has become of the leaders of that enterprise who have gone into the Army?'[74]

By January 1918 Haig's complaints about 'the failure to maintain and increase the Army in France' were appreciated by few sources of opinion formation outside the *Morning Post* and the *Globe*. Lieutenant-Colonel Repington, beleaguered military correspondent at *The Times*, was invited by Haig, who cared little for his methods, to his home at Kingston Hill on 6 January, 1918, where their conversation was dominated by Haig's tendency to identify all disputes as undermining his authority and *ipso facto* of the 'spirit of the army, which was a 'delicate plant'. [75] Shortly afterwards, Repington referred to the 'shameful poltroonery' of the War Cabinet and assumed that Conservative members were 'mere ciphers'. [76] This was far from the case during the series of upheavals which culminated in the dismissal of Robertson in February 1918 and the replacement of Lord Derby by Lord Milner at the War Office in April 1918. At the *Morning Post* its editor, H.A. Gwynne, produced rancorous attacks on politicians who were guilty of 'incomparable treachery to the fighting men', largely by failing to apply military conscription to Ireland.[77]

Haig expressed his appreciation of the *Morning Post's* support[78] but his place in the higher conduct of the war, once so confident, was battered by reaction to the Passchendaele offensive and the reverse at Cambrai and the onset of the German spring offensive. Haig's reaction to the onslaught on 21 March, 1918, was slow and by early April he expected to be recalled to England.[79] Further, the dismantling of the Haig-Robertson-Derby triumvirate was now completed. Haig's close working relationship, and unity of purpose, with Robertson waned in the weeks before the latter's dismissal in February 1918 because the War Office secured so few recruits and Haig was prepared to work under schemes which emanated from the Supreme War Council.[80] However, Haig had no deep regard for Lord Derby and welcomed Lord Milner's arrival at the War Office. Otherwise, Charteris noted, Haig had few friends at the War Office or in the War Cabinet by June 1918.[81]

Insight into the necessity for the War Cabinet to obtain an overview was apparent in April 1918 as signified by the absence of sustained popular criticism, beyond Parliament, of the Prime Minister for reducing the despatch of drafts to France in the first quarter of the year. On the home front reasons for the retention of skilled labour of military age in protected occupations was understood, particularly in relation to the complex process of shipping the American Expeditionary Force to France. In April 1918 Lloyd George took control of the programme for reinforcing British divisions in France.[82] Thereafter Lloyd George, Lord Milner and Wilson, Chief of the Imperial General Staff, supervised the strategic direction of the war in the 'X' Committee so that the new equilibrium obtained in civil-military relations in December 1917 remained in place to the Armistice.[83]

Lord Milner's arrival at the War Office, as a "like minded" colleague of the Prime Minister, depersonalized much of the friction between Lloyd George and senior military advisers. Ministerial authority at the War Office was regained as Lord Milner took executive responsibility for the reconstitution of broken divisions and for the monitoring of advances after August 1918 with Wilson to ensure that there would be no more Passchendaele's as the Hindenburg Line was reached. As the general election drew near Haig hoped that Lord Milner would retain 'supreme direction of the Army'.[84] More explicitly, the War Cabinet became far less of a monolithic Lloyd George 'dictatorship' than Repington, Gwynne, Esher, Charteris and even Haig would have us believe.

After April 1918 Haig's qualified subordination to Marshal Foch and encouragement of plans submitted by army commanders, who gradually took the operational initiative from GHQ, has led to the suggestion that he 'retained only a symbolic form of leadership'.[85] For example, in September 1918 Haig was 'struck' by the tactical skill demonstrated by corps and divisional commanders. Otherwise, his correspondence continued to contain vignettes such as the German troops who no longer obeyed their officers on becoming prisoners.[86] This statement echoed remarks of one year before and appeared alongside the injunction 'we must keep at them'. Haig remained committed to 'wearing out' battles.[87] This change-resistant singleness of purpose, which required the government to accept a self-denying ordinance in matters of inspection, debate and review of policy, was a conceptual luxury which could no longer be afforded in 1918.

Late in 1917 and certainly throughout 1918 it became arguable whether a young fit man should, as a matter of course, be in the trenches in the Ypres salient or harvesting corn or constructing merchant vessels. As improvised procedures on manpower allocation were replaced by systematic priority statements on vital war work, the sustenance and social fabric of the home front became as central to the conduct of the war as the wearing out battles. The British armies in France became part of an Allied war effort which owed much to the maintenance of British naval and mercantile power. Haig's formative experiences and professional training did not prepare him for the decline of the hegemonic military institutions and the grim irony of 1917–1 8, namely, that the management of total war constrained the jurisdiction of 'men on horseback' because the army no longer embodied (literally) the national interest.[88] The reduction of his role and influence in 1918 was inversely related to the enlarging significance of British shipping, coal and munitions as a transatlantic policy was invoked. In December 1917 Britain stood on the threshold of continuing to dissipate resources for no obvious gain for another year. Instead, although the problem was inadequately explained to the generals, the existence of the army as a 'self-contained, separate entity' was necessarily curtailed.[89] Trial-and-error changes were made to civil-military relations to apportion dwindling resources for more precisely stated and definitely agreed objectives in which the vagaries of 'wearing out' rhetoric had no place. In this way victory was not postponed; it was rendered achievable within an Allied context.

As part of a traditional, military hierarchy, Haig's hostility to Lloyd George and most War Cabinet ministers remained constant from May 1917 to the end of the war. In April 1918 Lord Esher reminded him, 'Since the Somme battle these old gentlemen have been undoing the work of the youth of England under your command'.[90] On first sustained contact Haig found Lloyd George 'flighty' in planning and thinking, 'unpunctual', unduly interested in French ideas, un-gentlemanly and publicity-minded. Haig's own personality was revealed in this listing of antithetical character traits. He concluded with damning emphasis 'you will gather that I have no great opinion of L[loyd] G[eorge] *as a man or a leader*'.[91] After the Beauvais con-ference in April 1918 Haig wrote 'L.G. is a fatiguing companion in a motor. He talks and argues so! And he appears to me to be a thorough impostor'.[92] From the vantage point of muscular christianity Haig never accorded Lloyd George the accolade 'He's a man', so prevalent in his empathetic descriptions of 'supportive' public figures.[93]

To the end of the war and beyond Lloyd George and Haig would fail to agree on the course and significance of their militant co-operation. On 17 November, 1918, Haig observed that 'our rulers' instead of electioneering ' should be on their knees, thanking God for having preserved the Old Country and our liberties in spite of the Government'.[94] For Haig, Lloyd George's conceit and swagger knew no bounds and on being requested to participate in a triumphant Allied pageant in London, choreographed by the Prime Minister, and informed that he would be in the fifth carriage with Wilson, he furiously noted, 'The real truth, which history will know, is that the British Army has won the war in France in spite of L.G.'.[95] In 1940 Lloyd George ruminated on the necessity for honest appraisals of prospects from advisers in wartime. Thomas Jones recorded, 'L.G. has a rooted distrust of the military leaders carried over from the last war. "They were always exaggerating our gains and the enemy's losses. They lied to me. Haig lied to me. Charteris deceived me"'.[96]

Lloyd George and Haig had no affinity with each other's spheres of life and employed very different ways of justifying their actions. Haig commanded authority, enjoyed unanimity of military opinion, demanded sacrifice and assumed that the country was behind the army. Under his gaze single minded subordinates, with fixity of purpose, played a straight game. Lloyd George conjured consent, co-ordinated disparate resources, calculated wastage rates and hoped that the people maintained faith in victory. Their opinions diverged more often than they coalesced and their moods rarely coincided on the spectrum of confidence to gloom. Yet in 1918 they managed to sustain an exhausted British army as a vital ingredient of Allied victory. On his welcome home Haig noted 'the people of England realize what has been accomplished by the Army and myself'.[97] Since 1918 an assessment of this statement has, increasingly, become more problematic. Consequently, debates initiated at the time on the changes in civil-military relations in the crucial emergent years of total war, 1916–18, look set to continue as a lively historiographical dimension of Passchendaele and its aftermath.

Notes.

1   R Blake (Ed.) *The Private Papers of Douglas Haig 1914–1 919*, London, Eyre and Spottiswoode, 1952, Haig to Lady Haig, 6 December, 1916, p. 184.

2   *Ibid.*, Haig diary, 2 December, 1916. In particular, Haig's admiration for Asquith was not translated into hostile remarks about Lloyd George during his rise to the premiership.

3   *Ibid.*, Haig diary, 23 November, 1916, p. 182.

4   Lord Riddell *War Diary 1914–1918*, London, Ivor Nicholson and Watson, 1933, 20–22 November, 1916, p. 236.

5   T Wilson (ed.) *The Political Diaries of C.P. Scott 1911–1 928*, London, Collins, 1970, 20–22 November, 1916, p 230.

6   Lord Riddell *War Diary 1914–1 918*, 21–25 October, 1916, p. 216

7   A.J.P. Taylor (ed.) *Lloyd George. A Diary by Frances Stevenson*, London, Hutchinson, 1971, 23 November, 1916, p.127.

8   P. Fraser *Lord Esher. A Political Biography*, London, Hart-Davis, MacGibbon, 1973, War journals, 17 September, 1916, p. 331.

9   *Ibid.* War journals, 17 September, 1916, p.331.

10 Lord Northcliffe to D. Lloyd George, 6 August, 1916, Add.Ms.65157, Northcliffe mss., British Library (BL).

11 *Daily Mail*, 13 October, 1916.

12 J.M. McEwen 'Northcliffe and Lloyd George at war, 1914–1 8', *The Historical Journal,* Vol. 24(3), 1981, p.659.

13 D.R. Woodward (ed.) *The Military Correspondence of Field-Marshal Sir William Robertson, Chief Imperial General Staff, December 1915-February 1918,* London, The Bodley Head, 1989, W. Robertson to D. Haig, 24 December, 1916, p. 132.

14 A.J.P. Taylor *Lloyd George. A Diary by Frances Stevenson.* 15 January, 1917, p. 139.

15 R. Blake (ed.) *The Private Papers of Douglas Haig 1914–1 919*, Haig diary, 1 February, 1917, p. 194.

16 G.J. De Groot *Military Miscellany I The Rev. George S. Duncan at GHQ, 1916–1918*, Stroud, Gloucs, Sutton Publishing, 1996, Duncan diary, 25 February, 1917, p. 325.

17 See the full collection of papers on the subject of 'Haig's alleged interviews with the French press', in 27/2, Derby mss. Liverpool Record Office (LRO).

18 J. Charteris *At GHQ*, London, Cassell, 1931, 20 February, 1917, p. 194.

19 P. Fraser *Lord Esher. A Political Biography*. Memorandum by Lord Stamfordham, 12 March 1917, p. 357; A.J.P. Taylor (ed.) *Lloyd George. A Diary by Frances Stevenson*, 16 March 1917, p. 147; W. Robertson to D. Haig, 6 March 1917, I/23/11, Robertson mss, LHCMA.

20 D. Haig to W. Robertson, 15 April, 1917, I/23/19, Robertson mss, LHCMA.

21 J Turner, *British Politics and the Great War. Coalition and Conflict 1915–1918*, London, Yale University Press, 1992, p. 165.

22 A.J.P. Taylor (ed.) *Lloyd George. A Diary by Frances Stevenson*, 15 January, 1917, pp. 135 and 139.

23 S. Roskill, *Hankey. Man of Secrets*, London, Collins, 1970, Vol. 1, 1877–1918, Hankey diary, 26 February, 1917, p. 363.

24 P. Fraser *Lord Esher. A Political Biography*. War journals, 7 March, 1917, p. 355.

25 K. Grieves *The politics of manpower, 1914–18*, Manchester, Manchester University Press, 1988, p. 217.

26 W. Robertson to D. Haig, 7 February, 1917, I/23/4, Robertson mss., LHCMA. See also W. Robertson to D. Haig, 14 April, 1917, I/23/18, Robertson mss., LHCMA.

27 A.J.P. Taylor (ed.) *Lloyd George. A Diary by Frances Stevenson*, 16 March, 1917, p. 147.

28 Haig diary, 16 July, 1916, No. 107, Acc. 3115, Haig mss., National Library of Scotland (NLS).

29 L. Kiggell, 10 January, 1917, quoted in Gerard J. De Groot, *Douglas Haig, 1861–1928*, London, Unwin Hyman, 1988, p.286. See also J. Charteris *At GHQ.*, 1 March, 1917, p. 195.

30 J. Turner *British Politics and the Great War* p. 164; on Lloyd George's inability to impose his wishes on military advisers in 1917 see D. French ' 'A One-Man Show' ? Civil-Military Relations in Britain during the First World War' in P. Smith (ed.) *Government and the Armed Forces in Britain 1856–1990*, London, Hambledon Press, 1996, p.77.

31 J. M. Bourne *Britain and the Great War 1914–1918*, London, Edward Arnold, 1989, p. 151; A.J.P. Taylor (ed.) *Lloyd George. A Diary by Frances Stevenson.* 12 May, 1917, p.157.

32 Quotations in this paragraph are taken from D. Haig, 'The Present Situation and Future Plans', May, 1917, with Haig's letter to W. Robertson, 1 May, 1917, 27/5, Derby mss., LRO.

33 Lord Milner to D. Haig, 9 June, 1917, F.130–1 , dep. 354, Milner mss., Bodleian Library, Oxford (BLO)

34 D. Haig, 'The Present Situation and Future Plans', May, 1917, 27/5. Derby mss., LRO.

35 Memorandum by D. Haig, 22 June, 1917, 1/50, Kiggell mss., LHCMA. On the socio-economic conditions of the home front during this period see the excellent coverage in D. French *The Strategy of the Lloyd George Coalition 1916–1918*, Oxford, Clarendon Press, 1993, pp. 82–92.

36 J. Smuts to D. Lloyd George, 21 June, 1917, F/45/9/9, Lloyd George mss., House of Lords Record Office (HLRO).

37   See Haig's comment on being questioned by members of the War Cabinet, 'all tending to show that each of them was more pessimistic than the other' R.Blake (ed.). *The Private Papers of Douglas Haig 1914–1919*, Haig diary, 19 June, 1917, p. 240.

38   Lloyd George's misgiving was recorded by Haig in his memorandum of 22 June, 1917, II/11/2, Kiggell mss. LHCMA. See also Minutes of the Cabinet Committee on War Policy, 19 June, 1917, CAB 27/6, Public Record Office (PRO); Lord Riddell *War Diary 1914–1918*, 5 August, 1917, p. 263.

39   J. Charteris *At GHQ* 28 June, 1917, p. 233.

40   J. Turner *British Politics and the Great War* p. 204.

41   Haig's memorandum, 22 June, 1917, II/11/2, Kiggell mss., LHCMA. See also D Haig to D. Lloyd George, 28 July, 1917, F/44/3/17, Lloyd George mss., HLRO.

42   W. Robertson to D. Haig, 18 July, 1917, I/23/38, Robertson mss., LHCMA. See also D. French *The Strategy of the Lloyd George Coalition 1916–1918*, p. 290.

43   R. Blake (ed.) *The Private Papers of Douglas Haig, 1914–1919*, Kitchener's instruction to Haig, 28 December, 1915, p. 121.

44   D. Haig to W. Robertson, 9 August, 1917, I/23/43b, Robertson mss. LHCMA.

45   D. Haig to W. Robertson, 21 July, 1917, No. 115, Acc 3155, Haig mss., NLS.

46   See W. Robertson to Lord Milner, 7 August, 1917, f.247, dep. 45, Milner mss., BLO.

47   L. Kiggell to H. Gough, 7 August, 1917, 4/1–129, Kiggell mss., LHCMA.

48   See D. French. *The Strategy of the Lloyd George Coalition 1916–18*, p.92.

49   D. Haig to W. Robertson, 13 August, 1917, I/23/44, Robertson mss., LHCMA.

50   D. Haig to Lord French, 20 August, 1917, Box 75/46/11, French mss., Imperial War Museum.

51   R. Blake (ed.) *The Private Papers of Douglas Haig 1914–1919*, Haig diary, 7 May, 1917, p.229.

52   Lord Milner to Lord Curzon, 19 October, 1917, f. 225 dep. 354, Milner mss., BLO. Lord Milner told Sidney Low 'Almost all high military opinion is against us, and the majority of the Cabinet bow – not always with conviction – to the unanimity of military opinion. I hope we are both wrong', 17 October, 1917, f. 26 dep. 354, Milner mss., BLO.

53   A. Bonar Law to D. Lloyd George, 18 September, 1917, 84/6/127, Bonar Law mss., HLRO.

54   Haig diary, 13 September, 1917, No. 117, Acc. 3155, Haig mss., NLS.

55 Gerard J. De Groot *Military Miscellany I, Rev. George Duncan at GHQ*, Duncan diary, 19 September, 1917, pp. 383 and 384.

56 Lord Riddell *War Diary 1914-1918*, 9 September, 1917, p.271.

57 Haig diary, 14 and 18 September, 1917, No. 117, Acc. 3155, Haig mss., NLS.

58 Lord Robert Cecil to A. Bonar Law, 10 September, 1917, 82/4/9, Bonar Law, mss., HLRO. Privately, Robertson was assured of support but the situation had changed. W. Robertson to D. Haig, 9 October, 1917, No. 118, Acc. 3155, Haig mss., NLS. See also J. Turner *British Politics and the Great War* p. 223.

59 G. Barnes to D. Lloyd George, 29 October, 1917, F/4/2/14, Lloyd George mss., HLRO.

60 A.J.P. Taylor (ed.) *Lloyd George. A Diary by Frances Stevenson*, 5 November, 1917, p. 163.

61 H. Wilson to L. Kiggell, 25 October, 1917, III/5, Kiggell mss., LHCMA. On Wilson's informal work for Lloyd George see C.E. Callwell *Field Marshal Sir Henry Wilson .His Life and Diaries*, London, Cassell, 1927, Vol. 2, pp. 16-17; S. Roskill, *Hankey Man of Secrets* Vol. 1, p. 442; J.M. McEwen ' "Brass-hats" and the British press during the First World War', *Canadian Journal of History* Vol. 18(1), 1983, p. 59.

62 R. Blake (ed.) *The Private Papers of Douglas Haig, 1914-1919*, Haig diary, 4 November, 1917, p. 263.

63 Enclosure to written draft of 'Paris Speech' F/234, Lloyd George mss., HLRO; M. Hankey *The Supreme Command, 1914-1918*, London, Collins, 1961, Vol. 2, p. 728; *Spectator* 17 November, 1917; Haig to Lady Haig, 14 November, 1917, No. 148, Acc. 3155, Haig mss., NLS; D. Woodward *Lloyd George and the Generals* Newark, New Jersey, Associated University Press, 1983, pp. 224-6.

64 D. Lloyd George *War Memoirs*, London, Odhams Press, 1938, Vol. 2, pp. 1408-9 and 1468-9.

65 T. Wilson *The Political Diaries of C.P. Scott 1911-28*, Diary entry for 16-19 October, 1917, pp. 321-3.

66 Lord Northcliffe to Major-General Charteris, 11 December, 1917, Add. Ms. 62159, Northcliffe Mss., BL. See also W. Robertson to H. Plumer, 10 December, 1917, I/34/41. Robertson mss., LHCMA.

67 D. Haig to Lord Derby, 10 December, 1917, 27/3, Derby mss., LRO. See also J. Charteris *At G.H.Q.*, 12 December, 1917, p. 273.

68 P. Fraser *Lord Esher. A Political Biography*, War Journals, 1 December, 1917, p. 375.

69 Minutes of the Man-Power Committee, 10 December, 1917, CAB 27/14, PRO.

70 K. Grieves *The politics of manpower, 1914-18*, p. 174., J Turner 'Lloyd George, the War Cabinet and High Politics' in P.H. Liddle *Passchendaele*

in Perspective. The Third Battle of Ypres, London, Leo Cooper, 1997, p. 24.

71   T. Wilson *The Political Diaries of C.P. Scott*, 28 December, 1917, p. 325.

72   J. Charteris *At GHQ*, 26 January, 1918, p. 282; W. Robertson to D. Haig, 7 January, 1918, I/23/77, Robertson mss., LHCMA.

73   C. Addison *Politics from within 1911–1918*, London, Herbert Jenkins Ltd., 1924, Vol.2, pp. 234–8.

74   Lord Northcliffe to Sir Philip Sassoon, 17 January, 1918, Add Ms. 62160, Northcliffe Mss., BL.

75   C à C Repington *The First World War 1914–1918*, London, Constable, 1920, Vol 2, p.173, 6 January, 1918.

76   *Ibid* Vol. 2, p. 180, 10 January, 1918.

77   K. Wilson (ed.) *The Rasp of War. The Letters of H.A. Gwynne to the Countess Bathurst*, London, Sidgwick and Jackson, 1988, H.A. Gwynne to Lady Bathurst, 30 December, 1917, p. 236.

78   *Ibid*. H.A Gwynne to Lady Bathurst, 22 May, 1918, p. 282.

79   *Ibid*. H.A. Gwynne to Viscount Esher, 9 April, 1918, p. 264.

80   Philip Sassoon sought to counter the impression that 'D.H. did agree positively to the scheme whereas in fact he did not and only said he would try to work *whatever* was settled'. H.J. Creedy to Lord Derby, n.d. 27/8, Derby mss., LRO.

81   J. Charteris *At GHQ*, 18 June, p. 314.

82   See D. Lloyd George to A. Bonar Law, 10 April, 1918, F/30/2/31. Lloyd George mss., HLRO; Minutes of the War Cabinet, 29 March, 1918, CAB 23/5 PRO.

83   J Turner 'Cabinets, Committees and Secretariats: the Higher direction of War' in K Burk (ed.) *War and the State. The Transformation of the British Government, 1914–1919*, London, George Allen and Unwin, 1982, p.166; K.O. Morgan 'Lloyd George's Premiership: A Study in "Prime Ministerial" Government', *The Historical Journal* Vol 13 (I), 1979, p. 138; D. Woodward *Lloyd George and the Generals* pp 304–305.

84   D. Haig to Lord Milner, 20 November. 1918, F. 87, dep 46, Milner mss., BLO.

85   T. Travers *How the War was won. Command and technology in the British Army on the Western front 1917–1918*, London, Routledge, 1992, p.175.

86   The preceding quotation and remarks are drawn from D. Haig to Lord Milner, 5 September, 1918, f. 162–3, dep. 355, Milner mss., BLO

87   T. Travers *How the War was won* p. 32. See, for example, R.Blake (ed.) *The Private Papers of Douglas Haig 1914–1919*, Haig to W. Churchill, 3 October, 1918, p.329.

88   On the soldiers' lack of understanding of alliance diplomacy see J. Gooch 'Soldiers, Strategy and War Aims in Britain 1914–18' in B. Hunt and A.

Preston (eds.) *War Aims and Strategic policy in the Great War*, London, Croom Helm, 1977, p.27. See J.M. Bourne *Britain and the Great War 1914–1918*, p.153; S.E. Finer *The Man on Horseback*, Harmondsworth, London, 1975, pp. 30–34.

89 D. French *The Strategy of the Lloyd George Coalition 1916–1918*, p. 106. See also T. Travers 'The Evolution of British Strategy and Tactics on the Western Front in 1918; GHQ, Manpower and Technology', *The Journal of Military History*, Vol. 54, 1990, pp 177, 199.

90 P. Fraser *Lord Esher. A political biography*, Lord Esher to D Haig, 29 April, 1918, p. 393.

91 Haig diary, 13 and 15 September, 1916, No. 131. Acc. 3155, Haig mss., NLS.

92 Haig diary, 8 April, 1918, No. 125, Acc. 3155 Haig mss., NLS. See also Lady Cynthia Asquith *Diaries 1915–18*, London, Century Hutchinson, 1987 reprint, 23 May, 1918, p. 44.

93 G.J. DeGroot *Military Miscellany I*, Duncan diary, 8 July, 1917, p. 362. See also the entry for 22 July, 1917, p.364.

94 R Blake (ed.) *Private Papers of Douglas Haig 1914–1919*, D. Haig to Lady Haig, 17 November, 1918, p. 407.

95 Haig diary, 30 November, 1918, No. 132., Acc. 3155, Haig mss., NLS.

96 T. Jones *A Diary with Letters 1931–1950*, London, Oxford University Press, 5 September, 1940, p. 469.

97 R Blake (ed.) *The Private Papers of Douglas Haig 1914–1919*, Haig diary, 19 December, 1918, p. 349.

Chapter 8

Haig and Britain's European Allies

William Philpott

Amongst the principal responsibilities of a commander in a coalition war is liaison with allies. This was especially the case in the special circumstances of the campaign on the Western Front. Sir Douglas Haig's army was deployed along a section of a static joint front for most of his period of command, alongside the French army, the principal army of the coalition; moreover, the British army was quartered and in action on French soil, with the declared objective of liberating it from enemy occupation. An analogous situation existed on the extreme northern flank, where Haig concentrated his offensive effort. Here the small Belgian army commanded by its strong willed monarch, King Albert I, clung on to the last corner of unoccupied Belgian territory with British and French support. Thus Haig was obliged to work on a daily basis with Britain's allies, in a situation in which his freedom of military action might be constrained by the demands of allied politics. This aspect of Haig's command responsibilities, essentially a political function, has been played down in studies which concentrate on Haig's military role and his relations with his political masters in London. Therefore an assessment of Haig's relations with his allies in the principal theatre will contribute to understanding the full nature of the Commander-in-Chief's duties.[1]

In an assessment of Haig's relations with his allies, as in any attempt to evaluate Haig's abilities and limitations, the principal contemporary source is Haig's own diary and correspondence.[2] While the diary inevitably gives a rather one sided view, there is no equivalent source for the other side of the relationship. The diary's value lies in the fact that within it Haig was able to vent his spleen at his allies with more candour than was ever possible in the formal correspondence, meetings and conferences through which inter-allied business was conducted.

For example, after attending the Versailles Supreme War Council on 2 July, 1918, Haig typically wrote:

> I found the [Prime Minster] very angry with the French because they were taking too large a share in the direction of the war, and gave little credit to Britain for what she was doing. The latest enormity is that a M. Tardieu, a journalist on the staff of *Le Matin*,[3] had taken up the question of bringing American troops to Europe and had allotted British tonnage for this purpose without any preliminary discussion with London! I was glad to see that Lloyd George was at last angry with the French because the French have acted in this style since the beginning of the war, only Mr. L. G. and others in the Government thought it necessary to give the French a free hand for fear that they would make peace if they did not.[4]

This extract effectively demonstrates the basic nature of the alliance in which Haig was a key figure; one beset by suspicion, antagonism and double-dealing, that was barely masked by the shared commitment to holding together to defeat their common enemy.[5] Haig's attitude and actions need to be understood in this context.

Haig approached this aspect of his duties with his customary determination and narrow-mindedness, although not without a certain degree of common sense.[6] Respect, flexibility and empathy are perhaps the key to effective coalition warfare, characteristics lacking on both sides of the Entente for much of the First World War. In this Haig was no exception. Haig's underlying suspicion of French methods and intentions is obvious from his diary record. Haig detected political influence and interest behind much French military decision making, especially in relation to Allied co-operation,[7] a tradition abhorrent to the constitutionally minded British officer. His allies in his view were determined to get all that they could from the British, by underhand methods if they could get away with them.[8] They paid no heed to British sensitivities – Haig felt he had to be constantly on his guard against schemes to assert French authority over the British army, or even to break it up and amalgamate it with the French army.[9] All this he felt was motivated by inherent resentment: 'Some Frenchmen find it hard to conceal their jealousy of Great Britain. They hate to think that the British army is on French soil saving France!!'.[10] In these circumstances Haig felt his primary responsibility was to defend the interests of his army in a sometimes fraught coalition campaign;[11] although his uncompromising attitude must be recognized as one of the factors which contributed to the indifferent management of the joint campaign on the

Western Front in particular, and more generally to inter-allied tensions in the broader coalition war effort.

Haig's role in the alliance was twofold, both military and political. On a day to day basis Haig had to liaise with the French high command about the preparation and conduct of joint operations. Such issues as when and where to launch offensive operations, the integration of British planning with that of *Grand Quartier Général* (GQG – French General headquarters), the defensive security of the front, and the extension of the British line, were constant preoccupations. Less frequently, Haig participated in the politico-military conferences and correspondence which governed the higher direction of the war in its non-military or non-European aspects; in 1916 and 1917 at the series of intermittent co-ordinating conferences that stood in for effective alliance management, and from the end of 1917 at the allied Supreme War Council which superseded them.

There were some who doubted Haig's suitability for the supreme command, since he had acquired a reputation for not getting on with the French.[12] Having served a lengthy apprenticeship, both as a corps commander in the war of movement in 1914, and as an army commander in the trench battles of 1915, Haig was already well acquainted with both the personalities and the methods of the French army when he moved to General Headquarters (GHQ) in December 1915. Both these earlier commands necessitated frequent liaison with the French units flanking Haig's troops, either to co-ordinate offensive effort, as at Guise in 1914 and Loos in 1915, or to conduct the defensive battle, as at Ypres in 1914. Unfortunately Haig's first experiences of co-operation with the French, during the retreat from Mons, were disastrous. They appear to have prejudiced Haig's attitude for the rest of the war. Ever after he held an irrational grudge against the 'decadent' race who in his opinion no longer possessed the martial qualities of their ancestors. The declining fighting ability of the French army, and their ever-growing need for firm British support and guidance, is a constant refrain throughout Haig's diary.[13] Indeed Haig's chaplain's diary hints at inherent francophobia on Haig's part.[14] While it might be going too far to accuse Haig of xenophobia,[15] there is no doubt that, typical of the jingoistic Briton of his day, commanding the mass army of the world's greatest empire gave him an innate sense of superiority over the foreigner. Such an outlook is reflected clearly in Haig's practical dealings with his allies.

On a more mundane level, it is clear from Haig's diary that at times the differences in operational and administrative methods of the two allied armies were a cause of tension.[16] In the heat of battle operational disagreements might arise, and individual Frenchmen might cause offence.[17] Certainly Haig had learned from experience that the French could be demanding and domineering in their approach to joint operations, and Haig took this impression with him to GHQ. For his part, he was not prepared to capitulate to French pressure if he thought it would compromise the interests of the British army, and had a poor opinion of British officers who were.[18] Nevertheless, it is evident that he intended to respect his ally's experience and sensibilities in the exercise of his command; Lord Kitchener's briefing before Haig took command had made this point clear:

> I was ... to keep friendly with the French. General Joffre should be looked upon as the Commander-in-Chief in France, where he knew the country and general situation well. .... we must do all we can to meet the French Commander-in-Chief's wishes whatever our personal feelings about the French Army and its Commanders.[19]

As far as personal feelings went, Haig was a close observer of character, and knew what he liked in a Frenchman. Indeed, in the pen portraits that Haig made of the individual Frenchmen that he met, it is clear that the Frenchmen that Haig liked best were those who were most like Englishmen! In this Haig demonstrated the traditional social and class prejudices of the turn of the century British officer corps. Reticence, gentlemanliness and breeding were qualities that he appreciated. French bluster, and their lackadaisical approach to joint arrangements, he deplored.[20] His description of his well-liked liaison officer Colonel des Vallières after their first meeting clearly illustrates his preferences: 'I am quite impressed with him. So quiet and silent for a Frenchman – and such a retiring gentlemanly man. Yet he has seen much and read much'.[21] Compare this with his attitude to General Nivelle after the latter had tried to give orders to the British army after the signing of the Calais command agreement in February 1917: 'it is a type of letter which no gentleman could have drafted .... N[ivelle] asked me to go to lunch, but I am glad of a real excuse for refusing – it will make him understand that he cannot play the "cad" one day, and expect me to be as friendly as before next week'.[22]

What is also apparent from Haig's pen portraits is that his opinion of individual Frenchmen would change according to whether they were supporting or opposing Haig's own objectives. Nivelle on their first meeting had been 'a most straightforward and soldierly man', an energetic replacement for Joffre in whom Haig had lost confidence.[23] Joffre in his time had been an agreeable collaborator: 'Not clever but reliable I should think and most ready to listen to any suggestion which I had to offer ... '.[24] Haig came during the course of 1916 to dislike his manner and resent his methods. Joffre was adopting the usual pattern of ungentlemanly behaviour typical of a Frenchman. For example, attempting to make a bargain with Haig that the latter would provide the French army with British workmen in exchange for a loan of French field guns provoked the typical comment: 'The truth is that there are not many officers in the French staff with gentlemanly ideas. They are out to get as much from the British as they possibly can.'[25] More worryingly, by the spring, when the shock of the opening of the battle of Verdun had caused GQG to panic and make frantic demands for British support, it appeared to Haig that Joffre was no longer up to the heavy responsibilities of his position.[26] The rest of the year was marked by growing tension between the two.

As well as having to deal on a day to day and month to month basis with individual Frenchmen, Haig had to have the broader military picture clearly in mind. Unlike Sir John French before him, Haig was well aware when he assumed command that Britain was the junior military partner, and that there was a need to work within appropriate parameters.[27] Yet over the years of Haig's command the two allied armies were to change, and with them the nature of the alliance relationship. The British army expanded, and grew in experience and confidence, and was ultimately to become the principal fighting force of the coalition. Meanwhile, the French army, as Haig was only too well aware and dwelt on at length in his diary, shrunk and declined in confidence and effectiveness. Haig was well aware that the war would be lost if the French army collapsed, and struggled to balance this fundamental truth with his own inclinations and personal opinions of the French. When faced with difficult strategic choices in the summer of 1917 following the breakdown of French morale, Haig neatly summed up his stance on alliance relations:

> We could see Italy and even Russia drop out, and still continue the war with France and America. But if France drops out we not only cannot continue the war on land but our armies in France will be in a very difficult position.
>
> To keep France in does not entail our following her advice blindly, or committing further mistakes to please her politicians. But we must be prepared to lighten the burden on her Army, by taking over all the line we can take *during the winter*, without detriment to our offensive next year.[28]

It was this paradoxical position with which he struggled until the British government resolved it by accepting the reality of the military position on the Western Front and formally subordinated Haig to the recently appointed French generalissimo, Foch, in the summer of 1918.[29]

Although well aware that the French were the political and military lynchpin of the alliance, having been given a mission to perform by the British government which did not involve subservience to the French, Haig resented political or allied interference in his arrangements for conducting the British military campaign. To this end Haig developed a style of negotiating with his allies which involved judicious concession over details coupled with a careful defence of his own, and his army's, interests.[30] In the negotiations over the battle of the Somme in the early months of 1916 this style was honed and entrenched.[31] Haig neatly summarized his methods when recording the crucial meeting with Joffre on 14 February, 1916: 'I had an anxious and difficult struggle. I had to be firm without being rude to gain my points.'[32]

By December 1915, when Haig assumed command of the British armies in France and Flanders, relations between the British army and their French allies were already troubled. This was partly a consequence of the British government's preoccupation with operations outside the main, western, theatre and the consequent slow build up of Britain's military forces there. But it mainly resulted from the fact that Haig's predecessor Sir John French had, owing to his obstinate demeanour and volatile temperament, helped to create a climate of misunderstanding and mistrust between the allied commands.[33] Taking command at the end of a year in which the French army had borne the major offensive burden, with casualties in proportion, Haig was anxious about the French army's staying power if the war was prolonged, and felt that the British had to give firm support and clear guidance to their wavering allies.[34] Haig recognized that one of his first tasks was to restore harmonious military co-operation, which involved steering a fine line between: 'put[ting] the British case and co-operat[ing] with the French in aiming at getting decisive results in their plan of operations'.[35]

Haig was to find these two objectives hard to reconcile when it came to negotiating with the French. As a loyal comrade Haig was happy to accept French directions magnanimously; but as an independent commander Haig was not prepared to be ordered about by the French. This distinction lay at the root of many of the disagreements Haig had with his French opposite number. When appointed he made it clear to des Vallières that, 'I am *not under* General Joffre's orders, but that would make no difference, as my intention was to do my utmost to carry out General Joffre's wishes on strategical matters, as if they were orders'.[36] In the short term this approach produced a great improvement in allied empathy. At the first meeting of French army group commanders that Haig attended the French premier, Briand, remarked that 'if the present good feeling had existed between us from the commencement the situation would now be very different'.[37]

However, in the detailed negotiations over the 1916 offensive campaign which followed, Haig's determination to put the British army's case led to considerable friction. Having formed a low opinion of the fighting qualities of the inexperienced British army during 1915, Joffre proposed that in the coming joint offensive the British army should carry out the attrition of the enemy before the French army delivered the decisive blow. The prospect of an attritional offensive, on a front dictated by Joffre, did not appeal to Haig, especially as it appeared to him that the French were prepared to sacrifice British lives to economize on French casualties.[38] It took two months of patient negotiation, in which Haig's diplomatic abilities were tested to the full, before an agreement was reached over the nature of the forthcoming western offensive. Haig was not to carry out the attritional offensive which Joffre had expected, but the British army was obliged to attack alongside the French on the Somme, suggesting that Haig had failed to convince Joffre that his army was capable of independent offensive action. It had been a painful initiation into the realities of coalition war-making. Haig confided to his wife when the negotiations had finished: 'The French are really very tiresome, but one has to keep on friendly terms. The truth is that we are too much of gentlemen for them. They mean to get all they can out of us and some of them don't stick at a lie to benefit their case! However, I try to do what is right.'[39] Yet French testimony suggests that it was not only Haig who had a hard time during these negotiations. Des Vallières' correspondence with Joffre demonstrates a growing exasperation with Haig's attempts to rewrite the allied battle plan in his favour. Ultimately he was recommending strongly to Joffre that a firm hand should be taken with the awkward British Commander-in-Chief to ensure he fell into line with French intentions.[40]

Tensions were experienced in the conduct as well as the planning of joint operations. There is no clearer example of Haig's prickly attitude when dealing with the pretensions of the French Commander-in-Chief than during the first week of the Somme offensive. After the disastrous first day the joint plan had to be reviewed. For Haig, the need to conform to French strategic directives had to be reconciled with main-taining tactical independence. From Haig's diary entry of his meeting with Joffre on 3 July one gets the impression that Haig had to defend his point of view against the domineering French commander (admit-tedly this is a fault which Joffre often showed in dealing with his allies). On Haig suggesting that the British exploit their partial success on the right of their front only, Haig records:

... Joffre exploded in a fit of rage. ... I waited calmly until he had finished. His breast heaved and his face flushed! ... When Joffre got out of breath I quietly explained what my position is relatively to him as the "Generalissimo". *I am solely responsible to the British Government for the action of the British Army*; ... I was most polite. Joffre saw he had made a mistake and next tried to cajole me. ... I smoothed old Joffre down. He seemed ashamed of his outburst. ... However, I have gained an advantage through keeping calm. My views have been accepted by the French ....[41]

However, on this occasion we have an account of the meeting from the French side which paints a rather different picture. Since the British failure on 1 July only confirmed Joffre's belief that the British had not yet mastered offensive tactics, Joffre reverted to his original conception of the joint offensive – that the British army should wear down the enemy on their front while the French exploited the gains they had made on the first day. Joffre's official diary records that at their meeting on 3 July, after Haig proposed to reduce the scope of British operations north of the Somme, it was only 'with difficulty and by using [my] authority, that Haig was persuaded to give up his project'. Joffre's point of view would seem to have prevailed; following the meeting, Joffre recorded that the British were now to carry out a methodical attack all along the line 'rather than trying to break through and push cavalry through the breach'. Yet the next day, when des Vallières reported his impressions of the meeting to Joffre, it was clear that Haig had not been won over; he was complaining that 'one does not treat a gentleman this way', and proposing once again an attack on the British right. Although Haig did not deny that he was under orders to obey Joffre's general strategic directives, he continued to assert his complete liberty to determine the tactical means of executing them. Eventually Joffre gave in despite disapproving of the British plan, feeling that after the initial British failure it was necessary to allow Haig a chance of success.[42]

The immediate consequence of this particular incident was that Joffre left Haig to work out the tactical details of the offensive with his subordinate Foch, with whom Haig was on rather better terms,[43] and for the next two-and-a-half months the allied armies were effectively conducting separate offensive operations side by side, rather than the co-ordinated strategic operation they had prepared. This detailed example, the only one in which both sides of the story were recorded at the time, clearly illustrates the delicate relationship between the allied commanders in the field.

Things could get even worse when politicians intervened. At the

Calais conference in late February 1917, probably the most unfortunate episode in the history of the Alliance, the British and French governments tried to spring on Haig a formula that would formally subordinate the British army to the French. Haig's reaction can be predicted. It was not so much the Calais agreement itself which Haig resented, for Haig felt that this only confirmed in writing the existing command relationship: 'I have always acted on General Joffre's "General Instructions" as if they had been Orders, but retained absolute freedom of action as to how I carried them out'.[44] But, as detailed above, Nivelle's haughty and ungentlemanly interpretation of the agreement aroused Haig's indignation.

After Nivelle's offensive failed, the Calais agreement was quietly forgotten, and Haig and Pétain, Nivelle's successor, were left to sort out their own arrangements for joint operations. Pétain was the kind of Frenchman whom Haig could get on with: 'most clear-headed and easy to discuss things with . . . businesslike, knowledgeable and brief of speech. The latter is, I find, a rare quality in a Frenchman!'[45] Their working relationship proved close enough to check political interference with military affairs. For example, the Versailles Supreme War Council was unable to overcome their concerted opposition to the further extension of the British line and the creation of an allied general reserve in the winter of 1918.[46] But it proved a brittle comradeship, and when it broke down in the face of the 1918 German offensive it exposed the allies to the prospect of defeat.

Now Haig exposed the better side of his nature. At the moment of greatest danger he was willing to sacrifice his own personal interests to ensure the cohesion of the alliance. To ensure co-ordination he willingly subordinated himself to General Foch's overall strategic direction at the Doullens conference on 26 March. After the German spring offensive had broken through at the junction of the allied armies Haig recognized that something had to be done to ensure the allied armies were not divided. For all his obstreperousness, Haig was well aware that in France a Frenchman must command.[47] Since Pétain had shown himself 'upset, almost unbalanced and anxious' in the face of the crisis, and Foch was 'sound and sensible . . . [and] has brought great energy to bear on the situation', it was 'essential to success that Foch should control Pétain'.[48] If it meant that he had to control Haig as well, that was a sacrifice worth making in the greater allied cause.[49]

Generally Foch's style of command, which he had learned after nearly four years of close association with the British army – to lead rather than command, as he himself described it[50] – was agreeable to Haig, even if he had always had a rather ambivalent relationship with the man himself. Although they still had frequent disagreements over strategy and tactics,[51] Foch always made a point of consulting Haig for his opinion, even if he would often overrule it. Consequently their relations were based on mutual understanding and respect.[52] Nevertheless Haig's relations with Foch could still be fractious when the former's hackles were up. There is a real sense of *déjà vu* on reading Haig's record of his meeting with Foch to discuss following up the successful British offensive at Amiens: 'I spoke to Foch quite straightly and let him understand that *I was responsible to my Government and fellow citizens for the handling of the British forces*'.[53] Foch was clearly, Haig later carped as the allied armies pushed on to victory under his leadership,'suffering from a swollen head, and thinks himself another Napoleon!'[54]

As for Britain's lesser European allies, Haig was even less understanding, and felt little need for the restraint and tact which he himself expected from the French. Haig raised no objection to the Portuguese Expeditionary Force being subordinated to the British command in exactly the sort of relationship that he refused to contemplate with the French! It is clear that he held the small Portuguese contribution to the allied cause in contempt; their presence was a necessary political gesture rather than an asset to the alliance.[55] The troops he felt were unreliable – they 'ran away' during the German spring offensive, stealing bicycles from the British reserves to speed their retreat! Their officers were even more contemptible – mostly 'conceited wretches' in Haig's considered judgement.[56]

Haig thought little better of the Belgian army.[57] Haig was constantly anxious about whether their troops would be able to hold their line in the event of a German offensive in the north.[58] Their offensive potential seemed no better. Their staff officers, whom Haig met on a regular basis, did not impress. Their Chief of Staff, General Wielemans, Haig commented, was 'a nice kindly old man, but quite stupid and I should say very lazy. He was chosen by Baron de Broqueville (Minister of War) on account of those qualities I believe.'[59] General Ruquoy, his successor, 'talked a great deal with a Walloon accent, and seemed very ignorant of a soldier's work. He gave me the impression he is in a funk of the Germans and that he could not expect his troops to withstand a German attack! I formed a poor opinion of the man as a soldier and of his determination as a man.'[60] Haig's real problem with the Belgians was with their Commander-in-Chief and King, Albert I, who was totally opposed to the idea of an allied offensive into Belgium for fear of the damage it might cause. As the sovereign of an allied nation the King could not be browbeaten into submission, and Haig returned empty-handed and bitter from his visits to Belgian headquarters when the question of offensive operations in Flanders was on the agenda.[61]

Haig, like many of the alliance's leaders, reserved his greatest contempt for the Italians. Following an allied conference on 21 March, 1916, he observed: '*Son Excellence le General Porro* from Italy impressed me badly. He read out at intervals lengthy documents bearing on various points as they arose, with the one object of showing why Italy can do *nothing*! ... The Italians seem a wretched people, useless as fighting men, but greedy for money. Moreover, I doubt whether they are really in earnest in this war. Many of them too are German spies.'[62] Given that this is typical of his comments whenever he encountered them it is probably a good thing that he only met Italians at the occasional conference and never had to co-operate with them in the field.[63]

While Haig's day to day business was with allied generals, on occasion he would have to deal with allied politicians. Haig had a rather difficult relationship with British politicians, and the same might be expected when he was faced with French statesmen. He always believed that in dealing with politicians the military should hold a united front, and therefore adhered strictly to the principle that he would not furnish French politicians with information that might undermine the authority of French military leaders.[64] Yet, somewhat two-facedly, Haig was not himself averse to using his contacts with French politicians to advance his own interests with respect to the French military leaders.

As with French generals and British politicians, Haig's relations with French politicians (perhaps the worst possible combination) were volatile and often antagonistic. Haig naturally took to French politicians who seemed genuinely interested in helping the British, and took against those, such as the French President, Raymond Poincaré, who seemed to be out to get all they could from the British, and would put political self-interest above military considerations.[65] Of all the French politicians Haig had to deal with, he had the most regard for General Lyautey, Minister of War in late 1916 and early 1917. Lyautey was the sort of Frenchman Haig could understand – 'a thorough gentleman whom I can trust' – and Haig was not afraid to share with him his problems with Nivelle and his staff.[66] He empathized with Lyautey as a fellow soldier stoically doing his duty 'in a Government of political jugglers with a Chamber of semi-lunatics', and was genuinely saddened when the French Chamber forced his resignation in March 1917, especially as he was to be succeeded by a revolutionary socialist.[67]

Things were less simple when it came to civilian politicians. In fact, the revolutionary socialist, Paul Painlevé, who soon became premier, proved to be 'a pleasant bright little man ... most anxious, he says, to keep on the most friendly terms with the British'. Yet despite being given the opportunity to air his grievances about the Calais agreement and its consequences, Haig loyally responded with nothing but praise to Painlevé's questions about Nivelle's suitability for his task.[68] Haig was keen to ensure that Painlevé supported his views on strategy before the French commander-in-chief, while declining to get involved in French military politics, which he feared would undermine close relations with the French in the field and hence compromise the success of joint operations.[69] Haig was more suspicious of the less genuine French politicians, such as the French premier in the early period of his command, Aristide Briand. Briand was 'a very charming but a cunning and quick-minded man ... thoroughly French'.[70] Briand showed his true colours at the Calais conference, after which Haig was only too happy to refuse his invitation to lunch.[71] Yet there was one French politician with whom Haig got on well from the start, Georges Clemenceau. He was impressed by 'the Tiger's' energy and common sense'.[72] During the last year of the war when Clemenceau was premier their close relationship proved useful when Haig enlisted Clemenceau's support to solve his problems over the General Reserve proposed by the Supreme War Council.[73]

Haig did not find dealing with allies easy. At the height of his difficulties, following the Calais conference, he had occasion to lament, 'all would be so easy if I only had to deal with the Germans!'[74] Yet he himself believed that he dealt with the special pressures of coalition war effectively. In the post-war memorandum on his command which Haig prepared for posterity he assessed the nature of relations between the allied armies:

French Generals had undoubtedly made some serious miscalculations at the outset of the campaign and subsequently. It was impossible for the British Commander in Chief not to realise this and while it did not detract from his respect and friendship for our Allies, from his admiration for all they had done, or from his determination to co-operate loyally and whole heartedly with them, as he did, it made it a very serious matter for him to submit his judgement to theirs. His men and his country looked to him for their welfare and he could not be wholly relieved by anyone of that responsibility.[75]

When it came to matters of detail:

the right and duty of independent judgement conferred on him, with the assurance of the support of the British government behind it, enabled him to take a firm, though courteous, stand whenever he was urged to any procedure which he judged unwise, detrimental to his own and there-fore to the Allied Armies, or unlikely to advance the object in view. Such occasions ... were rare, thanks partly to the readiness with which Sir Douglas Haig complied with all the demands made on him to which he saw no vital objection, and thanks also perhaps to our Allies being aware of his independent position and of the trust reposed in him by the govern-ment.[76]

Although an anodyne and self-serving document, which fails to convey the lively and sometimes troubled nature of the relationship which resulted, it clearly states the principles and practice which in his own mind governed Haig's dealings with the French army. While Haig attempts to assume the moral high ground, detailed examination of events has suggested that this attitude was not conducive to allied harmony.

It cannot be denied that a great deal of the misunderstanding which characterized Haig's relations with his allies was the product of differing national characteristics as well as conflicts of personality. But Haig's dealings with the French do not reveal his better side. Nivelle's frustrations, his British liaison officer recorded, were rooted in the fact that Haig 'attached undue importance to matters of prestige and was lacking in that spirit of co-operation without which work between allies was so difficult'.[77] Certainly Haig's relations with the French were very formal, and rarely cordial. Foch commented caustically on his relation-ship with Joffre: they 'exchange letters every 15 days, and as neither says anything they are in "perfect" agreement'.[78] Haig clearly had a highly developed sense of moral superiority and self-importance. Even when he did not get his own way, his diary tends to dress up compro-mises as successes. While it is to his credit that he was able to compromise, if rarely with good grace, as his predecessor Sir John French could not, his attitude at times smacks of hypocrisy. Through bitter experience, Haig had by the summer of 1916 made sure that GHQ 'always had everything in writing in their dealings with France'.[79] But he was later to complain that: 'we trusted in [French] good faith without any written documents, while they never would believe us but invariably wanted "an agreement in writing" duly signed'.[80] Moreover, Haig was fickle in his affections when it came to individual Frenchmen. The list of those who went down in his estimation once they had let him down is long. Perhaps, fundamentally, Haig felt he had been let down by the whole French nation as early as August 1914 and the retreat from Mons, when he had been left in the lurch by the French troops on his right flank,[81] and nothing in his future dealings with the French was to assuage this disillusionment.

While historians might criticize Haig for being difficult with his allies, they might have criticized him more for being subservient to them. As a professional soldier, Haig's loyalty was to his army not his allies, and his primary focus was on following his orders and doing his duty. After battling with Foch near the end of the war to regain command of the British Second Army, he felt obliged to tell him 'a few "home truths", for when all is said and done, *the British Army has defeated the Germans this year*, and I alone am responsible to the British government for the handling of the British troops'.[82] Such an attitude was never going to endear Haig to his allies or improve the efficiency of the alliance.

Notes

1   His chaplain, the reverend George Duncan, neatly summed up the true nature of Haig's role when he recorded that beating the Germans was the least of Haig's problems compared with his troubles from 'the unstable and unreliable French and interfering and character-less politicians'. Duncan diary, 23 October, 1917, 'The Reverend George S. Duncan at GHQ, 1916–1 8', in A.J. Guy, R.N.W. Thomas and G.J. De Groot (eds), *Military Miscellany I*(Stroud: Sutton Publishing Ltd for the Army Records Society, 1997), p. 399. It has been suggested that this aspect of Haig's command was played down in the 1930s by historians anticipating a future coalition war to avoid harming the Anglo-French relationship. See R. Blake (ed.), *The Private Papers of Sir Douglas Haig* (London: Eyre & Spottiswoode, 1952), pp. 51–2.

2   The diary is most accessible in the published edition, R. Blake (ed.), *The Private Papers of Sir Douglas Haig*, hereafter cited as Blake. The full diary and correspondence are to be found in the Haig papers in the National Library of Scotland, Edinburgh.

3   In fact Tardieu was high commissioner for foreign affairs with special responsibility for Franco-American relations.

4   Haig diary, 2 July, 1918, Blake, pp. 317–8.

5   The nature of the alliance is examined in W.J. Philpott, *Anglo-French Relations and Strategy on the Western Front, 1914–1918* (London: Macmillan, 1996), especially pp. 161–5.

6   For examples see Haig diary, 23 and 29 June and 31 August, 1915, Haig papers.

7   Haig diary, 12 February, 1916, Haig papers.

8   For examples see Haig diary, 17 November, 1914, 6 August, 1915 and 24 February, 1916, Haig papers.

9   His attitude is neatly summarized in Haig to Robertson, 11 March, 1917, Haig papers, 111.

10 Haig diary, 20 February, 1916; see also Haig diary, 8 September, 1917, Haig papers.

11 Haig diary, 8 March, 1917, Haig papers.

12 Report on visit to France and Belgium', by Wedgewood, Mottistone papers, Nuffield College Oxford, file 3, fol. 17; Wilson diary, 21 December, 1915, Sir Henry Wilson papers, Imperial War Museum, London.

13 Duncan diary, 29 April and 1 October, 1917, in 'Duncan at GHQ', pp. 349 and 395–6. See the introduction in Blake, pp. 51–6.

14 Duncan diary, 29 April, 1917, *ibid.*

15 In assessing Haig's relations with the French Blake concluded, 'occasional outbursts of annoyance' on Haig's part 'were never judgements of value upon the character of the French people', and relations with senior French figures generally remained cordial. Blake, p. 56.

16 Haig diary, 7 November, 1914, Blake, p. 77.

17 See for example, Haig diary, 9 November, 1914 and 24 April, 1915, Blake, pp. 77 & 91.

18 Notably the chief liaison officer between the Allied headquarters in 1915, Lieutenant-General Sir Henry Wilson. Haig diary, 18 December, 1914, Blake, p. 81.

19 Haig diary, 3 December, 1915, Blake, p. 115.

20 Haig diary, 24 September and 19 and 20 November, 1914, Haig papers.

21 Haig diary, 1 January, 1916, Blake, p. 122. Des Vallières it would seem grew rather less fond of the British. E.M. Spears, *Prelude to Victory* (London: Jonathan Cape, 1939), p. 132.

22 Haig diary, 28 February, 1918, and Haig to Lady Haig, 3 March, 1917, Blake, pp. 203 and 207.

23 Haig diary, 20 and 28 December, 1916, Blake, pp. 187–8.

24 Haig to Robertson, 3 January, 1916, Robertson papers, Liddell Hart Centre for Military Archives, Kings College London, I/22/6.

25 Haig diary, 28 March, 1916, Blake, p. 136.

26 Haig diary, 25, 27, 28 and 29 February, 8 March and 7 April, 1916, Blake, pp. 133–5 and Haig papers.

27 Haig diary, 1 January, 1916, Blake, p. 122.

28 Notes, 22 July, 1917, Haig's emphasis, Blake, p. 247.

29 W.J. Philpott, 'Britain and France go to War: Anglo-French Relations on the Western Front, 1914–1918', *War in History*, II (1995), 43–64: pp. 49–53.

30 Philpott, *Anglo-French Relations and Strategy*, p. 100. See also 'Notes for CGS on taking over more French line', 21 December, 1915, Haig papers, 104.

31 For details see Philpott, *ibid.*, pp. 112–21.

32 Haig diary, 14 February, 1916, Blake, p. 129.

33 Philpott, 'Britain and France go to War', pp. 55–6.

34 Haig diary, 11 November, 1915, Blake, p.112, and introduction, pp. 52–3.

35 Haig diary, 17 October, 1915, Blake, p. 109.

36 Haig diary, 1 January, 1916, Haig's emphasis, Blake, p, 122.

37 Haig diary, 29 December, 1915, Haig papers.

38 Haig diary, 2 February, 1916, Haig papers.

39 Haig to Lady Haig, 23 February, 1916, Haig papers, 156.

40 See correspondence in the Joffre papers, especially Des Vallières to Joffre, 10 January and 5 February, 1916, Service Historique de l'Armée de Terre, Vincennes, 1K268/3.

41 Haig diary, 3 July, 1916, Haig's emphasis, Blake, pp. 154–5.

42 Joffre journal, 2, 3 and 4 July, 1916, G. Pedroncini (ed.), *Journal de Marche de Joffre, 1916–19* (Vincennes: Service Historique de l'Armée de Terre, 1990), pp. 31–8.

43 Joffre journal, 2 July, 1916, *ibid.* p. 36.

44 Haig diary, 27 February, 1917, Blake, p. 202.

45 Haig diary, 3 and 18 May, 1917, Blake, pp. 226 and 232.

46 Philpott, *Anglo-French Relations and Strategy*, pp. 151–3.

47 Haig diary, 2 May, 1918, Blake, p. 308.

48 Haig diary, 24, 26 and 29 March, 1918, Blake, pp. 297–9.

49 Haig diary, 3 April, 1919, Blake, p. 360.

50 Sir G. Aston, *The Biography of the Late Marshal Foch* (London: Hutchinson and Co., [1929]), pp. 227–8.

51 For example during the second German spring offensive in Flanders. Haig diary, 9, 10 and 14 April, 1918, Blake, pp. 301–3.

52 The nature of their relationship is examined more fully in Philpott, *Anglo-French Relations and Strategy*, pp. 156–60. See also, Philpott, 'Britain and France go to War', pp. 59–60.

53 Haig diary, 14 August, 1918, Haig's emphasis, Blake, pp. 323–4.

54 Haig diary, 27 October, 1918, Blake, p. 207.

55 Duncan diary, 8 July, 1917, 'Duncan at GHQ', p. 362.

56 Haig diary, 9 and 18 April and 20 September, 1918, Blake, pp. 301–3 and 328.

57 Duncan diary, 8 July, 1917, 'Duncan at GHQ', p. 362.

58 Haig diary, 28 November, 1917, Blake, p. 269.

59 Haig diary, 12 March, 1916, Blake, p. 136.

60 Haig diary, 25 January, 1917, Blake, p. 194.

61 Haig diary, 7 February, 1916 and 25 May, 1917, Haig papers; King Albert diary, 7 February, 1916 and 3 February, 1917, M. R. Thielemans (ed.), *Albert Ier: Carnets et Correspondance de Guerre, 1914–1918* (Paris and Louvain-la-Neuve: Editions Duculot, 1991), pp. 59, 77–9, 248–9 and 298–9. For a detailed examination of the relations between the Belgians

and their allies see W.J. Philpott, 'Britain, France and the Belgian Army', in B.J.Bond (ed.), *Look to Your Front: Studies on the First World War by the British Commission for Military History* (Staplehurst: Spellmount books, 1999).

62 Haig diary, 12 March, 1916, Haig's emphasis, pp. 135–6.
63 When the prospect of Italian troops serving on the Western Front did arise Haig made strong representations that they should go to the French sector of the front. Haig to Robertson, 4 November, 1917, Haig papers, 119.
64 See for example, Haig diary, 2 and 4 May, 1916, Blake, pp. 141–2.
65 Haig diary, 11 and 15 October, 1917, Blake, pp. 260–1.
66 Haig diary, 12 March, 1917, Blake, p. 210.
67 Haig diary, 16 and 17 March, 1917, Blake, pp. 213–4.
68 Haig diary, 24 March, 1917, Blake, pp. 214–5.
69 Haig diary, 26 and 27 April, 1917, Blake, pp. 220–2.
70 Haig diary, 24 June, 1916, Blake, p. 149.
71 Haig diary, 27 February, 1917, Blake, p. 202.
72 Haig diary, 4 May, 1916, and Haig to Lady Haig, 31 January, 1918, Blake, pp. 141–2 and 281.
73 Haig diary, 24 February and 2 March, 1918, Blake, pp. 289–91.
74 Haig diary, 8 March, 1917, Haig papers.
75 'Summary of Operations on the Western Front, 1916–18', Haig papers, 213.
76 *Ibid.*
77 Spears, *Prelude to Victory*, p. 67.
78 Wilson diary, 12 May, 1916, Henry Wilson papers.
79 War Committee minutes, 7 June, 1916, Cabinet Office: Cabinet papers, 1915–16, Public Record Office, Kew (CAB 42): CAB 42/15/6.
80 Haig diary, 14 March, 1917, Blake, p. 211.
81 Haig diary, 26 and 27 August, 1914, Haig papers. The incident still rankled in 1917. Duncan diary, 22 April and 1 October, 1917, 'Duncan at GHQ', pp. 349 and 395–6.
82 Haig diary, 24 October, 1918, Haig's emphasis, Blake, p. 336.

Chapter 9

Haig and The Tank

J.P. Harris

One of many criticisms made of Haig's command of the British Expeditionary Force during operations on the Western Front from December 1915 to November 1918 is that he failed to understand and exploit the potential of the latest technology. In particular he is accused of not having made the fullest use of a significant British military innovation – the tank. This type of criticism was levelled at him by some contemporaries, including Ernest Swinton and Winston Churchill (early advocates of cross-country armoured fighting vehicles) by Sir Eustace Tennyson d'Eyncourt and Albert Stern (who were involved with tank design and development) and by JFC Fuller, the GSO1 of the Tank Corps.[1] The same sort of accusation is still occasionally raised by historians, Professor Tim Travers having built the most scholarly case against Haig along these lines.[2]

Of all the literary passages containing attacks on Haig's generalship, one of the most swingeing, probably one of the most influential in terms of public opinion, and, arguably, one of the least well-founded, is to be found in Winston Churchill's *The World Crisis*:

> "It has been necessary to the whole argument of this volume to dwell insistently upon . . . the Battle of Cambrai. Accusing as I do all the great ally [sic] offensives of 1915, 1916 and 1917, as needless and wrongly conceived operations of infinite cost, I am bound to reply to the question, What else could have been done? And I answer it pointing to the Battle of Cambrai, 'This could have been done'. This in many variants, this in larger and better forms, ought to have been done and would have been done if only the Generals had not been content to fight machine-gun bullets with the breasts of gallant men and think that was waging war".[3]

This passage attacks, of course, not just Douglas Haig but all the Allied generals of the 1915–1917 period. The British readership would, however, have identified Haig, commander-in-chief of the British Expeditionary Force for two thirds of this period, as the principal butt of Churchill's strictures. And while Third Army's attack towards the city of Cambrai on 20 November, 1917, involved a sophisticated mix of operational and tactical methods, the aspect of it which most caught the public imagination was the mass employment of tanks.

The use of the tank was a subject in which Churchill had a strong personal interest. No one can really be said to have invented the tank, but Churchill, despite his rather limited technical knowledge, was the man most responsible for its development in Great Britain. Armoured fighting vehicles for the British armed services were first developed on the initiative of the Royal Naval Air Service. In August 1914, as the Germans were overrunning Belgium, a squadron of this service was sent to the Continent by Churchill, then First Lord of the Admiralty. After Ostend, to which it was originally despatched, became untenable, the squadron based itself at Dunkirk and undertook a variety of reconnaissance duties. As the war, at this period, was still fluid, it began to undertake some of these duties using cars as well as aircraft and began to improvise armour on some of the cars. Its commander informed the Admiralty of these activities and requested that purpose-built armoured cars be sent to it. Churchill encouraged the idea and, early in 1915, the excellent Rolls-Royce armoured car became available for service. By that time the war on the Western Front had, however, become an entrenched stalemate. Armoured cars of that type were of very little use under those conditions. Undeterred, on 20 February, 1915, Churchill ordered the formation of a committee at the Admiralty under the Director of Naval Construction, Sir Eustace Tennyson d'Eyncourt, with the express purpose of designing an armoured fighting vehicle which could move cross-country and break into trench systems. It was this Director of Naval Construction's Committee, also known as the Landships Committee, which hired the engineers, Walter Wilson and William Tritton, whose collaborative effort produced a workable tank prototype by the end of 1915.[4]

Churchill also has the distinction of first bringing the tank to Haig's attention, which he did in a paper entitled *The Variants of the Offensive*,[5] Churchill had been forced to resign as First Lord of the Admiralty in May 1915. It was while he was serving as an infantry officer on the Western Front towards the end of the year that he framed and despatched to GHQ this grandiose memorandum, suggesting, as its title indicates, a number of methods of taking the offensive under the entrenched conditions then existing. The only one of these methods relevant here was "The Attack By Armour", in which Churchill suggested the use of a combination of caterpillar-tracked landships which, he indicated, had already been developed in England, and infantry advancing behind armoured shields.

Haig's reaction to *Variants,* when he read it in December 1915, certainly does not indicate a closed mind. Churchill was a fallen, and, to a great extent, a discredited, statesman. He was widely condemned for initiating the Dardanelles campaign, a humiliating failure. Ill-planned and arguably ill-conceived, that venture had diverted resources away from the crucial Western Front. Yet having arrived on the Western Front himself, Churchill was not content with learning the business of being a humble infantry officer. He was trying to teach the British High Command its business. Given the pressures he faced, having just taken over as commander-in-chief, Haig could almost have been forgiven had he tossed Churchill's memorandum straight into the waste-paper basket. But he did nothing of the kind. He read it carefully and asked, in a marginal note, whether anything was known of the caterpillar-tracked vehicles which Churchill had described.[6]

Haig's follow-up of the matter was, moreover, brisk and business-like, showing that the proposal had very much caught his interest. Discovering that an armoured, caterpillar-tracked, trench-crossing vehicle had indeed been designed and was ready for official trials, he sent Major Hugh Elles, a Royal Engineers officer at GHQ, to observe the trials on his behalf. The quasi-rhomboidal prototype variously called "Big Willy", "The Slug" and, subsequently, "Mother", success-fully negotiated an obstacle course, including a mock trench system, on Lord Salisbury's estate at Hatfield Park. Almost all the numerous VIPs who saw the display were impressed, though not Lord Kitchener, the Secretary of State for War. Elles' opinion, however, mattered more than anyone else's. He reported favourably to Haig and Haig demanded that he be supplied with 150 or so for the start of his big offensive on the Somme. None, however, was ready in time for the initial onslaught of 1 July, 1916. Their debut was performed, in smaller numbers than Haig had requested, in the attack of 15 September, 1916, later designated the start of the Battle of Flers-Courcelette.[7]

The British Mark I tank used in that battle, like subsequent British heavy tanks of the First World War, came in two versions – male and female. Males had both six-pounder guns (mounted in sponsons at the side) and machine guns. Females had machine guns only. Effective gunnery was usually difficult. No-one's field of vision was very good from inside a Mark I tank. They were capable of less than four miles per hour, slower than infantry over most types of ground, and they were also very bulky, making them conspicuous targets. This mattered as they could be destroyed by a direct hit from any type of shell and were not even entirely bullet proof. Ergonomically they were appalling. Their eight-man crews worked in sweltering interior temperatures and breathed an atmosphere thick with petrol fumes and carbon monoxide. Crew members were hammered around as their machines moved over broken ground, on tracks which lacked any system of springs, and thus were sometimes badly injured. Mechanical problems abounded. In particular the tracks tended to snap. When they did not break down mechanically, they often became stuck in ditches or on tree stumps.[8]

The British attack on 15 September, 1916, has been described too many times elsewhere to need a review here. Less than fifty tanks were available of which several failed to cross their start lines. In some parts of the battlefield on 15 September the attempt to integrate tanks into the plan of attack turned out to be more of a hindrance to the infantry than a help. In some instances the tanks did good work. But it was on the basis of much faith and rather slender evidence that Haig followed this very mixed debut with an order for 1,000[9] and encouraged the growth of a large and complex new branch of the army to handle the new weapon. These actions may be considered examples of the extraordinary, chronic and sometimes irrational optimism so characteristic of Haig as a commander. With the benefit of hindsight we know that the tank had a great future in warfare and so no historian attacks him for these decisions. Yet Haig's critical role in the introduction of the tank into the British Army, and in the creation of what became the Tank Corps, is rarely accorded the appreciation it deserves.

Haig, sometimes accused of being slow on the up-take with new technology, was attacked by some contemporaries for being too hasty in using tanks. Both Winston Churchill and Ernest Swinton, another early advocate of the tank idea, accused Haig of having wasted a golden opportunity. If tanks had been withheld from combat until a really impressive number were available great things, Churchill and Swinton argued, might have been achieved. These arguments, endorsed by the influential journalist and military historian, Basil Liddell Hart, are, to say the least, dubious. They were somewhat laconically dismissed by J.F.C. Fuller, the principal staff officer at the Tank Corps' headquarters in France for much of the war. Fuller, who, in other respects, was one of Haig's bitterest critics commented as follows on a draft history of the First World War by Liddell Hart:

"The use of tanks on 15 September, 1916, was not a mistake. Serious mechanical defects manifested. No peace test can equal a war test."[10]

Given the strain that the British munitions industry was under, it was perhaps inevitable that the growth of the Heavy Branch Machine Gun Corps (as the British Army's tank corps was designated until summer 1917) was slow. Small numbers of tanks did good work at Beaumont Hamel in the final phase of the 1916 Somme campaign. A few were used at the Battle of Arras, starting on 9 April, 1917. The record of tanks up to the middle of 1917 was mixed. There had been no very clear indication that they could play anything other than a minor, auxiliary role which would scarcely justify the great effort which had been expended upon them. Yet Haig kept the faith and continued the expansion of his tank forces. He reported to the War Office on 5 June, 1917, that:

> ". . . events have proved the utility of Tanks . . . both as a means of overcoming hostile resistance . . . and as a means of reducing casualties in the attacking troops and I consider that sufficient experience has now been gained to warrant the adoption of the Tank as a recognized addition to the existing means of conducting offensive operations."[11]

Haig clearly hoped for considerable assistance from tanks in his forthcoming offensive in Flanders. He was much interested in the development of faster tanks for pursuit and exploitation which were to be added to improved versions of the heavy breakthrough tank.[12]

Some of the new Mark IV heavy tanks, better armoured and more reliable than their predecessors, were available for use at Messines on 7 June, 1917. A few did good work despite the uphill advance and the very heavily cratered nature of the ground.[13] But it was not until later that summer that the possibility of using several hundred in one battle arose. Unfortunately for the Tank Corps (as the Heavy Branch became on 27 July, 1917) the battle into which they were pitched on 31 July, 1917, was Third Ypres. Heavy rain began that day and continued through much of August. The drainage system of the area had been shattered by the three-week preliminary bombardment and much of the battlefield became a morass. The Tank Corps quickly found itself nearly useless in these circumstances and began to lobby to be withdrawn from the Ypres battle and employed elsewhere. Voices from the home front joined this chorus and Haig found himself involved in a controversy over tank use.

On 22 August, Sir Eustace Tennyson d'Eyncourt, the civilian naval architect who had chaired the committee which had been responsible for the initial development of tanks, wrote to Haig offering suggestions on the employment of tanks. Rather than constantly requesting the Ministry of Munitions to provide tanks with equipment which would enable them to negotiate difficult ground, as was tending to happen up to the late summer of 1917, why, d'Eyncourt asked, did Haig not carefully select a battlefield which would be more suitable to tank use. The mass employment of tanks, with the benefit of surprise, on suitable ground, might, d'Eyncourt believed, pay considerable dividends.[14]

Haig's Flanders offensive was clearly in very serious trouble at this point. In its waterlogged condition, the battlefield was posing practically insuperable problems for all arms, not just for tanks. Haig's relationship with the Lloyd George government was under considerable strain as a result. Haig must have resented this intervention in the conduct of military operations by d'Eyncourt, a civilian who was not even of cabinet rank. But it is likely that d'Eyncourt had indirect channels of communication with Lloyd George and Haig, a great survivor with considerable political guile, may have suspected this. Whatever his motive, he handled the matter with considerable care and courtesy, replying to d'Eyncourt within a week and presenting a carefully worded argument in his own defence. He pointed out that:

> "... the choice of front on which to make an attack has to be made with regard to many considerations, tactical, strategical, political and so forth. In making this choice the tank, at any rate in its present state of development, can only be regarded as a minor factor. It is still in its infancy as regards design. It is of uncertain reliability. Its true powers are more or less a matter of conjecture. The troops are not yet fully accustomed to it, nor do they place sufficient faith in what it can accomplish to be willing to accept it in lieu of artillery preparation and support. As time goes on and the designs improve the tank will probably become a more important factor in the choice of battlefield but under present conditions it must be, as I have said, a minor factor.
>
> ... The question which I have to decide as matters stand is whether to use or not to use the tank under conditions which are unavoidably unfavourable. I have decided that, on the whole, it is advisable to make use of them; even under such conditions they have done valuable service more than sufficient to justify this decision."[15]

Though there were a few, very small-scale tank successes, even at Third Ypres, it is difficult to identify many. But Haig's argument that the potency of the tank was not such that an entire campaign could be planned around its characteristics was a reasonable one, not really discredited by the experience of the Battle of Cambrai the following November.

Yet d'Eyncourt's letter, when considered in conjunction with the pleas of the Tank Corps itself was not, perhaps, without some influence on Haig. Within about a fortnight of replying to d'Eyncourt he did in fact authorize the withdrawal of the bulk of the Tank Corps from Flanders. A number of ideas were already in the wind for the employment of tanks in other sectors further south. The one which was eventually acted upon was a Third Army scheme for a major attack towards Cambrai.

Brigadier-General Hugh Elles, who commanded the Tank Corps in France, seems to have been first informed about the Third Army scheme of attack in September. In brief the idea was for a surprise attack on a quiet sector of the front which, though heavily fortified, was relatively weakly held by the Germans. The attack would, as usual, be carried out mainly by infantry, supported by a powerful concentration of artillery. But there was to be no preliminary artillery bombardment and, to be sure of achieving as much surprise as possible, artillery moved into the area especially for this attack would be obliged to register silently without firing ranging shots. The reasonably accurate silent registration of artillery, which was a crucial ingredient of the Third Army plan for the Battle of Cambrai, only became feasible as a result of a vast range of improvements in artillery technology and techniques during the course of the war. It is doubtful whether it could have been achieved much before the middle of 1917. (This is one of the reasons why the passage from Churchill's *World Crisis* quoted above must be treated sceptically.) A large number of tanks was needed to lead the infantry attack at Cambrai mainly for one reason. Without a preliminary bombardment the huge belts of barbed wire which covered the German positions in front of Cambrai would be uncut at Zero hour for the infantry assault. The primary role of the tanks, therefore, was to crush the wire.[16]

Haig cannot take any credit for devising the scheme for an attack used at Cambrai. That belongs to General Sir Julian Byng and his Third Army staff. Indeed he only gave final approved for the Third Army scheme as the Third Battle of Ypres was drawing to a distinctly unsatisfactory conclusion. The Cambrai scheme gave him some hope of snatching a victory before the winter of a very disappointing year set in. Such a victory he desperately needed in order to drag his reputation out of the Flanders mud. Yet Haig does deserve some credit for approving a very unconventional operation, conceptually ahead of anything any other national army had yet tried on the Western Front.

A total of 478 tanks were assembled for the Battle of Cambrai. These included some which were fitted with radio as signals stations, some which were used for carrying supplies and a couple which were designed to lay bridges. More than 300 Mark IV fighting tanks led the attack. The first day of the battle, 20 November, 1917, did not entirely live up to expectations. There was not a sufficient breakthrough to enable the cavalry to "go through". But an advance of about four miles was achieved in some places, a striking success compared to most of the Third Ypres campaign. Haig's mistake was in insisting on the continuance of the offensive far beyond the point of diminishing returns. By doing this he tended to exhaust his forces and left them vulnerable to the devastating German counter-stroke of 30 November. When the battle came to an end in mid-December it could be considered at best a draw from the British point of view and Haig's prestige was but little enhanced by it.[17]

Tanks were basically offensive weapons and no one had a very clear idea of how they should be used in a situation in which the British were standing on the defensive on the Western Front. Yet as Haig had realized by 4 December, 1917 that was bound to be the situation in the early months of 1918, the Russian front having collapsed and the Germans being thus free to transfer large forces to the West. The concept which the Tank Corps principally advocated for its role in meeting the expected German offensives was large-scale counter-attack. It was a role which GHQ approved but which the Tank Corps was rarely able to execute in practice. Mark IV heavy tanks (the great majority of the tanks available in spring 1918) were really too slow and too lacking in manoeuvrability to be an effective instrument for operational counter-stroke, or even tactical counter-attack, in fluid warfare. Yet fluid warfare set in on the Somme with, for the British, alarming speed after the Germans mounted their "Michael" offensive on 21 March . Many tanks, having broken down or run out of petrol, had to be abandoned by their crews as the war passed them by. Whole tank battalions were practically without tanks by April. With the British Expeditionary Force facing its most desperate crisis since 1914, Haig insisted that tankless Tank Corps personnel should not remain idle, but rather should join the fighting as Lewis gunners. JFC Fuller chose to interpret this as an attack by Haig on the Tank corps as an institution. In fact Haig was happy enough to allow the continued expansion of the Tank corps once the spring crisis had passed.[18]

The period at which the British Expeditionary Force made the most effective use of tanks was the "Hundred Days" campaign , starting with the Battle of Amiens on 8 August, 1918, and concluding with the Armistice on 11 November. It is in this period, especially, that Professor Travers believes tanks and other relatively new forms of technology were insufficiently utilized, Haig and other senior British officers having a bias in favour of a more traditional, manpower-centred approach to warfare. Though this is an interesting thesis, it is not altogether convincing. For one thing it is clear that the British made more dramatic and successful use of the tank at this period than any of the other national armies – hardly indicative of a bias against this particular form of technology, one which Haig had played a large part in introducing into the British Expeditionary Force in the first place. Secondly, though the Mark V tank, the type which predominated in the British Tank Corps during the Hundred Days was a little faster and considerably more manoeuvrable than the Mark IV, it was still acutely vulnerable to artillery used in the direct fire role. As the Germans took the threat of tanks more seriously during the Hundred Days, they deployed more artillery in this way. Though useful in big assaults, the Mark V was, moreover, not really a suitable instrument for the more fluid warfare which arose from time to time during the final campaign. The faster Medium A Whippet tank was never available in large numbers. Its slightly greater speed made it only a little less vulnerable to German artillery and it had difficulty in operating without the support of infantry and artillery. These generally could not keep up with it when it was engaged in pursuit and exploitation. Serious ergonomic problems, moreover, continued to plague all British tanks. The Mark V was even worse ventilated than the Mark IV and, in action, its crews tended to be progressively poisoned by their own machines. Finally the very high casualty figures for Tank Corps' personnel during the Hundred Days scarcely suggest that the Corps was an under-utilized asset.[19]

Haig's generalship can, doubtless, be faulted in many areas. Attacks on him on grounds of bias against, or under-utilization of, tanks seem, however, to be ill-founded.

Notes

1   J.P. Harris, *Men , Ideas and Tanks* (Manchester University Press) 1995, pp. 4–194.

2   T. Travers, *How The War Was Won: Command and Technology in the British Army on the Western front 1917–1918* (Routledge) 1992, passim.

3   W. Churchill, *The World Crisis* (Sandhurst Edition, Thornton Butterworth) 1933, p. 379.

4   Harris, op. cit., 4–46.

5   "The Variants of the Offensive", Churchill to GHQ, 3 December, 1915, PRO WO 158/831.

6   B.H. Liddell Hart, *The Tanks, Vol. I* (Cassell) 1959, p. 48.

7   For a summary of these events see Harris op. cit. pp. 30–57.

8   For a summary of British tanks used in the First World War see D. Fletcher, *Landships: British Tanks In The First World War* (HMSO) 1984, passim.

9   "Recommendations For The Expansion of the Heavy Section, Machine Gun Corps. Conference Held On The 19th and 20th September 1916", p. 1, and Haig to War Office, 2 October, 1916, PRO WO 158/836.

10 Fuller to Liddell Hart, 22 September, 1926, LH 1/302/100, Liddell hart Centre for Military Archives (LHCMA), King's College London.

11 Haig to War Office, 5 June 1917, para. 1. PRO MUN 4/2791.

12 Harris, op. cit., p. 97.

13 "Messines, Details of the Assistance Rendered by Tanks" (undated) PRO 158/858.

14 D'Eyncourt to Haig, 22 August, 1917, BC1/12, Fuller Papers, LHCMA.

15 Haig to d'Eyncourt, 27 August, 1917, BC 1/13, Fuller papers, LHCMA.

16 Harris, op. cit., pp. 105–113.

17 Harris, op. cit., pp. 120 – 126 and J.L. Gibot and P. Gorczyinski, *En Suivant Les Tanks: Cambrai 20 November – 7 December, 1917* (privately printed) 1997, passim.

18 Harris, op. cit., pp. 133–153.

19 Harris, op. cit., pp. 157–194.

Chapter 10

The Impact of Technology on the BEF and its Commander

Michael Crawshaw

SETTING

There is an apocryphal story of a member of the Ordnance Board in the late nineteenth century defending its record of turning down practically every idea or invention submitted to it on the grounds that ninety-nine out of every hundred were of no practical use to the military and if in the process the members also turned away the one valuable proposal, a failure rate of only one percent was not a bad performance.[1] In assessing the extent to which the gentleman's tongue was in his cheek one should remember that this was also the period of W S Gilbert; however, the story strikes a chord as bearing out the popular view of the military establishment of the time as Luddites to a man, an attitude which extends to include the period of the Great War.

In fact the judgement is manifestly unfair, whether applied to the Victorian or the later Army. From the period of the Great Exhibition of 1851 onward, Victorian society, including substantial elements of the Armed Forces, was enthusiastically interested in applying the *products* of advancing technology.[2] Regrettably, it was much less interested in the *how and why* of the design and manufacture of those products – a tendency which can be found in the Army to this day, although the Victorian/Edwardian lexicon did not include the word 'anorak'.[3]

The result was, and continues to be, that technology-driven (and other) progress in any walk of life tends to be rapid when it is evolutionary – 'doing the same thing only better' – where the effects are easily and directly comprehensible to the non-specialist mind (which description tends to apply to the majority of highly-placed decision-makers and leaders). Where there is a step change – 'doing things differently' – there is a need for two sorts of individual: on the one hand the specialists responsible for developing the new way, on the other the generalists with the ability to grasp and decide how the new can be adapted to serve the needs of the system. Good performers in the second category are harder to come by, for they require openness of mind nicely balanced by a finely developed critical facility, coupled with the courage to act on their decisions. If the balance is right, the result is an ability to pick winners. In Douglas Haig, the British Army in the Great War was fortunate in finding a leader who, contrary to caricature, possessed an openness of mind to technical innovation and the clarity of vision to concentrate on the applications which offered the best prospects of success.[4] Unfortunately, the ethos of the Regular Army, reflecting the society from which it sprang, was not conducive to producing the numbers of specialists required for the new warfare.[5] Nevertheless, as an example of what could be done within the limits of evolutionary progress, one has only to look at the rapid succession of changes of the Service rifle in the sixty years between 1850 and 1910[6] to realize that the British military establishment was capable of at least keeping up with the leaders in adopting the best of technology in this field.

It had to be so. Technological advance in the 19th Century was running at such a pace that wherever a new development in materials, chemistry, and all kinds of engineering appeared which could be adopted or adapted for military use, some nation would pick it up. And if this happened, the remainder had to follow suit or risk disaster as a consequence of being technologically outflanked.[7] The favourite example here is the impact of the Prussian needle gun, publicized as the chief agent of victory against the Austrians in 1866, though there was a substantial amount of spin involved in the claims.[8] However, the rest of the list of significant developments, even in the purely military field and hence easily comprehensible by the most allegedly hidebound of soldiers, is formidable. The 19th century saw the introduction of Congreve's rockets; the replacement of flintlock by percussion cap ignition; the general replacement of smoothbore muskets by rifles, made possible by expanding (Minié) bullets; breech loading small arms; brass cartridge cases making first, magazine small arms, and then machine guns, practicable weapons; the application of steel construction, rifling, and breech loading to artillery; smokeless propellants and high explosive shell fillings to supplant nearly 600 years of black powder; a reduction of small arms calibres by a factor of 60 percent; impact fuzes for artillery shell; and quick-firing artillery with on-carriage recoil firing brass-cased ammunition – meteoric progress, given that the only significant innovation in the preceding century had been Shrapnel's spherical case shell. Tactically, the result was a transformation of the battlefield, as the effective ranges of weapons increased by an order of magnitude, while rates of fire and the terminal effects of projectiles improved in proportion. On the human side, exploitation of (or even coping with) these developments called for a new breed of military men – the 'educated soldiers'.

As significant were the application to military purposes of progress in civilian transport and telecommunications technology visible in all the European wars of the late middle of the century, and more so, in their coupling with the full mobilization of national human and industrial resources seen for the first time in the American Civil War. The British Army showed a commendable interest in the operations of that war, thanks particularly to the efforts of Henderson at the Staff College, but the very detailed study which ensued tended to neglect the importance of the industrial dimension.[9]

This last gives an important indicator as to the strengths and weaknesses of the Edwardian Army. Inherited from the previous century was an undeniable competence in the business of 'small wars', which had been seen at its best in the River War in the Sudan (1896–99),[10] and the contemporaneous campaign on the North-West Frontier.[11] Tactics, equipment, and staff procedures effective in such operations had been found seriously wanting in South Africa, and considerable energy was expended to rectify these shortcomings. The resulting surge of reform and restructuring produced an excellent small army, well-educated, equipped and trained for an expeditionary deployment in a limited war against a capable enemy, backed by a Territorial Force designed for home defence only, and with minimal reserves of personnel, equipment, and consumables. More critically, the means of production for the force's sustainability were geared to low-rate peacetime output.[12] Haldane's Army reforms were conducted in a climate of 'doing good by stealth', where it was politically impossible for a Liberal administration to countenance a major continental commitment and its implications for personnel numbers and industrial production. Circumstances (and some individuals) conspired to bring about a situation where Haldane's force would be committed into the high intensity war for which it and its supporting organizations were totally unfitted. Additional to the problems of sustaining the original strength of the BEF at rates of expenditure undreamt of in the pre-war period were the demands of re-equipping the Territorial Force for full-scale war and the enormous expansion brought about by the raising of the New Armies. The impact of technology on the British Army in the Great War must therefore be viewed under more than one heading: not only innovation in the design and introduction of new weapons and equipment into service, but also the development of techniques and organizations to make better use of resources already available, and finally the mobilizing of the means of production to provide both existing and new items of equipment and supply in the astronomical quantities necessitated by the war of materiel.

The BEF of 1914–18 still remains the greatest single enterprise ever mounted by the British peoples. Its maximum strength was close to two million. It was located in a friendly foreign country, which had its drawbacks as well as its advantages from the point of view of host nation support (the Germans did not have to ask nicely). The task of housing, moving, clothing, feeding, doctoring, paying, and disciplining this community set down in the middle of a first-world country was a totally new experience for the British Army, both in qualitative and quantitative terms – and a far cry from doing it with much smaller forces in a colonial setting. This basic requirement of organizing and provisioning the 'living' aspects of the BEF had to be set alongside the 'operational' requirement – to equip, train, deploy, command, control and sustain in action the combat element of the force. In both areas Haig and his subordinates had to learn as they went along, and learn the living and the operational aspects simultaneously – there was no question of being able to get the one right and then progress to the other. It is arguable that the pressure of administrative concerns at all levels from the Commander-in-Chief downward was a significant factor in the slow development of operational expertise in the BEF,[13] and that the greater operational fluency apparent in the second half of 1918 was a consequence, *inter alia*, of the higher commanders needing less to be involved in administrative matters as staffs became more competent.[14] From the point of view of this essay, the 'living' aspects of the BEF were as shaped by available technology as were the 'operational'. Haig's solution to these quasi-civilian problems was to import civilian experts into GHQ as quasi-soldiers, not as advisers but with executive powers; Geddes, as head of railways and transportation, being the prime example.[15]

STATE OF THE ART

The process of technological advance sees, in any area, the rise, plateauing and fall of successive dominant systems or solutions. In the first decade of the twentieth century steam technology had reached its apogee with the widespread use of the turbine for marine propulsion and power generation; the adoption of oil firing for the most modern warships such as the *Queen Elizabeths* of the Royal Navy's 5th Battle Squadron made oil a strategic material, starting an engagement with the Middle East whose geopolitical effects remain in place to this day. The internal combustion engine was a quarter of a century old, was maturing as an automotive power plant, and had made heavier than air flying machines feasible, while by 1910 the diesel engine was established for marine applications – its application to submarines making the long range submersible a practical weapon of war. Materials technology was progressing from iron and steel into the first uses of aluminium – although aeroplanes were almost exclusively of wood and fabric construction, the Zeppelins which represented the most advanced stage of practical aircraft development by 1914 had aluminium structures. The chemical industry, in which field Germany was the acknowledged leader, was moving on from processes based on extraction and modification of natural materials into synthesis; the development of aniline dyes and the fixing of atmospheric nitrogen being of particular relevance to the production of military explosives independent of supplies of natural nitrates. Organic chemistry was still predominantly coal-based, but coal products include the benzene derivatives which still form the basis of present-day high explosives. Electrical power was another area of technology which, although still developing fast and with a long way to go before standardization of supplies would be achieved, had reached a practical level of maturity.

This progress was, however, not matched in the field of telecommunications. Global long-haul communications were based on submarine cables carrying telegraph traffic only, supplemented by the beginnings of an Empire-wide wireless telegraphy (W/T) network. There were extensive national telephone networks, but long-distance telephony was held back by the non-availability of effective amplifiers. Radio telephony in 1914 was still in the laboratory stage, while the application of W/T to mobile applications was limited by the size of the sets and power supply requirements. Where these limitations were less of a restriction, as in the case of static stations, on board ship, and in airships, W/T was capable by 1914 of providing reliable communications over tactically useful ranges.[16] But even W/T could not be packaged into mobile vehicle stations, let alone manpack sets. In summary, by 1914 the technology for the infrastructure and the weaponry, the skeleton and the muscles of modern industrial warfare, was in place. Technology for command and control, the nervous system, had not reached a comparable plane of evolution. This mismatch of capability is one of two defining factors in so many of the events of the Great War – the other being the lack of an effective mobile arm of exploitation.

By 1914, British industry was paying the price for its place as the leader in the First Industrial Revolution. Emphasis on practical rather than theoretical attainments at management level, the categorization of science and technology as second-class fields by the academic establishment, low levels of education among the mass of the workforce, and labour relations routinely based on confrontation, all contributed to a failure to update as both the United States and Germany first closed up on and then overtook Britain, both in terms of production quantity and in the areas of research, design, and (particularly in the case of the United States) the technology of volume production.[17] The British remained very good at the high quality one-off product involving a large input of skilled labour. They were much less good at repetition production of medium-sized equipments or mass production of smaller goods and components to tight standards. This characteristic applied to critical items of military equipment – many of which would be required in vast quantities for expanding forces. Thus the Short Magazine Lee Enfield, although possessed of the sweetest bolt action ever incorporated into a Service rifle, achieved this at the expense of an inordinate amount of hand fitting which made it highly unsuitable for mass production.[18] Similarly, anyone who has ever stripped a Vickers machine gun will be lost in admiration at the workmanship, but aghast at the complexity of the mechanism from the production point of view. And the enhancement of ammunition production by 1916 was offset by poor quality fuzes which resulted in dudding rates of one-third during the preparatory bombardments for the Somme offensive. The peacetime-based procurement system performed miracles given its shortcomings, but the formation of the Ministry of Munitions was essential to solving the supply problem. It was not, however, until mid-1917 under Churchill that the Ministry's efforts began to produce quality matériel on a war-winning scale.

EXPERIENCE

The four key areas of technology affecting the fighting forces of 1914–18 were weaponry, transportation, aviation, and telecommunications

Weaponry

The technology, as opposed to the availability, of weapons themselves did not advance enormously during the course of the War. At first sight this may be thought surprising. There are exceptions, but not many; the most significant are tanks, trench mortars and gas, to which enthusiasts for minority interests might add portable flame weapons and the first sub-machineguns, eg the German MP18. Tanks are the subject of a separate article in this book, so only two points are appropriate: the first, that the tank may be considered as a weapon in its own right, but also as a means of protected transport of extremely conventional weaponry; and the second, that the whole history of the tanks of the Great War is one of continuous support from the Commander-in-Chief, support which did not waver even in the days of their worst fortunes.

In general, however, the weapons with which the Great War would be fought were largely defined by the beginning of the century. By 1900, personal weapons in all armies were settling down as bolt action magazine rifles of 6.5–8mm calibre, supplemented by a variety of revolvers and automatic pistols for officers and specialist troops. The Maxim pattern belt-fed machine gun had proved itself in battle and had been widely adopted.[19] The French 75mm field gun Modèle 97, the first to have an effective on-carriage buffer-recuperator system, had set the benchmark for all other field artillery weapons and every national arms industry was racing to provide a matching product.[20]

The immediate pre-war period was typified by refinement of what was already in existence. Rifles in the British, German, and US armies were shortened to carbine length to obviate the need for a separate cavalry weapon – thereby, fortuitously, improving their suitability for trench warfare. Rapid recharging of magazines, pioneered by Mauser (charger) and Männlicher (clip) became the norm. Machine guns were lightened – the weight of the Maxim gun alone and empty (not including its tripod mount) was 27kg, which limited its utility as an infantry weapon other than in static fighting. Its replacement in British service, the Vickers, weighed (also gun only) 18kg. Unfortunately the Vickers was accepted for service only in 1912, and only 90 had been delivered by July 1914.[21] Fortunately the Lewis had been accepted as aircraft armament in 1913 and was produced as a supplement to the Vickers, tripod-mounted in the medium MG role.[22] The utility of the true light machine gun – bipod-mounted – was identified by Haig in mid–1915 and its battle-winning value, as scalings approached one per platoon, was emphasized by him at an Army Commanders' Conference in March 1916.[23] The importance of the LMG to the development of the platoon-based tactics of 1917 (and later) cannot be over-emphasized.[24]

Artillery design trends in the period illustrate the conflict between the demands of fire performance – range and weight of shell – calling for heavier construction – and those of mobility with horse traction. The British 13- and 18-pdr field guns, influenced by experience in South Africa and the Sudan, illustrate the effect of design balance favouring mobility, the later 4.5-inch howitzer, with a shell weight twice that of the 18-pdr, inevitably coming out as a heavier equipment. Its designers employed a very small propellant charge and accepted limited range to keep the weight down.

German artillery thinking was based more on the need for reduction of fixed defences than on the open-warfare concerns of the British, and the consequent need for a greater proportion of heavy-calibre weapons. Not only did this give rise to the excellent German/Austrian siege artillery, but also the brilliant design which produced, in the 150mm field howitzer (the notorious 'five-nine'), a medium artillery weapon (listed as a 'heavy' by the standards of its day) with mobility characteristics little worse than those of a normal field gun, and some very good weapons at calibres intermediate between the five-nine and the siege howitzers. The British situation with regard to artillery holdings was a reflection of the sort of war that it had intended to fight – a conflict of fast-moving open warfare for which a small professional army equipped with an adequate scaling of (mostly) light weapons. Once into a war of static operations involving massed forces, Britain was faced with multiple deficiencies. First, there were the deficiencies in quantity, against the demands of vast expansion (not only in numbers of units and formations but also in terms of increased equipment and supply scalings). Second there were qualitative deficiencies. These included the requirement for large numbers of heavy weapons, the need for HE shell instead of shrapnel, for more effective fuzes, and for the maintenance of acceptable standards of quality control.[25, 26] To some extent the problem was ameliorated by the fact that at the outbreak of war prototypes were available of some of the heavier artillery pieces which were to enter into service in ever-increasing numbers over the next four years.[27] But there is all the world of difference between prototypes and series production – of ammunition as much as of guns. The greater part of the difficulties facing the BEF consisted not so much of identifying solutions to its problems as in the production of the hardware components of those solutions. In October 1914 even that most basic commodity of war – .303-inch small arms ammunition – was in desperately short supply.[28]

Weaponry, of course, goes beyond the basic elements dealt with here, and the circumstances of war on the Western Front brought into being developments in both orthodox and unorthodox weaponry going beyond peacetime anticipation. Trench warfare imposed demands for short range HE weapons – grenades, trench mortars,[29] which were either non-existent or in such short supply that expedients of doubtful utility and even more dubious safety had to be pressed into service, while as better weapons came forward the ever-present production questions limited their effect. What is inescapable is that by the time of the Somme all the weapons with which the war would be won were in place – but not until late 1917 would the command and control and support systems be in place to make full use of them, and not until the summer of 1918 would they be available in sufficient quantity to give the operational flexibility that facilitated the victories of the Hundred Days.[30]

It is in the control of indirect fire, more than in the development of the weapons themselves, that the true measure of the Great War firepower revolution can be taken. Prior to the War, artillery techniques in the British Army were driven by an ethos of very close support, to the extent that indirect techniques were still frowned on as unmanly.[31] The experience of the 1914 battles caused this view to be rapidly modified, and the history of artillery support in the remainder of the War is one of development and refinement of indirect fire techniques. The Battle of Cambrai is always considered as a landmark in the development of combat arm tactics with the first use of tanks in mass, but the artillery plan for the operation is justifiably considered as representing a greater technical achievement. For the first time, with the enthusiastic backing of the Third Army Commander (Byng), a major fireplan was put into effect without prior adjustment of fire. As a result operational surprise for a major British Western Front attack was achieved for the first time (a measure of tactical surprise having been achieved at Arras and Messines). This was the result of a combination of multiple technical achievements and the extension of 'garrison artillery' techniques to the Royal Field Artillery (not without protest): the production of reliable mapping based on both ground and aerial survey; accurate survey of battery positions onto the grid; location of enemy positions by ground and aerial observation, flash spotting, and the new technique of sound ranging; measurement of individual gun performance characteristics; and the application of meteorological data. Individually, these methods had been maturing over the years, but it was the use of all the techniques in concert which produced the outstanding performance at Cambrai, which became the norm for the last year of the war.[32] The same techniques were essential to the success at Amiens in August 1918, and although the production of precise data became more difficult as static warfare gave way to mobile during the Hundred Days, the artillery arm remained the battle winner to the end of the war. Nevertheless, procedural control by timed programmes had to remain the norm for the major attacks; the lack of mobile radio continued to limit the ability of artillery to react to actual, as opposed to planned, events on the ground. During the Hundred Days solutions were found in the more laterally-thinking formations involving unconventional deployments which at times saw 6-inch howitzers in action forward of divisional 18-pdrs, and fireplans being worked out on the spot between the infantry and whichever Gunners happened to be present.[33]

It has been suggested that the advances in artillery during the First World War amount to a 'revolution in military affairs', that presently overworked term.[34] Certainly there was a technical revolution with major operational implications; it is perhaps better to leave the discussion there rather than indulge in semantics.

Supply, Transport and Mobility

The state of the art with regard to transport in 1914 is one of competing technologies. For land movement of commodities and of personnel rail remained unrivalled for large quantity movement, even over relatively short distances.[35] Mechanical road transport was in a state of flux, with a variety of prime mover and load carrier combinations available, ranging from steam traction engines to motor trucks, passing through steam lorries and petrol tractors of various types (including tracked) on the way. Horse-drawn wagons continued to play a large part in distribution systems. The key to a successful military supply and transport system lay in making best use of the characteristics of all the available modes of transport. Rail's capability for bulk lift and reasonable speed was offset by its inflexibility. The motor truck of the period could maintain a good speed over hard surfaces but had a poor off-road performance, while the typical capacity of one-and-a-half tonnes (the '30-cwt') limited MT's capability for bulk movement. Mechanical prime movers with an off-road capability, such as the Holt tractor, were too slow on roads for use in logistic roles, but found use as gun tractors. For the forward area, where a combination of reasonable on-road speed with cross-country mobility was as necessary eighty years ago as it is today, the horse-drawn GS wagon remained the practical solution. The BEF therefore went to war with a very logical system of mechanical transport being used for supply from railhead to refilling points from which horse transport-based divisional ASC trains supplied forward to unit echelons. This had an added advantage in that the still small pool of trained motor vehicle drivers was concentrated in specialist units – in 1914 there were many more people able to drive a horse-drawn than a motor vehicle. The resilience of the system was immediately proved under the stress of the 1914 retreat, where supply of the BEF held up surprisingly well under the severest conditions. The decisions which produced this system indicate a commendable level of common-sense and appreciation of what would and what would not work on the part of those responsible.

Once the front stabilised the disadvantage of rail technology – its inflexibility – was less of a disadvantage. The highly developed rail systems in Northern France were a major factor favouring the defensive, in that a defender could move reinforcements to a threatened point more rapidly by rail than the attacker could build up across a shattered battlefield. For practically the whole duration of the War, this factor worked in the Germans' favour, given that the strategic imperative for the Allies of evicting the enemy from France and Belgium dictated a continuous offensive posture. Even in the last days of the War, the Germans were retreating over an intact rail system while the advancing Allies had to contend with the effects of a thorough programme of demolition and denial.

As well as the standard gauge system substantial use was made of narrow-gauge rail (the 60-cm Decauville system) to meet the demands of the artillery war. The beauty of light rail is that once it is in place, large loads can be moved by small horsepowers – the 20 BHP Simplex locomotive could haul 20 tonnes of payload or more, and unlike standard-gauge track, 60-cm was easy to lay and equally important, to maintain and repair.[36]

Mechanical transport was not, of course, confined to load-carrying duties. The staff car had replaced the horse for road movement of commanders and staffs by the beginning of the War, and the use of motor buses for troop lift dates from a successful trial in 1908. By November 1914 a total of 360 buses, each capable of carrying 25 fully equipped troops, had already been taken into service. Motor ambulances speeded up casualty evacuation, saving lives,[37] and motor cycle despatch riders supplemented line communications. Tactically, armoured cars operated on an improvised basis in the early mobile fighting and were a feature of the 1918 battles, together with motorised machine-gun units and lorried infantry. However, all these tactical developments foundered on the lack of off-road mobility of Great War wheels.

Even in 1918, off-road mobility was limited to the track and the horse, and the track had not yet developed the speed and the range to supplant the horse as the cross-country mobile arm. Given the near-impossibility of horsed cavalry operating successfully in an offensive role on the Western Front, this 'hiatus'[38] in the availability of an arm of exploitation remains the second defining factor in the texture of the Great War, the shortcomings of contemporary telecommunications technology being the first.

Aviation
Aviation and telecommunications represent the two most glamorous fields of technological development during the twentieth century. Just nine years cover the period from Orville Wright's first hop at Kittyhawk

to the outbreak of the Great War. The period of the War is one of progress at a breakneck rate, but progress which is nevertheless evolutionary. Initially, military views of the aeroplane were sceptically inclined; these were, after all, the pioneering days of flying for fun and the very business of getting airborne being an end in itself (it should also be remembered that even in 1914 airship technology was far more mature than that of aeroplanes, to the extent that 37,250 passengers had already been carried by Graf Zeppelin's creations).[39] Haig was one of those early sceptics, but after an unfortunate experience at the hands of aerial observation by the opposing side's airship in the 1912 manoeuvres,[40] became a convert to the principle of aircraft as observation platforms. The RFC therefore arrived in France with a clear mandate as to its primary role, which was actually the only sensible role for the aircraft of the period; this clarity of purpose was initially lacking in both the French and German air arms.

If one makes an objective examination of the primary use of aircraft throughout the Great War, 'observation' is the key, covering reconnaissance, terrain mapping, target acquisition, and control of fire. Applying Field Marshal Slim's criterion from a later war, to the effect that an aircraft is simply a vehicle for carrying things from A to B,[41] in the Great War the vital 'things' were the trained eyes of the observer, together with cameras to record images and wireless communications for immediate reporting. Although offensive support of the ground battle grew in importance as the campaign progressed, a single aircraft controlling artillery could accurately deliver a far greater weight of fire than could a bomber force equipped with the relatively puny ordnance of the day, or ground strafing aircraft, however effective their individual contributions proved at critical moments in the battle.

So the key image of the British aircraft of the Great War is not one of Sopwith Camels mixing it with the Richthofen Circus, or the Handley-Page o/400s of the Independent Air Force taking their first steps towards a strategic bombing capability. It is more the lumbering RE8 – the 'Harry Tate' – with its observer craning over the side with his camera or tapping back fall-of-shot information on his primitive wireless transmitter, while he and his pilot pray that the more glamorous departments of the RFC will keep the Albatross or the Fokker off their backs for long enough to let them get the job done and go home. The great fighter clashes were devoted to this aim – to maintain the use of enemy air space by our own observation aircraft while denying access to ours by theirs.[42] The material provided by the observation aircraft permitted the production of up-to-date and extremely accurate mapping, which was an essential ingredient of the new way of artillery warfare introduced by the British at Cambrai in November

1917. The greatest contribution of the air arm to final victory lay in perhaps its least glamorous, its most integrated with the ground war, and certainly the most technically dominated of all its applications – an application which led back to the clearsightedness of the Commander of I Corps in August 1914.

Telecommunications

It has become a truism that the supreme technological deficiency in all armies of the 1914–18 era lay in the field of telecommunications. Telecommunications technology lagged behind weapon and sustainability developments to the extent that the full capability of the weapon systems available could not be used. The absence of mobile communications made it impossible for higher HQ to keep track of a developing battle. As a result, fire support could not be directed to where it was needed, and the absence of situation reports made it difficult to deploy reserves to the decisive point. Procedural solutions had therefore to be applied – the production of meticulously detailed battle and fire plans which, as is the habit of plans, rarely survived contact with the enemy. Up to the end of 1917, this placed the BEF and its Commander in an impossible bind; the plan for a major attack would probably continue to hold together reasonably well and yield results for up to three days. After that, diminishing returns applied and closing down the battle was the sensible thing to do. The problem then became – what next? To replan, move the artillery forward, wind up the clockwork and go again in the same place was to forfeit surprise and give the enemy time to strengthen his defences. To redeploy elsewhere (particularly the mass of artillery) would be to accept very limited gains for a large investment in time and effort. Only in mid–1918, when the vast increase in available materiel permitted the adoption of an operational concept based on short battles fought in rapid succession on separate Army fronts without the need for such redeployment did the procedural solution come to fruition, and even then the need for rigid adherence to plan limited flexibility. However, by then radio technology was offering the possibility of breaking out of the dilemma

The lack of mobile communications was a fact of life, based not just on technological shortcomings but on the deficiencies of pure science at the time. The BEF's communications were line-based, overlaid by a radio net extending, even by 1916, down to brigade level, by despatch riders where a motor cycle could go, and by runner where one could not. Line was only survivable if dug in to a depth of around two metres, duplicated, triplicated and cross-connected – 'laddered' – an approach which was very much attuned to static warfare and which itself was impossible to implement forward of battalion. Line, particularly the more rickety circuits found in the extreme forward area, was also very prone to intercept; severe restrictions were imposed on its use below battalion level, and screened balanced pair cables were used in conjunction with the Fullerphone to achieve secure telegraphy in clear. The circumstances of static warfare were highly conducive to interception of both line and wireless communication, to the extent that COMSEC (communications security) measures were so rigorously enforced by GHQ as to inhibit the use of radio and even telephones – when by 1918 the available technology was on the verge of solving the communications problems of the BEF.[43] The BEF, in common with other armies, seems to have fallen into the trap of being so concerned as to the risk of compromise of traffic that it failed to take full advantage of wireless, and even line, capabilities, at a time when the air defence organization in South East England was showing what could be done with two-way radio used on a lavish scale.[44]

Nevertheless, the exploitation of available telecommunications technology, not only in the field of communications themselves but in terms of the application of COMSEC measures, the acquisition and exploitation of COMINT (communications intelligence), and the use of electronic deception measures as in the preparation for the Battle of Amiens, indicate an approach to information warfare on the part of GHQ which was advanced for its day.

TECHNOLOGY AND THE COMMANDER IN CHIEF

The high command has to be judged on the basis of the use it made of technology, first as it existed prior to the outbreak of war, secondly on the speed and effectiveness with which it took advantage of developments during hostilities, and finally on the extent to which capability gaps were identified and technical solutions sought.

The responsibility for the application of technology to war is not one to which the actual holders of high command appointments can necessarily devote a great deal of their working time. Research, design, development, production are functions which are exercised in peace and war by branches of ministries. However, a commander in the field does bear responsibility for the identification of a need and its rapid communication, supported by a senior signature, to the agencies that can put action in hand to meet the need. As important, under the stress of war, is a receptive attitude towards innovation, even to 'solutions looking for problems'. The Great War was notable for the large number of such innovations which were of no use whatsoever,[45] bearing out the view of the anonymous Victorian which begins this essay. Some, such as the Stokes mortar, were winners; others, such as cloud gas techniques, might not fulfil their initial promise but might fill a capability gap until the real answer came along.[46] Others, such as Haig's own proposal for tank landing craft for use in operations against the Belgian coast,[47] were overtaken by events.

Second only to Haig's strength of will, in the array of qualities fitting him uniquely among his contemporaries for his post, was his ability to apply his mind effectively to a span of concerns which would have brought lesser men down. His insatiable curiosity and enthusiasm for new ideas have already been mentioned (see note 4). This was not merely a matter of noting ideas for the record, but of putting his personal weight behind them in his correspondence with the people and organizations with the power to make things happen. His intelligent layman's understanding of weapon principles shows him to advantage as compared with some more modern figures. Haig's listening and information-gathering service was excellent; his body of liaison officers visiting forward formations kept him abreast of happenings in the real world. His luncheon and dinner-tables, where he entertained both subordinates and high-placed visitors, provided him with other opportunities for direct contact. His personal intervention at critical junctures was instrumental in the development of the RFC, of the gas weapon, of the Lewis in the light role, of the No 5 (Mills) grenade, of light and heavy trench mortars, and of the tanks. And his tireless persistence in pressing for quantity in both new and existing equipments was proved correct, as abundance of materiel provided the long-denied operational flexibility which gives the fighting of the last six months of the War its texture, different from anything that had gone before. Although the BEF had survived the first two German offensives of 1918, survival alone is no guarantee of good morale. But when equipment losses are immediately made good with new and shiny replacements, with the assurance that there is more where that came from, tails lift. The spring of 1918 did not quite bring defeat for the BEF, but defeat twice came too close for comfort. That the same BEF, despite its depleted ranks (and manpower deficiencies, unlike equipment losses, could never be made up) came back to play the principal role in running the German Army out of France and out of the War, is a tribute to those who equipped it and those who identified and pressed for the equipment it needed. Douglas Haig did not fail in that duty of a commander – the duty of ensuring that his troops had the right tools for the job, and, in the end, enough of them.

ACKNOWLEDGEMENTS

My thanks to John Hussey for reading the manuscript and suggesting a number of amendments (most of which have been incorporated); to David Porter for help with research and ideas; and to the staff of the Prince Consort's Library, Aldershot, for their helpfulness to the rusticated researcher and their incredible speed of reaction.

Notes

1   Ian V Hogg, *German Secret Weapons of the Second World War*, Greenhill Books, London 1999, p 11.

2   The excesses of enthusiasm for technological progress recently highlighted (somewhat heavy-handedly) in James Cameron's film *Titanic* (Fox 1997).

3   For a contemporary gloss on these attitudes, see Rudyard Kipling, *McAndrew's Hymn* (1893).

4   Any assessment of Haig as being of limited intellect must be torpedoed by the fact that Haldane, who was most certainly nobody's fool, asked specifically for his services as DMT/DSD to implement the reform programme of 1906 onward, retained him in post for three years, and spoke in glowing terms on his departure – 'the most highly equipped thinker in the British Army'. John Terraine, *Haig – The Educated Soldier*, Hutchinson, London 1963 pp 40–45 and title page to Part 1. For Haig's enthusiasm for the cutting edge of technology, *ibid*, pp 95–96. Haldane's regard for Haig's intellectual qualities remained undimmed through the war years: see Robert Blake (ed), *The Private Papers of Douglas Haig 1914–1919*, Eyre and Spottiswoode, London 1952, p 188, for Haldane's letter of congratulation on Haig's elevation to Field-Marshal.

5   The lack of technically educated officers to fill what would now be termed weapons staff posts was a serious shortcoming during the Great War; see *History of the Ministry of Munitions* Vol 9 Pt II p 105. For a present-day perspective see P W Merriman, 'The Importance of Being Purple', *British Army Review* No 120, December 1998, p 31, where avoidance of the technical leg of the Joint Services Command and Staff Course is still viewed as an advantage by the author.

6   Minié, Enfield, Snider conversion, Martini-Henry, Lee-Metford, long Lee-Enfield, short Lee-Enfield. In contrast, the SMLE then lasted in Regular Army service until the end of the 1950s. Similarly, and as another tribute to the abilities of the pre-Great War designers, the Vickers remained in operational use in the British Army up to 1964 (Confrontation with Indonesia).

7   William McElwee, *The Art of War from Waterloo to Mons*, Weidenfeld & Nicolson, London 1974, *passim*. McElwee's thesis is that success in

19th Century warfare went almost exclusively to the side which had gained the technical advantage.

8   *Ibid*, p 138.

9   For example, few overviews of the Civil War stress Richmond's vital industrial capacity, which was at least as important a factor as its status as the capital of the Confederacy in ensuring that the Army of Northern Virginia would stand and fight to defend it – the essential aim of Grant's fixing operations of 1864. The city contained not only the Richmond Ironworks but the South's main small arms production line.

10 For a recent and accessible account of the Sudan campaign see Edward M Spiers, *Wars of Intervention: A Case Study – The Reconquest of the Sudan 1896–99*, The Occasional No 32, Strategic and Combat Studies Institute, Camberley, 1998.

11 This allegedly 'small' war actually involved British and Indian Army forces equivalent in strength to two corps. See Michael Barthorp, *The Frontier Ablaze: The North West Frontier Rising 1897–98*, Windrow & Greene, London 1997 for a modern account of these operations.

12 John Hussey, 'Without an Army, and Without any Preparation to Equip One: The Financial and Industrial Background to 1914', *British Army Review* No 109, April 1995, p 76. Not only is this article a brilliant summary of the subject covered by its title, but it also carries the story through to the mid-war period, and is full of useful statistics.

13 The BEF, and the British Army as a whole, were far worse placed than their Continental Allies and their main adversary in this regard; the business of raising and sustaining great armies being already familiar to the nations with long experience of fielding large conscript forces. Editorial article, 'The High Tide and the Turn', *British Army Review*, No 119, August 1998, p 83.

14 And simply to improved competence on the part of commanders and staffs at all levels. Professor Tim Travers overstates the case when he suggests (*How the War Was Won*, Routledge, London 1992, pp 175–177) that the last phase of the war saw an 'abdication of responsibility' on the part of Haig in favour of the Army Commanders; it does show an unqualified willingness on Haig's part to trust the subordinates whom he had trained – not such a bad thing, viewed from the standpoint of an Army which today embraces the principle of mission command?

15 John Terraine, *Educated Soldier*, pp 176–177, quoting *Diary* 27 October, 1916.

16 John Terraine, *The White Heat*, Leo Cooper, London 1992, pp 39–41. The Royal Navy had installed three shipboard W/T sets in 1899, over 400 by 1914. The Army had successfully trialled airship installations in 1911; 1912 saw successful transmission from a seaplane.

17 Correlli Barnett, *The Collapse of British Power,* Alan Sutton, Gloucester 1984, *passim.*

18 So much so that the pattern 1914 (P14) rifle was preferred to the SMLE for mass production in the United States, despite being a much less suitable weapon for combat (it was much beloved by the 'gravel bellies' – the target shooting fraternity – as being everything that the SMLE was not). Ian V Hogg and John Weeks, *Military Small Arms of the 20th Century,* Arms and Armour, London 1991, p 105.

19 Kitchener's Anglo-Egyptian force at Omdurman had included 44 Maxims (W S Churchill, *The River War,* Longmans, London 1899, quoted in Spiers, *op cit*). Imperial forces in South Africa held 315 Maxims (John Terraine, *The Smoke and the Fire,* Leo Cooper, London 1992, p 135). In 1914 the British Army's total holdings were 1963 (Hussey, op cit, p 79). The weapon had been a 'given' in military thinking long before the Great War; the problem remained how to integrate a weapon that was too heavy for the infantry battalion, yet was not an artillery piece, into the order of battle. The organizational implications were still causing heart-searching at the time of the Kirke Committee in 1931 (Kirke Committee Report, WO33/1297, pp 15–16).

20 The characteristic of the 75 and its equivalents in other armies having the most far-reaching implications was the increase in rates of fire. Not only did this transform the battlefield in terms of fire effect, but the resulting vast increase in ammunition expenditure had not been factored into stock holdings or production planning even by 1914.

21 Weights Hogg and Weeks, *op cit*, pp 283, 286. Numbers Hussey, *op cit,* p 80.

22 The Lewis had the advantage that it required only one-sixth the production cost and man-hours of the Vickers (Hogg and Weeks, *ibid,* p 284). There is no doubt that on first acceptance it was seen as another means of meeting the demand for 'machine guns, class unspecified'.

23 Haig to Ministry of Munitions fact-finding mission June 1915 and at Army Commanders' conference March 1916 (Terraine, *Smoke and Fire, op cit,* pp140–141).

24 If one has to select a single reference as the leader of the pack, Paddy Griffith, *Battle Tactics of the Western Front: The British Army's Art of Attack 1916–18,* Yale University Press, London 1994, pp 129–34.

25 Both the 13-pdr of the RHA and the RFA 18-pdr were designed as 'galloper guns', driven by the requirement to provide direct fire support to cavalry or infantry with shrapnel at limited ranges. The design of both was based on a light, pole trail carriage with cross-axle traverse which limited elevation of the 18-pdr to 16 degrees and its maximum range to 6525 yards. Both guns look old-fashioned when set against the 4.5-inch howitzer, despite there being only 5 years between the dates of their entry

into service (1904 and 1909) (for a superbly detailed record of these weapons see Len Trawin, *Early British Quick-firing Artillery*, Nexus Special Interests, Hemel Hempstead 1997). Until the arrival of the box trail Mk 3 carriage in 1918, which permitted 30 degrees elevation giving a range in excess of 9000 yards, 18-pdr batteries paid the penalty by being always dragged forward to gun positions where they were highly vulnerable to counter-battery fire. In the later stages of Third Ypres, their short range forced the 18-pdrs so far forward that obtaining stable gun platforms in the morass was well-nigh impossible, and ammunition supply often reduced to what could be carried up on the man. As a result, after Broodseinde (4 October, 1917) artillery support for attacks was severely limited.

Range limitations were not confined to the field guns; the 60-pdr gun, itself a primary counter-battery weapon, went through the greater part of the War with range limited to 10000 yards. An update increased this to 16000, but again not until 1918 (Ian V Hogg, *British and American Artillery of the Second World War*, Arms and Armour, London 1978, pp 23, 44 – a useful source of statistics on Great War legacy equipments still in service in 1939 and after). These performance shortcomings can be traced without difficulty to the urgent need for volume production of existing equipments from limited production facilities, and the unacceptability of a break in production while new designs were introduced. By 1918 the necessary production capacity had become available.

26   18-pdr HE was first used at First Ypres on a trial basis (Shelford Bidwell and Dominick Graham, *Fire-Power*, Allen & Unwin, London 1985, p 68 fn 80). British HE filling at the outbreak of war was Lyddite (picric acid – trinitrophenol) which had the advantage that phenol provided a cheap and readily available feedstock, but Lyddite was over-sensitive in itself and chemically aggressive, its reaction products being even less safe. German HE used TNT: very safe, to the extent that serious effort has to be put into making it explode; much easier to fill into shell than Lyddite; but derived from toluene, which the British chemical industry was not able to supply in quantity at the outbreak of war. TNT-based fillings entered British service in quantity from 1916 onward; the defects of Lyddite were illustrated at Jutland when fillings of armour-piercing shell detonated on impact.

Early-war percussion shell fuzes were slow-acting so that projectiles buried before exploding, limiting their splinter effect. The introduction of the direct-acting Fuze No 106 in the spring of 1917 dramatically increased lethality – and wire-cutting ability – while simplifying fire planning; creeping barrages using shrapnel called for a high degree of expertise in fuze-setting.

27   The 'heavy' element of the BEF's artillery on first deployment in 1914 was

provided solely by the four 60-pdr guns in each divisional heavy battery. One 9.2-inch howitzer had been delivered, which became the design parent for all the super-heavy howitzers. Heavier weapons, of various calibres and degrees of antiquity, first reached the BEF on the Aisne in September 1914 (Bidwell & Graham, *op cit*, p 80).

28   Hussey, *op cit*, p 80, states that on 2 Oct 14 reserve stocks of .303-inch SAA stood at three million rounds only. This was one week's production from Woolwich and just under half a week's worth from all sources.

29   For intervention by Haig to encourage development of Stokes mortar, see extract from *Diary*, entry for 20 Jul 15, reproduced in Terraine, *Educated Soldier*, facing p 367. For need for heavy trench mortars and reliable grenades, *ibid* p 95

30   Bidwell & Graham record Birch's statement that Haig tasked him to 're-organise and strengthen the artillery so that it could . . . be able to make a surprise attack at any point in the line instead of having to concentrate the whole of the artillery in one place . . .' *op cit*, p 151.

31   Lyn Macdonald, *1914*, Michael Joseph, London 1987, p 162.

32   Jonathan Bailey, *The First World War and the Birth of Modern Warfare*, The Occasional No 22, Strategic and Combat Studies Institute, Camberley 1996. The development of artillery techniques in the Great War ably summarized, pp 7–17.

33   Bidwell & Graham, *op cit*, p 140.

34   Bailey, *op cit*, pp 17–21.

35   Material for this section drawn from John Sutton (ed), *Wait for the Waggon: The Story of the Royal Corps of Transport and its Predecessors, 1794–1993*, Leo Cooper for the Institution of the Royal Army Service Corps and the Royal Corps of Transport, London 1998, pp 50–75.

36   Light rail is something of a lost technology. The Museum of Army Transport at Beverley has a substantial display devoted to the subject; the characteristics which made it so effective in the conditions of the Western Front make it equally suitable for application to humanitarian operations today.

37   In the *Diary* entry for 4 December, 1914, Haig notes the advantages of motor over horse-drawn ambulances as being able to get closer to the front line. Blake, *op cit*, p 79.

38   C N Barclay, *Armistice 1918*, Dent, London 1968, p 90, quoted in Terraine, *White Heat*, p 93.

39   Terraine, *White Heat*, p 27.

40   Terraine, *Educated Soldier*, pp 53, 88.

41   FM The Viscount Slim, *Defeat into Victory*, Cassell, London 1956, p 165.

42   Bidwell & Graham, *op cit* p 143, for agreement between Haig and Trenchard on necessity of winning and maintaining air superiority. *Diary*, 27 November, 1916, has Haig putting the requirement for more powerful

aero engines as a pre-requisite to this end, second only to manpower needs in his overall priorities, to Bonar Law (Blake, *op cit*, p183). Also see Terraine, *Educated Soldier*, p 287, for Haig taking the same point up with Robertson in December 1916.

43 Bidwell & Graham, *op cit*, p 141–142 for a précis of the 1918 state of the art in telecoms. The authors stress the weight and fragility of most wireless equipment, so that forward area operation tended to be by line back to a semi-static 'wireless head'. Nevertheless there were cases of wireless being taken forward, with a continuous wave Woolwich valve set working back from Vimy Ridge in April 1917 at a range of 8000 yards off a five foot aerial – this at medium frequency; high frequency did not become generally available until 1924 (*Admiralty Handbook of Wireless Telegraphy 1938*, Part II, HMSO, London 1938, p K1). Despite the emphasis placed by John Terraine and other authors as to the lack of 'a walkie-talkie', the most serious deficiency in the Great War was an effective battalion rear link to brigade – which in WWII was provided by a *vehicle-mounted* set.

44 For UK air defence system, Terraine, *White Heat,* p 270. Detail on COMSEC from John Ferris (ed), *The British Army and Signals Intelligence During The First World War,* Alan Sutton for Army Records Society, Stroud 1992.The BEF approach to COMSEC failed to take into account the fact that the threat from interception was high during quiet periods but lower during intense operations, when the importance of rapid passage of information outweighs the risk of compromise, and leaky means of communication such as radio, the power buzzer, and any line which would work ought to have been used more freely. Users of present-day insecure voice radio may find a resonance here.

45 Eg the 'trench fans' foisted upon an unwilling BEF in the rush to provide countermeasures in the aftermath of the first German gas attacks at second Ypres. (Author's records).

46 First Army's attack at Loos in September 1915 relied on gas to compensate for the shortfall in artillery; *Diary* 16 September, 1915, (Blake, *op cit*, p 103). Also see entry for 7 July, 1915, (*ibid*, p 96), where Haig stresses the importance of reserving the first use of gas for a major occasion. Significantly, after Loos cloud gas was never used again as a key component of the support for any major attack.

47 *Diary*, 18 September, 1916; Blake, *op cit*, p 167.

Chapter 11

Haig and the Press

Stephen Badsey

Historians of the First World War, and of the career of Douglas Haig, have certainly not neglected the role played in both by the British Press. Robert Blake, in his introduction to the 1952 published edition of Haig's papers, noted the remarkable power exercised by Press magnates during the war, and the deference shown to them by politicians and generals.[1] But even at the other end of a 'media century', a full account of the Press in the First World War has yet to be written, and the extensive newspaper record of Haig's activities remains a misunderstood and under-used resource. Consequently, the manner in which Haig fought what is now called the 'Media War' has remained a neglected factor in assessing his achievements.[2]

The remarkable powers attributed in Britain during the First World War to the Press and its owners arose directly from the failure of established institutions to adjust to the political and social changes of the preceding years. Despite the extension of the franchise by the Reform and Redistribution Acts of 1884–85, Britain continued to be governed largely by patricians for another two decades. In 1914 many politicians whose fathers had feared both the Mob and the Revolution were still feeling their way towards understanding the new mass politics. In 1928, after two further extensions of the franchise had produced universal suffrage, Asquith wrote that 'The average party politician finds it difficult to realise the extent of the vague, floating, and dim formless elements which go to make up our vast electorate',[3] adding that things had become much worse since the granting of votes to women.

With the Press also, it was not until the early twentieth century that changes instituted decades earlier began to have their impact in Britain. The Education Acts (England and Wales) of 1870 and 1880 are now seen as the culmination, rather than the start, of the growth of working class literacy and newspaper reading.[4] But despite the more populist 'New Journalism' style introduced in the 1880s by the *Pall Mall Gazette*, the major changes in newspaper ownership and sales came only in 1894, from the Anglo-Irish Harmsworth family, led by Alfred (created Lord Northcliffe in 1905), whose success in founding the first mass circulation daily newspaper, the *Daily Mail* in 1896, also enabled him to buy *The Times* in 1908. By the start of the war, Northcliffe's newspapers accounted for around half the total daily sales in London alone.

In the nineteenth century, owners and editors of newspapers – and a few reporters – had been seen both as opinion formers, and as essential conduits of communication between the various national elites and interest groups; the actual size of newspaper circulation was much less important. This older type was still well represented by one of Haig's guests at GHQ in 1916, John St. Loe Strachey, the owner-editor of the weekly *Spectator*, who was also Lord Lieutenant of Surrey.[5] Northcliffe, as the self-styled 'Ogre of Fleet Street', was himself very much a journalist; but his success began a new trend of businessmen with little background in journalism founding or acquiring newspapers, often in syndicates rather than outright, solely for financial gain and as a means of exercising political influence. From a market utterly dominated by *The Times* fifty years before, by 1914 there were about eight major daily national newspapers, all based in London with the exception of the *Manchester Guardian*, together with about twice that number of influential weeklies and lower-circulation London newspapers. A close association with this kind of Pressman was a mark of political radicals, including particularly Lloyd George, who surrounded himself with newspaper owners such as Sir Henry Dalziel, Sir George Riddell, Lord Cowdray, Lord Rothermere (Northcliffe's brother), and Sir Max Aitken (who became Lord Beaverbrook in 1917). Part of the story of Lloyd George's wartime rise to power and premiership was his eventual success in bringing such men into his government by 1918, progressively alienating others as he did so.[6]

The power exercised by these men derived partly from their being rich enough to own newspapers, but also from a basic dilemma among politicians of how to measure and interpret public opinion in the mass. A fusion of the older beliefs, that a newspaper report or editorial spoke for an important section of public opinion, with the fact of the mass sales of newspapers like the *Daily Mail* or Beaverbrook's *Daily Express*, produced the simplistic view that the Press somehow held direct control over the views and voting powers of the new mass electorate. Beaverbrook's later assessment of Northcliffe, that 'His power was so considerable that it was of the utmost importance in all matters of public interest to secure his assistance or at any rate his neutrality',[7] was widely held during the First World War, not least by Northcliffe himself. In one entirely characteristic outburst to Haig in January, 1917, Northcliffe threatened, if they would not do his bidding, to bring down not only the British government, but the French government as well.[8] These beliefs were given formal expression as a weapon of war by Lloyd George in Spring, 1918, with the appointment of Northcliffe as Director of Propaganda in Enemy Countries and Beaverbrook as Chancellor of the Duchy of Lancaster heading the new Ministry of Information. The patrician Lord Esher wrote to Sir William Robertson that 'The [P]ress has taken over the powers that Parliament has abdicated' adding that this was 'a natural outcome of what is called "popular government"'.[9]

Chief in importance among the lower-circulation London newspapers was that bastion of die-hard Conservatism, the *Morning Post*, edited by H. A. 'Taffy' Gwynne, who was later active in the early British fascist movement.[10] The most famous of the accredited war correspondents at Haig's GHQ, Philip Gibbs of the *Daily Chronicle*, wrote that he found it necessary to talk to most generals 'on the lines of leading articles in the *Morning Post*'.[11] During the Curragh Incident, Gwynne acted as an adviser to Field-Marshal Sir John French;[12] and other senior Army officers with whom he had at least some contact or correspondence included Herbert Kitchener, Henry Wilson, William Robertson, Horace Smith-Dorrien, Henry Rawlinson, Hubert Gough, Julian Byng, Philip Chetwode and Ivor Maxse,[13] as well as Douglas Haig. Although Gwynne visited Haig at GHQ, written communication between them, and also between Haig and other prominent members of the Press, took place through either Haig's Brigadier-General Intelligence John Charteris, or his suave and secretive private secretary, Captain Sir Philip Sassoon.[14] Reporters visiting GHQ were also usually seen by Charteris, (who had worked for *The Times* in the past),[15] or even by one of his staff officers,[16] while Haig might see editors and proprietors himself.

Other than Gwynne, the newsman who enjoyed the most privileged status among senior Army officers was the military correspondent of *The Times*, Lieutenant-Colonel (Retired) Charles à Court Repington, whose involvement in the military politics of the war became notorious, not least through his own egotistical memoirs. In the early part of the war, Repington enjoyed the privilege of personal invitations to GHQ from Sir John French. Indeed, it was the sophistic claim that Repington was present at GHQ as a guest rather than a reporter which enabled both French and *The Times* to argue that Repington's 'Shell Scandal' report of 12 May, 1915, was not a violation of military regulations.[17]

Repington also listed French's two chiefs of staff, Archibald Murray and William Robertson, as 'two of my oldest and most valued soldier friends',[18] a relationship which deepened in significance when Robertson took over as CIGS. In contrast, Haig's dislike of Repington went back years before the First World War. When Repington asked to interview him at First Army Headquarters in May, 1915, Haig declined on the grounds that 'neither I nor my staff had the authority to see any newspaper correspondents and that all information for the Press must be obtained from GHQ'.[19] This was followed by an incident a few days later when one of First Army's observation posts was heavily shelled, something which Haig and his staff attributed to a further report in *The Times* by Repington which French had let pass uncensored.[20] Haig's first reaction was to demand from GHQ the exclusion of all reporters from First Army area; and the experience undoubtedly reinforced his underlying dislike of the Press.

In addition to the activities of proprietors, editors and reporters behind the scenes, described by Esher as having 'taken the place of the Jesuits of old',[21] the main political importance of the Press was the manner in which an otherwise hidden conflict or controversy could coalesce around a sudden public revelation or 'scoop' (a term which itself dates from the 1880s). In the course of the war such episodes included the Mons Despatch in *The Times* of August, 1914, Repington's Shell Scandal report of May, 1915, and the Maurice Letter of May, 1918. The newspaper interview in particular was in 1914 still seen as a recent practice, introduced into Britain from the United States as part of the 'New Journalism' style. A willingness to grant interviews was an indicator of political populism, and Asquith eventually made it a rule to give no Press interviews at all.[22] A common compromise, which Haig himself adopted at GHQ, was to allow occasional interviews but to forbid verbatim reporting, so that no actual quotations appeared. Charteris, who was usually present, contemptuously described the resulting pieces as '... "Union Jack over the door, cow grazing in the meadow, strong silent man, blue eyes, white moustache, raised [relief] maps", and such-like drivel'.[23] Given Haig's inarticulate style of speech, this was a wise precaution. In 1908 there had been a spectacular *gaffe* when an interview with Kaiser Wilhelm II intended to improve Anglo-German relations had appeared in the *Daily Telegraph* in verbatim form, beginning with the Kaiser's observation that 'You English are mad, mad, mad as March hares',[24] an incident which precipitated the fall of Chancellor von Bülow. Just as the assassination at Sarajevo was the occasion rather than the cause of the war itself, so during its course such newspaper dramas formed the occasions through which much wider issues found their particular form and substance.

By the First World War the convention was very well established that senior Army officers were permitted the same kind of informal contact with newspaper owners and editors as any other influential people. Even interviews were tolerated, although only rarely of the verbatim kind. But in their strict interpretation, military regulations made contact with the Press of virtually any kind an offence. Military censorship and tight control of the Press at the start of the war was not, as it is often portrayed, a personal whim of Lord Kitchener, (although he was deeply hostile towards war reporters), but a reflection of the most recent thinking on the subject, based on a genuine attempt to learn the lessons of previous wars.[25] Even the criticized use of Colonel Ernest Swinton as the military 'Eye Witness' during Autumn and Winter, 1914–1915, was just a late manifestation of the nineteenth century tradition of serving officers doubling as war correspondents. Military thinking on the Press reflected the views of civilian society: that what the war correspondent wrote was so powerfully influential that it must be rigorously controlled, not just to avoid giving secrets to the enemy, but to maintain civilian morale at home. In addition to wide-ranging government powers for control of the Press, starting in 1914 with the Defence of the Realm Act (DORA) and the creation of the Whitehall Press Bureau, the War Office had its own double censorship system for reports from the Western Front, which were censored first by the Press Section at GHQ (part of the Intelligence Branch) and then again at the War Office.

Despite this very strong range of legal sanctions available, the power and influence exercised by the London Press remained so great that in practice it was left to be largely self-regulating. Censorship was usually of the lightest kind, and regulations were enforced only in the very rare cases of direct confrontation or open defiance of the government, such as exhibited by the *Morning Post* in February 1918. In return, most of the London Press agreed with the historian of *The Times*, that 'their task was to sustain the morale of the nation in mortal combat', distinguishing this from 'fair criticism of the government of the day'.[26] On the fighting fronts, once the need for accredited journalists was accepted in early 1915, matters were left almost entirely in the hands of local senior commanders. The extensive provincial Press was both excluded from providing accredited war correspondents and largely ignored by the censorship regulations, as simply politically unimportant.[27]

In December, 1915, when Haig assumed command of the BEF, the *Sunday Times* ran a 'Character Sketch' which began 'There are spots on every sun and it must be confessed that the new Commander-in-Chief does not like journalists'.[28] Throughout his career, Haig's loyalties and power base depended on the political and social elite, and he disapproved of those who sought Press and public attention. Indeed, a large part of Haig's dislike of Lloyd George was what he saw as the Welshman's obsession with the Press and publicity.[29] Shortly after Haig assumed command on the Western Front, Sassoon replied on Haig's behalf to a letter of congratulations from Gwynne of the *Morning Post*:

> 'He [Haig] thinks it splendid of an Editor, and one that has so many journalistic interests like yourself, to praise him for what you call his disregard of the Press! It is that he feels – I am sure [inserted] – that every man should be judged by his own actions and merits and that it is wrong to try to influence other people's judgements. All editors, as you will admit, are not like yourself, nor all papers like the *Morning Post*, and for those who wish to steer a straight course there are too many rocks ahead without going into the back waters of intrigue.'[30]

The idea of Sassoon, a former MP from the famous Jewish financial family, writing to the rabidly anti-Semitic, politician-hating Gwynne, is certainly an incongruous one. But Haig was clearly at pains to put nothing in his own handwriting, nor to have any idea directly attributed to himself. However, Haig was by no means a complete Press novice. Earlier in his career he had seen Lord Roberts' deliberate cultivation of the Press at first hand; and he had himself played a part in publicizing the Cavalry Division in the South African War (1899–1902) through the journalist C. S. Goldmann.[31] While at First Army he was also kept informed of French's attempts to manipulate the Press against Kitchener.[32] The impressive collection of newspaper cuttings kept by his wife during the war, which form part of his papers, bears testimony to his role as a public figure. If his own Press contacts were largely indirect, then this was a matter of personal preference. His chief mistake on taking over at GHQ was that both he and Charteris believed that their relationship with the Press was one over which they could exercise complete control.

The accredited correspondents at GHQ under Haig, of which there were usually no more than six headed by Philip Gibbs, Percival Philips of the *Daily Express*, William Beach Thomas of the *Daily Mail*, and H. Perry Robinson of *The Times*, have received much criticism, including the often quoted judgement of Lord Rothermere at the end of Third Ypres that 'They don't know the truth, they don't speak the truth, and we know that they don't!'.[33] Much of this criticism, both at the time and since,[34] attributes to the reporters the considerable power to influence opinions in which they and their contemporaries believed. In reality, the reporters and their GHQ escort officers (who included the former *Manchester Guardian* journalist C. E. Montague)[35] found themselves as minor players trapped in a complicated hierarchical structure dominated by politicians, generals and newspaper owners.[36] In return for access to GHQ and to some of its secrets, they practised largely voluntary self-censorship and conformed to the military restrictions placed upon them, including pooling their reports and wearing uniform as honorary officers. Attempts to increase their number were resisted not only by GHQ, but also by the newspaper owners themselves.

As for the truthfulness of their reports, it is a matter of record that the GHQ correspondents – and Philip Gibbs in particular – wrote, and their newspapers published, vivid accounts of the fighting experiences of individual soldiers in battle, very much in the 'New Journalism' style; but always holding out hope of victory, and without criticism of the higher commanders.[37] As Gibbs put it, in an introduction to a collection of his articles which was published while the war was still being fought:

> 'There is no criticism in this book, no judgement of actions of men, no detailed summing up of success or failure. That is not within my liberty or duty as a correspondent with the Armies in the Field.'[38]

They were also too inclined to repeat uncritically information supplied by GHQ. According to Major Arthur Lee, one of the GHQ Press Section officers (who made no effort to hide his own distaste for the Press), the purpose of the GHQ daily briefings was to tell the accredited correspondents 'as much of the military situation up to date as was considered good for them'.[39]

Still, the reporters did have some independent influence, and their advice and knowledge on events in France were sought by senior officers and politicians in Whitehall. In November, 1917, when Gibbs was on leave in London, he impressed Lloyd George both with his high private opinion of Major-General Charles ('Tim') Harington, chief of staff of Second Army,[40] and by his description, given at a dinner in his honour, of the dreadful conditions of Passchendaele.[41] According to Gibbs, he 'told the naked truth that night',[42] to Lloyd George, something that he might reveal only among fellow members of the elite. It was not that the masses did not know about the casualty lists, but that the elite were convinced that the people's faith in their leaders would be shaken if any newspaper raised wider questions about the war.

On taking over at GHQ, Haig inherited a number of Press problems, including persistent complaints from the London newspapers that daily official GHQ *communiqués* were dull and unhelpful, and the correspondents' reports over-censored. Much of the pressure came from the War Office, particularly from Robertson who, unlike Haig, had no choice but to deal with the Press and its owners on a daily basis. 'He who lives by the river must make friends with the crocodile', as Charteris put it.[43] On 1 June, 1916, Haig had his first ever meeting with the GHQ correspondents, in one of those episodes which reveal the limitations of Haig's diary and letters as an accurate record of events. According to Haig, 'They all expressed themselves as thoroughly satisfied with the facilities given them',[44] and also 'Gibbs and Beach Thomas seem quite gentlemanly fellows'.[45] Gibbs remembered Haig's opening remarks as being something along these lines:

> 'I think I understand fairly well what you gentlemen want ... You want to get hold of little stories on heroism, and so forth, and to write them up in a bright way to make good reading for Mary Anne in the kitchen, and the man in the street.'[46]

Although Gibbs in particular never really forgave this insult, the correspondents gamely swallowed it. They explained their problems to Haig, who to his credit listened, agreeing to allow them greater freedom of movement and better briefings in future. Haig then briefed the reporters on the GHQ position for the forthcoming offensive, using a three-page 'Memorandum on Policy for the Press' which is one of the most important pieces of evidence on Haig's own views on the war at this stage. It began with a warning:

> 'A danger which the country has to face at present is that of unreasoning impatience. Military history teems with instances where sound military principles have had to be abandoned owing to the pressure of ill-informed public opinion. The [P]ress is the best means to hand to prevent the danger in the present war.'

There followed pages on the progressive weakening of Germany and the increasing strength of Britain, and estimates of the losses suffered by both Germany and France since 1914, concluding:

> '[T]he lessons which the people of England have to learn are patience, self-sacrifice and confidence in our ability to win in the long run. The aim for which the war is being waged is the destruction of German militarism. Three years of war and the loss of one-tenth of the manhood of the nation is not too great a price to pay in so great a cause.'[47]

It is not clear if the reporters were given copies of this critical document. But even the British Army's *Official History* devotes a few pages to Haig's relaxation of censorship and improvement of Press coverage of the Western Front.[48] The quality of official *communiqués* was also much improved, initially by the Foreign Office loaning Charteris the novelist John Buchan, who had also previously served as an official correspondent at GHQ.[49]

All this should be seen as just one more example of Haig's thoroughness, rather than any attempt to engage with the Press himself. After this first meeting, he scarcely saw the GHQ correspondents again for the duration of the war, leaving their handling almost entirely to the Press Section staff. Even so, what the GHQ correspondents wrote for the next two years may be taken as reflecting Haig's own views and wishes very closely indeed. Haig eventually trusted Gibbs and Beach Thomas enough to ask them to compose his own weekly Commander-in-Chief's reports on the war.[50] In a little ceremony held on the Hohenzollern Bridge in Cologne on 16 December, 1918, Haig gave each reporter his handshake and a small Union Jack, with the words, 'Gentleman, you have played the game like men!', perhaps the highest compliment in his vocabulary.[51] The five senior reporters also later received knighthoods.

Before the 1916 Somme offensive, Haig had successfully resisted pleas from Robertson to allow 'on your invitation 4 or 5 of our big newspaper proprietors', including Northcliffe, to visit GHQ.[52] But soon afterwards, Haig received his first lesson on the real power of the Press. On 4 July, Lord Esher wrote from Paris that Repington wished to visit GHQ, but expected a personal invitation from Haig such as he had received from French, and continued to receive from the Italian and French commanders. Haig's reaction was to snub Repington, replying that he could apply through Charteris like any other correspondent. Four days later, somebody had changed Haig's mind for him. He recorded in his diary:

> 'Among the correspondents [visiting the front] is Repington of *The Times* ... I was requested from London to receive Repington for the good of the Army, so I did so at about 10.30 a.m. I hated seeing such a dishonest individual, but I felt it was my duty to the Army to do so. Otherwise, he would have been an unfriendly critic of its actions.'[53]

The meeting was a little tense, neither Haig nor Repington quite managing to hide their mutual dislike.[54] But despite this, Repington remained a reluctant supporter of Haig, in keeping with his broader position of supporting the Army. Haig sought Repington's help, for example, in June, 1917 over the dispute about manpower for the forthcoming Third Ypres offensive.[55]

On 21 July, 1916, Repington's employer, Northcliffe of *The Times*, also made the visit to GHQ at Haig's invitation. Charteris, at least, realized the critical nature of this meeting, noting that unlike Kitchener, who had withstood attacks. by the Press, Haig had virtually no public *persona* or support on which to draw. 'A great deal depends on how he and D[ouglas] H[aig] get on together', Charteris concluded, 'they have very little in common'.[56] Astonishingly, the two men got on magnificently, Northcliffe even attending church with Haig that Sunday.[57] Haig gave Northcliffe complete freedom of access to information within GHQ, and in return Northcliffe wrote frequently to Haig through Sassoon. Shortly after this visit, Northcliffe went to the War Office and offered to put his whole Press empire at the disposal of the General Staff, apparently hoping to be placed in charge of British propaganda, for which he believed at the time he had Haig's support.[58]

Throughout Autumn, 1916, Pressmen and what Charteris called the 'Press war-lords'[59] continued to visit GHQ, only the most important being seen by Haig himself. However, a considerable network of informal contacts also existed, with which Haig was seldom directly involved, and which has left little record. A rare case of such a contact becoming visible occurred in October, 1916, when Haig was visited by Major-General Ivor Maxse, commanding 18th (Eastern) Division, whose younger brother L. J. ('Leo') Maxse was the owner-editor of the weekly *National Review*. Haig used the opportunity to put in his diary a very clear statement of his own official position regarding the Press:

'He had heard from his brother ... that [Attorney General] F. E. Smith and others have banded together with the object of having me removed from Command of the Armies in France. Gen[eral] Maxse wished to know whether I thought he ought to urge his brother to take action in the matter. I saw him along with Gen[eral] Kiggell and I said that I had no dealings with the Press personally. That my policy had always been to give the Press as free a hand as possible. To show them everything, to allow them to talk to anyone they chose, and to write what they liked, provided no secrets were given away to the enemy. In the present case, I saw no reason to depart from this policy. If his brother chose to come to France and go round the Army and see whether F.E. Smith's statements were true or false, he was free to do so in the ordinary way. I, at any rate, could take no part in a Press campaign against anyone. All my time was taken up in thinking out how to beat the enemy of Great Britain, I mean Germany.'[60]

Nonetheless, shortly after this incident, Sassoon wrote to Gwynne congratulating him on a *Morning Post* leader attacking F. E. Smith.[61] The exact connection between the *National Review* and the rise of Ivor Maxse under Haig must remain a matter of conjecture; but Leo Maxse did visit GHQ on at least three occasions, as well as corresponding with Haig.

The main persistent problem in Press coverage of the Somme, to which there was no obvious solution, was that with so few accredited reporters at GHQ both the Canadians (who had their own propaganda organization run by Aitken, himself a Canadian by birth) and the Australians received a higher Press profile than British troops, with corresponding friction and problems in neutral countries, particularly the United States. Haig reluctantly agreed to grant interviews to overseas journalists, as 'part of the British government scheme of propaganda in neutral and other countries'.[62] This continued for just over six months, until an episode which has parallels with that which befell the Kaiser nine years earlier, which again reveals Haig's close interaction with the Press, and which nearly cost Haig his career.

In early 1917, shortly after a further visit by Northcliffe, Haig finally bowed to pressure from Esher and the Foreign Office to grant interviews to some French political deputies who were also journalists.[63] These were supervised by Charteris, and by the Press Section officer responsible for liaison with the French, Major the Honourable Neville Lytton. 'He is not fluent in any language', the bilingual Lytton wrote of Haig, 'but he is not much less fluent in French than he is in English'.[64] Haig recorded only that the Frenchmen 'seemed very pleased at my receiving them',[65] while Charteris added that 'it was intended only as a formal presentation, but D[ouglas] H[aig] took the opportunity of giving them his views that the Germans were hard hit, and that this year's big attacks should be successful'.[66]

A day or so later, the reporters submitted their pieces to Lytton for censorship, but the head of the Press Section, Colonel Arthur Hutton Wilson, required them to be cleared by Charteris, who had gone home on leave. Rather than delay the pieces Lytton prevailed on Hutton Wilson to send them to Charteris at home in Britain, who barely glanced at them before returning them to the waiting messenger. From Charteris' description they had already been censored at the War Office, ordinarily the second tier of censorship; he later claimed that he expected them to go back to GHQ for clearance by Haig personally or by Kiggell, which was not normal procedure.[67]

No one thought anything of this matter until Charteris came back from leave on 15 February. On that day, Haig's interview appeared in several Paris newspapers, each version slightly different, and all giving long and ostensibly verbatim quotations from Haig on the critical importance of the Western Front, and the inevitability of victory there. The opinions were clearly Haig's, although the expressions were equally clearly not. To make matters worse, a translation of the version in the French newspaper *l'Information* also appeared in that day's *The Times* together with an editorial fully supporting Haig's views. Lytton felt that the problem lay in over-literal translation: what was simple rousing speech in French appeared as bombast in English.[68] Before the end of the day a Parliamentary question had been put down by the Labour MP Philip Snowdon, and the War Office was demanding an explanation.

Haig's response was first to deny that he had ever given such an interview; then to argue that he had been misquoted; and then, having obtained the French reaction (which was overwhelmingly favourable), to wonder what the fuss was about.[69] Charteris at first denied that he had ever seen the pieces, until Lytton and Hutton Wilson produced the written evidence.[70] Repington in London hugely enjoyed Haig's embarrassment, spreading completely false stories over the weekend that the French were incensed at Haig's statements, and that an unknown enemy of Haig in the War Office (whom he identified as 'Z') had deliberately passed the reports in order to bring Haig down.[71]

On Monday, 18 February, Robertson arrived at GHQ for lunch, and Lytton travelled back to London with the CIGS, briefing him on the way. Next morning, Lytton faced the War Cabinet with Robertson by his side. Neither Lloyd George, who Lytton described as 'in a towering passion'[72] nor Curzon was inclined to believe a word of Lytton's story. Bonar Law calmed the meeting down, and also spoke for the government in the Commons that afternoon. Lytton briefed Northcliffe at home on the episode, as a consequence of which *The Times* and the other Northcliffe newspapers took a conciliatory line next day. According to Lytton, 'Haig would have gone' without Northcliffe's backing.[73] Haig received letters of support from Northcliffe, and also from Aitken, (who had just accepted his peerage, having hoped for a cabinet post under Lloyd George), who wrote that 'A sort of attempt has been made to take advantage of what slipped through in the Press, but this has been frustrated entirely because no decent paper would touch it'.[74]

Lytton reported to Haig on his return, and all assumed that the episode was closed. But the greatest damage had already been done. Lloyd George had sensed a deliberate conspiracy (although a less likely military conspirator than the aristocratic aesthete Lytton – the brother of a peer and a notable society artist – would be hard to imagine), believing that Haig was challenging his new authority as Prime Minister with the backing of Northcliffe and *The Times*. Without waiting to check, on the afternoon that the first stories appeared, Lloyd George had visited the War Office together with Hankey, where he suggested to the French liaison officer the placing of the British Commander-in-Chief on the Western Front under French command, the idea which became the basis of the notorious Calais Conference later that month.[75]

This Press episode was not the cause of the bad relations between Haig and Lloyd George. Given the level of heightened tension and disagreement, any small incident might have produced a confrontation. But it was the spark that lit the bonfire, leading to that confrontation taking the particular form that it did, with all the consequences for 1917, and beyond. Major Lee – perhaps reflecting GHQ gossip rather than hard fact – wrote that Lloyd George saw Charteris as the root of the supposed conspiracy, and that it was this incident which convinced him that Charteris must be removed from Haig's side.[76]

The behaviour of the British Press and propaganda organizations in 1917, and the absence of any contemporary public debate over the Third Ypres offensive, have been discussed elsewhere.[77] The friction between GHQ and the War Office over Press policy had largely ceased; partly through the reforms instituted by Haig, which continued through 1917, separating the Press Section from GHQ's propaganda organizations; partly through further changes in London, and the bringing of newsmen into the government propaganda organizations by Lloyd George;[78] and partly by Northcliffe being appointed in May, 1917 as head of a British mission to the United States, keeping him out of the country for most of the year.

In September, 1917, Gwynne of the *Morning Post* visited Haig, following this up with a letter to Charteris arguing that Haig must improve his public profile in order to oppose anti-Haig sentiments in London.[79] Charteris' resulting *crie de coeur* shows how far he had come from the belief that the Press could be controlled from GHQ:

'But if we use the Press to crack up D[ouglas] H[aig] we shall have L[loyd] G[eorge] outing him at once. If we let the correspondents have an interview with him, we shall have a repetition of last February's episode. If we check Philip Gibbs writing his 'horror-mongering' stuff we shall have his paper down our throat. If we say the Boche is beaten, or even that his morale is being lowered, we shall have the W[ar] O[ffice] itself saying that we are over-optimistic and thus making it harder for Robertson to screw the necessary men and munitions out of L[loyd] [G[eorge]. All the same I have taken steps to do what I can to give some effect to Gwynne's views, for they are right and it is worth taking the risk.'[80]

Newspaper owners, some editors, and even Repington, visited or wrote to Haig during Third Ypres,[81] and there is just enough evidence to suggest GHQ's complicity in a deliberate Press campaign, which Lloyd George and his associates were convinced that Haig was orchestrating through Robertson.[82] Lloyd George raised the matter with Haig directly at an angry meeting in Paris in November, although apparently stopping short of an outright accusation.[83] This goes some way to explaining the remarkable Press and popular reaction to the Battle of Cambrai. It was not simply a spontaneous expression of hope after the failure of Third Ypres, but a conscious attempt to boost Haig's popularity by his supporters.

It was at this critical point, at the end of 1917, that Haig lost the support of Northcliffe, who had returned to Britain. The exact circumstances may have been appropriately trivial: Northcliffe visited GHQ on 7 December, but became angry and insulted when Haig showed boredom and irritation with his reminiscences about the United States.[84] The first sign of the break was criticism in the Northcliffe Press of British generalship over the German counter-attack at Cambrai. As a member of the GHQ enquiry board into the battle, Ivor Maxse (now commanding XVIII Corps), retaliated by blaming the Press for alleged false reporting, and suggested even greater military control at GHQ over the accredited correspondents, a suggestion which Haig wisely ignored.[85] However, the experience of Cambrai once more left Haig with little taste for greater involvement with the Press.

Whatever the immediate cause, the underlying motive for Northcliffe's change of allegiance was undoubtedly the prospect of political office. Northcliffe rejected Lloyd George's first tentative offer, that of the newly created Air Ministry, in the most public way imaginable, by posting his rejection in The Times before Lloyd George was informed of it.[86] His brother Lord Rothermere was given the job instead. Haig came to believe that Northcliffe's aim was nothing short of the War Office itself; a belief which formed an important part of Haig's continuing support for Lord Derby as Secretary for War in February, 1918, when Derby was contemplating resignation.[87] It was Northcliffe's change of allegiance which led Repington to leave The Times for the Morning Post, and to his involvement in the Maurice Letter in May, the sending of which Haig utterly condemned.[88]

The neglect of the BEF's achievements in 1918, which has increasingly pre-occupied modern scholars, can also be traced in part to changes in Press policy both in Whitehall and GHQ at the start of the year. While this also awaits further research, the broad shape of the story is reasonably clear. With Beaverbrook, Rothermere and (effectively) Northcliffe joining other Press magnates in government, newspapers increasingly reflected the Whitehall perspective that the war would last until 1919. Meanwhile, Charteris' successor as head of the Intelligence Branch, Brigadier-General E. W. Cox, had no wish to deal directly with Beaverbrook or Northcliffe, who were beginning to argue for direct control of GHQ's Press and propaganda apparatus. The Press Section, renamed the Censorship and Publicity Section, was transferred to the new Staff Duties Branch of GHQ under Major-General G. P. Downey, who also showed no interest in it. While the handful of GHQ correspondents remained quite inadequate in numbers, Haig did nothing to correct this, nor to win back Press support. In consequence, there was no policy or desire either in Whitehall or at GHQ to mitigate the claims of a rout by Fifth Army in Spring, 1918, nor to publicize the British victories of later in the year.

In September, 1918, in response to a letter of congratulation from Henry Wilson as CIGS, Haig wrote rather pointedly, 'I am not nor am I likely to be a "famous general". For that must we not have pandered to Repington and the Gutter Press?',[89] a remark which could serve as his professional epitaph. Haig's enforced interaction with the Press helped shape both his strategy and some of his battles; but his few attempts to deal with them directly were clumsy, and handicapped by his limited political understanding. His preferred practice of using only indirect methods was undoubtedly correct given his own personality and limitations; but it has left a legacy of ambiguity and fragmented evidence which has prevented this important aspect of his military life being understood and valued as it deserves. The only view of events which can be positively disproved from the available record is that which Haig himself sought to promote: that he continued the war as he began it, an apolitical soldier who engaged with the Press only when directly ordered to do so. At the other extreme, the view of Lloyd George, that Haig both initiated and directed a Press campaign to promote his own position against that of the government, remains now as it was then, a matter of opinion.

Notes

1   Robert Blake, *The Private Papers of Douglas Haig 1914–1919*, Eyre and Spottiswoode, London, 1952, Introduction, p. 64.

2   For the modern concept of the 'Media War' and its importance in warfare see John Pimlott and Stephen Badsey (editors), *The Gulf War Assessed*, Arms and Armour, London, 1992, pp. 219–246; and Philip M. Taylor, *Global Communications, International Affairs and the Media Since 1945*, Routledge, London, 1997, pp. 119–124.

3   The Earl of Oxford and Asquith, *Memories and Reflections 1852–1927*, Cassell, London, 1928, Volume II, p. 235.

4   For a brief and interesting summary of this complex subject see Peter Broks, *Media Science Before the Great War*, MacMillan, London, 1996, pp. 14–17.

5   Haig Diary, 1914–1918, Volume X, entry for 4 August, 1916. Entries in the Haig Diary that appear in Blake, *The Private Papers of Douglas Haig* are cited from that source for convenience. Otherwise, there are three versions of the Haig Diary. The original manuscript version is in the Haig Papers at the National Library of Scotland [NLS], and is also available on microfilm. The typescript version (to which all entries given in this chapter refer) exists in two copies, one also as part of the Haig Papers in the NLS, and another in the Public Record Office, Kew [PRO], held as document reference WO 256/1–37.

6   See for example [George Riddell], *Lord Riddell's War Diary 1914–1918*, Ivor Nicolson and Watson, London, 1933, especially p. 231.

7   [William Maxwell Aitken] Lord Beaverbrook, *Men and Power 1917–1918*, Collins, London, 1956, Introduction, p. xxii.

8   Blake, *The Private Papers of Douglas Haig*, p. 189.

9   Oliver, Viscount Esher (editor), *Journals and Letters of Reginald Viscount Esher, Volume 4, 1916–1930*, Ivor Nicholson and Watson, London, 1938, p. 175.

10 Philip Hoare, *Wilde's Last Stand: Decadence, Conspiracy and the First World War*, Duckworth, London, 1997, p. 211.

11 Philip Gibbs, *Realities of War*, William Heinneman, London, 1920, p. 46 (US edition *Now It Can Be told*, Harper & Brothers, New York, 1920).

12 See Ian F.W. Becket (ed.), *The Army and the Curragh Incident, 1914*, Army Records Society, London, 1986, passim.

13 Imperial War Museum [IWM]: 'The Military Correspondence of H. A. Gwynne' [Gwynne Papers], *passim*; C. E. Callwell, *Field-Marshal Sir Henry Wilson*, Cassell, London, 1927, Volume I, pp. 200, 241; David R. Woodward (editor), *The Military Correspondence of Field-Marshal Sir William Robertson, Chief of the Imperial General Staff December 1915–February 1918*, Army Records Society, London, 1989, pp. 56, 115; Jeffery Williams, *Byng of Vimy. General and Governor-General*, Leo Cooper, London, 1983, pp. 55, 85.

14 Stanley Jackson, *The Sassoons*, Heinemann, London, 1968, p. 166 et seq. Philip and Siegfried Sassoon are often described as 'cousins', but their relationship was not close either in terms of blood or friendship; Philip (the third baronet), was the grandson of Siegfried's grandfather's half-brother.

15 John Charteris, *At GHQ*, Cassell, London, 1931, p. 94.

16 'The World War I Diary of Lieutenant-Colonel A. N. Lee', unpublished type-script, p. 109 for early 1917, IWM: A. N. Lee Papers, 66/121/1. Lee served as a captain or major for most of the war, being promoted after its end.

17　[Anon.], *The History of The Times Volume IV. The 150th Anniversary and Beyond 1912–1948. Part I Chapters I-XII 1912–1920*, Times Printing House, London, 1952, p. 274. See also Repington's own account: Charles à Court Repington, *The First World War*, 2 Volumes, Constable, London, 1920, Volume I pp. 36–39, and for the most recent assessment Adrian Bristow, *A Serious Disappointment: The Battle of Aubers Ridge 1915 and the Munitions Scandal*, Leo Cooper, London, 1995, pp. 147–158.

18　Repington, *The First World War*, Volume I, p. 27.

19　Blake, *The Private Papers of Douglas Haig*, p. 93.

20　Blake, *The Private Papers of Douglas Haig*, p. 93; Charteris, *At GHQ*, p. 94. See also Repington's 'Shell Scandal' dispatch and other newspaper reports of the battle in Bristow, *A Serious Disappointment*, pp. 152–4, together with other comments on the Press coverage of the Battle of Aubers Ridge on pp. 173–4. Repington, *The First World War*, makes no reference to the allegation.

21　Esher, *Journal and Letters*, p. 166.

22　Asquith, *Memories and Reflections*, Volume I, p. 238.

23　Charteris, *At GHQ*, p. 193.

24　*Daily Telegraph*, 28 October, 1908; see also Robert K Massie, *Dreadnought: Britain, Germany and the Coming of the Great War*, Random House, New York, 1991, pp. 684–94; Zara Steiner, *Britain and the Origins of the First World War*, MacMillan, London, 1977, pp. 52–4; and the commentary by the two chief protagonists in the affair: Ex-Kaiser William, *My Memoirs 1878–1918*, Cassell, London, 1922, pp. 115–19; Prince von Bülow, *Memoirs 1903–1909*, Puttnam, London, 1931, pp. 340–50.

25　For a summary of this see Philip Towle, 'The Debate on wartime Censorship in Britain 1902–14', in Brian Bond and Ian Roy (eds.), *War and Society, A Yearbook of Military History*, Croom Helm, London, 1975.

26　*The History of the Times Volume IV Part I*, p. 218.

27　This meant that it was very much easier for soldiers to publish letters and photographs in their local newspapers, which are a valuable source of historical information. See the use made of such sources in, for example, Malcolm Brown, *Tommy Goes To War*, J.M. Dent, London, 1978, and J. M. Bourne, *Britain and the Great War 1914–1918*, Edward Arnold, London, 1989.

28　*Sunday Times*, 19 December, 1915.

29　Jackson, *The Sassoons*, p. 167; Reginald Pound and Geoffrey Harmsworth, *Northcliffe*, Cassell, London, 1959, p. 506.

30　Philip Sassoon to H. A. Gwynne, 6 January, 1916, marked 'Confidential and Private', IWM: Gwynne Papers, Folio 4, HAG/29.

31 See C. S.Goldmann, *With General French and the Cavalry in South Africa*, MacMillan, London, 1902, Preface, p. xi; L. S. Amery, *My Political Life, Volume I, England Before the Storm 1896–1914*, Hutchinson, London, 1953, pp. 128–33.

32 Blake, *The Private Papers of Douglas Haig*, p. 93.

33 Quoted in Lucy Masterman, *C. F .C. Masterman. A Biography*, Nicholson and Watson, London, 1929, p. 296.

34 For a particularly extreme position see Philip Knightley, *The First Casualty*, Quartet, London, 1982, pp. 79–96; for the most recent discussion of the role of the war correspondents see Martin J. Farrar, *News From the Front, War Correspondents on the Western Front 1914–1918*, Sutton, Stroud, 1998, passim.

35 See Gary S. Messenger, *British Propaganda and the State in the First World War*, Manchester University Press, Manchester, pp. 235–248. For a general account see also M. L. Sanders and Philip M. Taylor, *British Propaganda During the First World War*, MacMillan, London, 1982, passim.

36 For a very clear account of these men and their problems see Keith Grieves, 'War Correspondents and Conducting Officers on the Western Front from 1915,' in Hugh Cecil and Peter H. Liddle (editors), *Facing Armageddon, The First World War Experienced*, Leo Cooper, London, 1996, pp. 719–735.

37 Philip Gibbs, *The Pageant of The Years*, William Heinemann, London, 1946, pp. 162–9, 207, 226.

38 Philip Gibbs, *From Bapaume to Passchendaele, 1917*, Introduction, p. 21; also quoted and criticized in David Lloyd George, *War Memoirs*, Odhams Press, London, 1936, Volume II, p. 1319.

39 'The World War I Diary of Lieutenant-Colonel A. N. Lee', p. 93 for July, 1916, IWM: A. N. Lee Papers 66/21/1.

40 *Lord Riddell's War Diary 1914–1918*, p. 300.

41 *The History of the Times, Volume IV Part 1*, p. 345.

42 Gibbs, *The Pageant of the Years*, p. 208.

43 Charteris, *At GHQ*, p. 153–4, citing his diary entry for 8 July, 1916.

44 Letter from Haig to Robertson quoted in Woodward, *The Military Correspondence of Sir William Robertson*, p. 56.

45 Haig Diary Volume IX, entry for 1 June, 1916.

46 Gibbs, *Realities of War*, p. 24.

47 Haig Diary Volume IX, 'Memorandum on Policy for Press', appendix to entry for 26 May, 1916, (the entry for 1 July gives this memorandum as apparently written on 29 May, but the difference is not significant).

48 James E. Edmonds, *History of the Great War Based on Official Documents. Military Operations France and Belgium 1916, Volume 1*, HMSO, London, 1932, pp. 144–8.

49 Charteris, *At GHQ*, p. 170; Haig Papers Volume XI, entry for 27 September, 1916.

50 Gibbs, *The Pageant of the Years*, p. 168.

51 Gibbs, *Realities of War*, p. 24, and *The Pageant of the Years*, p. 239. The ceremony was also filmed by the official cine-cameramen; see Roger Smither (editor), *Imperial War Museum Film Catalogue Volume I: The First World War Archive*, Flicks Books, Trowbridge, 1993, p. 134.

52 Correspondence between Robertson and Haig quoted in Woodward, *The Military Correspondence of Sir William Robertson*, pp. 55–56.

53 Haig Diary Volume XA, entry for 8 July, 1916.

54 Repington, *The First World War*, Volume I, pp. 265–6; Charteris, *At GHQ*, p. 163.

55 Blake, *The Private Papers of Douglas Haig*, p. 241.

56 Charteris, *At GHQ*, p. 156.

57 Haig Diary Volume XA entry for 21–22 July, 1916; Charteris, *At GHQ*, pp. 156–8; Pound and Harmsworth, *Northcliffe*, 1959, pp. 502–6.

58 Pound and Harmsworth, *Northcliffe*, p. 503; Esher, *Journals and Letters*, p. 60.

59 Charteris, *At GHQ*, p. 225.

60 Blake, *The Private Papers of Douglas Haig*, p. 170.

61 Philip Sassoon to H. A. Gwynne, 8 November, 1916, IWM: Gwynne Papers Folio 4 HAG/29.

62 Haig Diary, Volume IX, entry for 29 July, 1916.

63 Haig's diary mentions one interview as taking place on 1 February; Charteris, who was present and based his account on letters home, also mentions only one interview but places it four days earlier. Other sources refer to 'interviews'. All sources are consistent that some kind of group interview took place.

64 Neville Lytton, *The Press and the General Staff*, Collins, London, 1920, p. 66.

65 Haig Diary Volume XIII, entry for 1 February, 1917.

66 Charteris, *At GHQ*, p. 192.

67 Charteris, *At GHQ*, pp. 192–194; Lytton, *The Press and the General Staff*, pp. 69–70.

68 Lytton, *The Press and the General Staff*, p. 69.

69 Haig Diary Volume XIII, entries for 15–18 February, 1917. Other papers relating to this episode including newspaper articles, accounts, and reports of the parliamentary debate, are appended to this section of Haig's diary. See also the two War Cabinet discussions of the incident, PRO CAB 23 1 pp. 244–249, War Cabinet 73 of 19 February, 1917, and War Cabinet 75 of 20 February, 1917, and the account in 'The World War I Diary of Lieutenant-Colonel A. N. Lee', pp. 118–119 for February, 1917, IWM: A. N. Lee Papers.

70 'The World War I Diary of Lieutenant-Colonel A. N. Lee', p. 119 for February, 1917, IWM: A. N. Lee Papers.

71 Repington, The First World War, Volume I, pp. 460–462.

72 Lytton, *The Press and the General Staff*, p. 70; PRO CAB 23/1 War Cabinet 75 of 20 February, 1917.

73 Lytton, *The Press and the General Staff*, p. 72.

74 Charteris, *At GHQ*, p. 194.

75 The French officer's report to his superiors is quoted as an appendix to Edward Spears, *Prelude To Victory*, Jonathan Cape, London, 1939, p. 546. For a recent assessment of the impact of the *Times* report see David R. Woodward, *Lloyd George and the Generals*, University of Delaware Press, Newark/Associated University Press, London, 1983, pp. 144–5.

76 'The World War I Diary of Lieutenant-Colonel A. N. Lee', p. 119 for February, 1917, IWM: A. N. Lee Papers.

77 See Stephen Badsey and Philip Taylor, 'Images of Battle: The Press, Propaganda and Passchendaele,' in Peter H. Liddle (editor), *Passchendaele in Perspective: The Third Battle of Ypres*, Leo Cooper, London, 1997, pp. 371–389; Farrar, *News From the Front*, pp. 148–152, 161–179.

78 Messinger, *British Propaganda and the State in the First World War*, pp. 85–98, 122–161; Nicholas Reeves, *Official British Film Propaganda During the First World War*, Croom Helm, London, 1986, pp. 23–32.

79 Charteris, *At GHQ*, p. 253, Blake, *The Private Papers of Douglas Haig*, p. 254.

80 Charteris, *At GHQ*, p. 254.

81 Repington, *The First World War*, Volume II, pp. 98, 100–2; Charteris, *At GHQ*, pp. 255, 260; Blake, *The Private Papers of Douglas Haig*, pp. 256, 263.

82 Lloyd George, *War Memoirs*, Volume II, pp. 1318–20; Repington, *The First World War*, Volume II, p. 148.

83 Blake, *The Private Papers of Douglas Haig*, p. 263.

84 Blake, *The Private Papers of Douglas Haig*, p. 65; Charteris, *At GHQ*, p. 273; Pound and Harmsworth, *Northcliffe*, p. 598.

85 PRO WO 158/53 'Cambrai Enquiry – File No. 1', Appendix L signed by Ivor Maxse; also quoted and criticized in Lloyd George, *War Memoirs*, Volume II, p. 1340. See also John Baynes, *Far From a Donkey, The Life of General Sir Ivor Maxse*, Brassey's. London, 1995, p. 182.

86 *Lord Riddell's War Diary 1914–1918*, p. 291.

87 Blake, *The Private Papers of Douglas Haig*, p. 287.

88 Blake, *The Private Papers of Douglas Haig*, p. 308.

89 Quoted in John Terraine, *Douglas Haig, The Educated Soldier*, Hutchinson, London, 1963, p. 43.

Chapter 12

Haig and Military Discipline

John Peaty

A comprehensive assessment of Douglas Haig and British military discipline during the Great War is rendered impracticable by the great dearth of primary evidence. Eighty years after the end of the Great War, only one in a thousand court-martial proceedings from the Great War survive. The surviving proceedings concern those executed for capital offences. All proceedings concerning non-capital offences, capital offences where a verdict of not guilty was returned and capital offences where a verdict of guilty was returned but the death sentence was commuted by Haig no longer survive. It is obvious that such a fragmentary record imposes enormous constraints on an assessment of Haig and discipline during the Great War. Inevitably, examination must be confined to those capital courts-martial where the death sentence was confirmed by Haig, being the only primary evidence available to us. Although unavoidably restricted, such an examination is not without interest or value. For, seventy years after his death, if Haig is known to the man in the street it is probably because of a high-profile campaign to obtain pardons for those executed during the Great War, three quarters of whom were executed on his orders. Both explicitly and implicitly, campaigners for pardons have characterized Haig as a brutal disciplinarian.

During the Great War, 9,496,170 men enlisted in the Armed Forces of the British Empire, of whom 947,023 were killed (including Indians).[1] Of those killed, 346 were executed (excluding Indians). In recent years an enormous amount of attention and concern has been focused on this tiny minority of men who, in the eyes of the vast majority of their contemporaries, let their country down, their comrades down and themselves down.

Interest in Great War executions was reawakened in 1974 by the publication of *The Thin Yellow Line* by William Moore. 1978 saw the posthumous publication of a memoir by Victor Silvester. 1983 saw the publication of *For the Sake of Example* by Anthony Babington (the phrase was coined by Wellington, one of Britain's greatest soldiers). 1986 saw the showing of the television series *The Monocled Mutineer* by Alan Bleasdale, based upon the 1978 book of that name by William Allison and John Fairley. 1989 saw the publication of, most influentially, *Shot at Dawn* by Julian Sykes and Julian Putkowski, which was reissued in a slightly revised edition in 1992 (the phrase was coined by Horatio Bottomley, one of Britain's most corrupt politicians). The publication of *Shot at Dawn* prompted, as was openly intended by its authors, the launching of a campaign to pardon those executed; a campaign which really took off following its reissue. In support of that campaign, Babington's book was reissued in a slightly revised edition in 1993. Further support came in 1995 with the publication of *For God's Sake Shoot Straight* by Leonard Sellers.

The campaign for pardons has been led by Andrew Mackinlay, Labour MP for Thurrock. On 15 June, 1992, Mackinlay tabled a Motion in the Commons urging the Prime Minister, John Major, to recommend a pardon for men executed during the Great War for offences other than murder or mutiny. After careful consideration, on 10 February, 1993, Mackinlay's call for a pardon was rejected by the Prime Minister in a firm but fair letter. The Prime Minister wrote that there were two main grounds on which pardons might be recommended. The first ground was "legal impropriety or procedural error. The files record each stage of the case, up to the final decision by the Commander-in-Chief. No evidence was found to lead us, including the Judge Advocate General, to think that the convictions were unsound or that the accused were treated unfairly at the time". The second ground was "humanitarian". The Prime Minister appreciated the distress of the relatives of the executed men and sympathized with them. "I do think it is essential, however, that full account is taken of the circumstances of the time. The First World War was probably the bloodiest conflict ever [sic. For Britain it certainly was; for many other countries it certainly was not]. At certain periods, troops from this country and those of our Allies were being killed at a rate of tens of thousands a day. Soldiers who deserted were sentenced against this background of heavy casualties amongst the vast majority of fellow soldiers who were carrying out orders. The authorities at the time took the view that deserters had to receive due punishment because of the effect of desertions on the military capacity and morale of the Allied armies. Millions of soldiers put their lives at risk and endured the most terrible sufferings. They had to be able to rely on the support of their comrades in arms". The Prime Minister concluded:

> "I have reflected long and hard but I have reached the conclusion that we cannot re-write history by substituting our latter-day judgement for that of contmporaries, whatever we might think. With the passage of time attitudes and values change. This applies as much to past civilian trials as to military ones, in which sentences were imposed based on the values of the time. I am sure that all people, when they think of this subject now, recognize that those soldiers who deserted did so in the most appalling conditions and under terrible pressures and take that fully into account in reaching any judgement in their own mind".

Undeterred, on 19 October, 1993, Mackinlay introduced in the Commons a Private Member's Bill to pardon men executed during the Great War for offences other than murder and mutiny. The Bill provided for two options: a blanket pardon (the favoured option) or a selective pardon. On 4 November, 1993, the issue was debated in the Lords, when the Government reiterated its opposition to pardons. Viscount Cranborne, the Parliamentary Under Secretary of State for Defence, told the Lords that an examination of the surviving records had shown that "the regulations at the time were not breached by the authorities". On 18 May, 1994, Mackinlay reintroduced in the Commons his Private Members Bill. On 1 July, 1994, Mackinlay presented to the Commons a petition calling for pardons. On 16 September, 1995, the Office of the Leader of the Opposition announced that a future Labour Government would consider the matter sympathetically. Following the election of a Labour Government, on 27 May, 1997, Dr. Reid, the Minister for the Armed Forces, announced a re-examination of the surviving records. On 24 July, 1998, following the completion of the re-examination, Reid told the Commons that the granting of pardons was impracticable but expressed regret for the executions. Mackinlay welcomed the expression of regret but reserved his position on pardons.

Prompted by Mackinlay's campaign, a detailed study of the surviving courts-martial proceedings from the Great War held and open to inspection in the Public Record Office (W071) was carried out over a two year period. I intend to outline its conclusions; I then intend to emphasize certain points which seem to me to be of particular importance; I then intend to discuss *Shot at Dawn* and *For the Sake of Example*; I then intend, finally, to address the question of pardons.

But first let me outline the key statistics.

It is important to note that these were compiled and published by the War Office as long ago as 1922.[2]

In the period 4 August, 1914, to 31 March, 1920, 5,952 officers and 298,310 men (a total of 304,262) were court-martialled. This resulted in the following findings: 270,927 convictions (89.04%); 24,166 acquittals (7.94%); 5,047 convictions quashed (1.66%); 4,122 convictions not confirmed (1.36%). The most common offences were: absence without leave (81,188); miscellaneous (51,186); drunkenness (41,762); desertion (38,630 – of which only 7,361 were committed in the field); insubordination (30,082); loss of property (28,754). The most common sentences were: 3 months detention (63,966); Field Punishment No. 1 (60,210); stoppages and fines (33,469); 6 months detention (27,668); reductions in rank (27,639); Field Punishment No. 2 (20,759). It is clear that during the Great War there was a lot of indiscipline in the British Army. However, it is equally clear that most of it was of a non-serious nature.

In the period 4 August, 1914, to 31 March, 1920, 3,080 men were sentenced to death by courts-martial under the Army Act. Only 346 of the sentences were confirmed and carried out – 11.23%. In other words, 88.77% of those sentenced to death were reprieved. Of the 324 British, Dominion and Colonial soldiers executed, 91 i.e. 28% were under suspended sentence for a previous offence (including 9 under two suspended sentences). Of these 91, 40 had been previously sentenced to death (in 38 cases for desertion, in 1 case for quitting his post and in 1 case for disobedience). One had been sentenced to death for desertion on two previous occasions. These figures scarcely suggest a harsh and unforgiving system of military justice. They suggest rather a system of military justice that could be tough but was usually prepared to give a man another chance.

Of the 346 men executed, the great majority (291, including 3 officers) were serving in Imperial (i.e. British) Forces; 31 were serving in Overseas (i.e. Dominion) Contingents (25 Canadians, 1 South African and 5 New Zealanders); 5 were serving in Colonial Forces; 10 were Chinese Coolies; 4 were Coloured Labourers; and 5 were Camp Followers. The great majority of those executed (322) were serving on the Western Front, where most of the Empire's forces were located. Under French (August 1914 to December 1915), 56 executions were carried out. Under Haig (December 1915 to April 1919), 258 executions were carried out. The considerable difference between the two figures is due to the fact that Haig commanded a much larger force than French and for a much longer period.

Contrary to popular belief, very few were executed for cowardice in the face of the enemy: there were a mere 18 executions for that offence. The great majority were executed for desertion while on active service.

Desertion was defined as the act of a man absenting himself without leave from his unit with the intention of permanently avoiding service. If a man was apprehended out of uniform and/or a considerable time after he had gone absent, this would be strong evidence of an intention never to return. It was also desertion for a man to absent himself with the intention of avoiding some important duty, such as proceeding with his unit overseas, even though he might intend eventually to return to the service. A man was declared a deserter after an absence of 21 days; however, if a man was apprehended within 21 days he could be charged with desertion just the same, if the circumstances suggested intent.

During the Great War desertion was a serious drain on manpower. Yet, remarkably, between the outbreak of war and the armistice – a period of fifty one months – only 266 men were executed for desertion.

In addition to those executed for cowardice or desertion: 37 were executed for murder; 7 for quitting their posts; 5 for disobedience; 6 for striking or showing violence to superiors; 3 for mutiny; 2 for sleeping at their posts; and 2 for casting away their arms. After the Armistice, the only executions which took place were for murder.

Contrary to popular belief, few of those executed were callow youths. As far as can be ascertained, the great majority were, in the eyes of the law, mature adults, i.e. over 21.

Sykes and Putkowski estimate that the average age of those executed was mid twenties. They also estimate that 40% of those executed had been in serious trouble before. They further estimate that (excluding non-combatants) 30% were regulars or reservists; 3% territorials; 40% Kitchener volunteers; 19% Irish, Canadian and New Zealand volunteers; and 9% conscripts.[3] There was of course no distinction between these groups as far as the Army Act was concerned, although the figures certainly suggest that there was a more indulgent attitude towards those who had not joined the Army, and thus submitted to its discipline, freely.

I want now to outline the conclusions of the study of the proceedings in the Public Record Office.

1. In every case studied the verdict and the sentence of the court-martial were confirmed by the Commander-in-Chief. Recommendations for mercy which were made in some of the cases studied were inevitably *not* acted upon, since all the cases studied resulted in execution. We do not know how many recommendations *were* acted upon because the files relating to cases where the death sentence was commuted do not survive. In the absence of the files, we do not know why the vast

majority of death sentences were commuted. We do not know the relative weight attached to recommendations for mercy, points of law, medical evidence, previous conduct etc. Not only are we without the files of those cases where the death sentence was commuted but we are also without the files of those cases where a verdict of not guilty was returned. It is therefore true to say that we have an extremely partial record of British military justice during the war.

2. Before confirmation by the Commander-in-Chief, courts-martial verdicts were scrutinised by the Judge Advocate General at GHQ with regard to the legality of both the findings and the sentences. It follows that in none of the surviving cases, all of which were confirmed, were material legal irregularities detected by the Judge Advocate General.

3. A large proportion of desertions did not take place in or close to the trenches. The emotive picture of scores of men cracking up under fire is a false one: some men did lose their nerve when under attack but many absented themselves when their unit came out of the line or when it was ordered up to the front, while others did not return from leave in Britain when they should have. It is a fact that those serving on the Western Front were not continually going over the top or being shelled: they enjoyed long periods either out of the line, or in quiet sectors of the line, or at home on leave.

4. Several of those executed for desertion were apprehended in Britain. Some men failed to return from leave. Two men deserted together at Waterloo Station while the draft was waiting for a train to take them to France i.e. they were under orders to proceed overseas (Privates Jennings and Lewis of the South Lancashire Regiment). They were arrested seven months later and taken to France for trial. All those who had deserted while on leave or under orders to embark and all those who had deserted in France and had managed to get back to Britain, were returned to their unit to be tried and their unit was invariably in France. No executions took place in Britain.

5. Few men were represented during the early years of the war, although during 1916 the files increasingly record the presence of an "accused's friend" or "prisoner's friend" (often a barrister or solicitor in civilian life), although he did not always choose to cross-examine witnesses. Remarkably, on one occasion the friend was the accused's own CO. Even more remarkably, the accused was facing three charges of desertion and one of striking an officer.

6. Medical opinion was called for when it was thought pertinent. Unless medical evidence existed from the time when the offence had been

committed, obviously medical opinion could only relate to the man as he was at the time of his court-martial. It usually took the form of an examination by either the man's own unit MO or by a doctor at a rear medical facility. Following the examination, the MO or doctor invariably stated that the man was responsible for his actions, or knew what he was doing, or was not suffering from mental derangement.

7. Formal medical boards were unusual. Where these were convened a record of their findings is to be found on file.

8. Specific reference to "shell-shock" was very rare. However, references to loss of memory, dizziness, "queer turns", nervousness, bad nerves, terror etc. were common.

9. Files for 1915–16 and for 1918 are quite full, containing not only the proceedings but also comments by superior officers up to and including the Commander-in-Chief. These were not wholly or always gratuitous, since the unit and brigade commanders were required to provide details of the man's disciplinary record as well as a view by, ideally, an officer who had known him for some time (not always possible given the scale of casualties) – of his personal character and his military worth. Comments by superior officers usually included the view of his CO whether the man's action was deliberate and the views of those further up the chain of command (especially at brigade and division) as to whether an example was necessary given the current state of discipline. Files for 1914 and, unaccountably, for 1917 are perfunctory, containing only the proceedings, Commander-in-Chief's confirmation, the man's conduct sheet and little else.

10. The files of those Canadians and New Zealanders executed are not held in this country. The files of several men are listed under their assumed names. The files of Lance Corporal Price and Private Morgan (both of the Welsh Regiment and both executed for murder) are not in the Public Record Office.

11. In all cases the courts-martial were properly constituted. Most were field general courts-martial and, as stipulated, they consisted of at least three officers, one of whom, not below the rank of captain, presided.

12. Acts of collective indiscipline were extremely rare in the British Army, although a very small number of cases did involve more than three accused. The notorious "mutiny" at Etaples in 1917 resulted in the execution of only one man: Corporal Short of the Northumberland Fusiliers. Nothing remotely similar to the mass mutinies in the French

Army and the mass desertions in the Russian and Italian Armies occurred in the British Army, not even during the dark days of spring 1918, when only two men were executed for desertion.

13. The overwhelming majority of the men executed were British soldiers. The next largest group was Canadian soldiers and after that Chinese coolies. The latter had an unusual propensity for murder. One of them committed suicide while awaiting execution.

14. The overwhelming majority of executions were for offences committed with the BEF; a small minority took place in other theatres. This reflects, firstly, the great imbalance of forces between the Western Front and other theatres and, secondly, the great difference in conditions between the Western Front and other theatres.

15. A large number of men, particularly during the last years of the war, were court-martialled for second, or even third, offences. The files relating to their previous courts-martial do not survive.

16. Many men elected to present no defence or declined to call witnesses or make a statement; these were not limited to repeat offenders.

17. Some of those executed pleaded guilty. For example: Private Byers of the Royal Scots Fusiliers pleaded guilty to desertion; Private Sabongidda of the Nigeria Regiment pleaded guilty to offering violence to a superior.

18. Almost invariably the basic facts of a man's offence were not disputed. The critical factors were the presence of intent, the man's disciplinary record (particularly whether he was a repeat offender) and the perceived need to set an example. Original conduct sheets (or certified copies) were available for the majority of the accused; some had been lost in action. Almost invariably the accused pleaded "not guilty". Where they elected to make a defence or plead mitigation, they invariably denied any intent. The presence of intent was therefore often based on the opinion of their officers and on evidence before the court – many deserters were not apprehended until months after they had gone absent, dressed in civilian clothes and many miles from where they had last been seen. The need to set an example was articulated by the chain of command in numerous cases, especially when discipline in the man's unit or brigade or division was thought to be bad or deteriorating.

19. The arrival of large numbers of conscripts at the front in the period 1916 to 1918 was not reflected in a large number of conscript executions.

In a nutshell, the study found no white cases, very many black cases and a handful of grey cases. The grey cases were those of Second-Lieutenant Poole of the West Yorks; Private McColl of the East Yorks; Privates Johnson and McClair (real name Chapman) of the Border Regiment. All were executed for desertion. In the case of Poole, a medical board ignored evidence that he had been suffering from shell-shock. In the case of McColl, medical evidence was requested but was unavailable. In the case of Johnson and McClair, a legal ruling was sought as to their status – both men claimed that they were no longer soldiers – but there is no evidence that it was given.

I want now to emphasize certain points which seem to me to be of particular importance.

As John Terraine has pointed out, British military justice during the Great War had been designed to cater for a small regular army, drawing its recruits from "the rougher elements of the population"; and the commuting of almost nine out of ten death sentences shows that this was appreciated by those in authority. Indeed, it demonstrates "reason and compassion" on their part.[4]

The fact that almost 90% of death sentences were commuted provides implicit evidence of Haig's attitude and approach to discipline. He was usually prepared to show mercy and give a man a second chance. However, when a man re-offended, or when his crime was blatant, or when the situation demanded an example be made, he was prepared to send a man to his death.

There is little explicit evidence of Haig's attitude and approach to discipline. As Commander of I Corps (August to December 1914) and Commander of 1st Army (December 1914 to December 1915), Haig was required to give his comments on death sentences passed by courts-martial within his command. As Commander-in-Chief of the BEF (December 1915 to April 1919), Haig was required to confirm or commute death sentences passed by courts-martial within his command. We have his comments on the court-martial proceedings made in his capacity as Corps and Army Commander, such as his comment in the Ward case. We have his comment as Commander-in-Chief on the court-martial proceedings in the Earp case. We have his diary entry as Commander-in-Chief regarding the Poole case.

In September 1914, as Commander of I Corps, Haig recommended that the death sentence passed on Private Ward of the Berkshire Regiment should be carried out. He wrote:

"I am of the opinion that it is necessary to make an example to prevent cowardice in the face of the enemy as far as possible".[5]

When confirming a death sentence, as a rule Haig did not write anything other than the single word "Confirmed" on the proceedings. One exception to this rule is the case of Private Earp of the Warwickshire Regiment in July 1916. Convicted and sentenced to death for quitting his post on the eve of the Somme offensive, the court-martial recommended him to mercy. However, Rawlinson considered that unless the sentence was confirmed "the standard of courage in the British Army was likely to be lowered". Haig obviously agreed, confirming the sentence and writing against the court-martial's plea for mercy:

"How can we ever win if this plea is allowed?"[6]

The truth is often unpleasant. Yet it is the truth that the British Army could not have survived and won the war if soldiers had been allowed to quit their posts or desert with impunity.

Of the 258 men executed on Haig's orders, three were officers: Second-Lieutenant Poole of the West Yorkshire Regiment, executed for desertion in December 1916; Sub-Lieutenant Dyett of the Nelson Battalion, Royal Naval Division, executed for desertion in January 1917; and Second-Lieutenant Paterson of the Essex Regiment, executed for murdering Sergeant Harold Collison DCM MSM of the GHQ Detective Staff while a deserter in September 1918. In his diary for 6 December, 1916, Haig recorded:

"This morning the AG brought me Court-Martial proceedings on an officer charged with desertion and sentenced by the Court to be shot. After careful consideration I confirmed the proceedings. This is the first sentence of death on an officer to be put into execution since I became C-in-C. Such a crime is more serious in the case of an officer than of a man, and also it is highly important that all ranks should realize that the law is the same for an officer as a private".[7]

In confirming the death sentences on Poole and Dyett, Haig clearly agreed with the view expressed on the respective proceedings by Plumer and Gough: if a private had behaved as the officer had done, he would in all probability have been shot.

Many of those executed were poorly educated, some even illiterate. However, neither poor education nor illiteracy is synonymous with an inability to distinguish right from wrong and neither is a defence under the law.

Very few men were executed for cowardice; the great majority were executed for desertion. Cowardice and desertion were distinct offences and the distinction is very important. What constituted cowardice was a subjective judgement, about which witnesses held different views. Desertion on the other hand had an objective reality: you were absent from your unit for three weeks or more. The facts spoke for themselves: if you were arrested miles behind the lines wearing civilian clothes weeks or months after you had left your unit without permission it was pointless to argue that you were not a deserter and hardly anyone bothered to do so. The only points at issue were the validity of any excuse and the weight of any mitigating factors. Of those who were executed for desertion, 6 had deserted in Britain (either on leave from France or under orders to embark for France) while 8 had deserted in France and had managed to get across the Channel and reach Britain. The fact that a man deserted in or to Britain did not give him any immunity. It did however provide strong evidence of intent.

The belief that all or almost all desertions were involuntary, the result of shell-shock – that is, all or almost all desertions took place in the front-line and under the impact of prolonged and numbing bombardment – is an enduring but a false one. In fact, many desertions took place away from the front-line and not under the impact of bombardment. Moreover, many deserters had not served in the front-line and had not been subjected to bombardment. Indeed, for several of those executed for desertion the first shot they heard fired in anger was also the last thing they heard. Take, for example, the case of Drummer Rose of the Yorkshire Regiment. Rose deserted as his unit was moving up to the line on 18 December, 1914. He lived comfortably with a Frenchwoman in Hazebrouck for very nearly two years before he was informed upon, arrested, court-martialled and sentenced to death. His Brigade commander wrote, with commendable restraint in the circumstances:

"I can discover no redeeming feature in this case nor any reason why the sentence should not be carried out".

Rose was executed on 4 March, 1917.

The Great War was not hell for every soldier; nor was it hell all the time. Indeed, in the opinion of the noted army psychiatrist Dr. Robert Ahrenfeldt, the stress experienced by British soldiers during the Second World War was "incomparably greater" than that experienced by British soldiers during the Great War.[8] I think Ahrenfeldt goes way over the top: I quote him primarily to discredit psychiatrists, who have done much to undermine a commonsense approach to crime and punishment.

Discipline is essential to Armies, for without it no Army can fulfil its primary function of fighting and winning battles. Armies consist of small teams: infantry sections, gun crews, tank crews and the like. Whether the team succeeds or fails, whether its members live or die, depends on every member pulling his weight, behaving himself and not leaving the others in the lurch.

During Haig's lifetime British military discipline underwent many changes, yet its basic tenets remained the same. Born only nine years after the death of Wellington, Haig shared his belief that discipline was essential to an army and was best upheld by the infliction of exemplary punishment. In 1814 Wellington declined to reprieve a soldier sentenced to death, writing to the court-martial:

"I consider all punishments to be for the sake of example, and the punishment of military men in particular is expedient only in cases where the prevalence of any crime, or the evils resulting from it, are likely to be injurious to the public interests. I beg the Court to consider their recommendations in this light and to apply it to the existing circumstances and situation of the Army, and to what is notorious in regard to this crime . . . I beg to inform the court martial that a very common, and a most alarming, crime in this Army is that of striking and otherwise resisting, sometimes even by firing at, non-commissioned officers, and even officers, in the execution of their duty. It will not be disputed that there is no crime so fatal to the very existence of an Army, and no crime which officers, sworn as the members of a general court martial are, should feel so anxious to punish, as that of which this soldier has been guilty. It is very unpleasant to me to be obliged to resist the inclination of the general court martial to save the life of this soldier; but I would wish the Court to observe that, if the impunity with which this offence, clearly proved, shall have been committed, should, as is possible, occasion resistance to authority in other instances, the supposed mercy will turn out to be extreme cruelty, and will occasion the loss of some valuable men to the service".

Wellington's belief in exemplary punishment remained a basic tenet of British military discipline until shortly after Haig's death in 1928. Indeed, Wellington's letter was quoted with approval in the Report of the Darling Committee on Courts-Martial in 1919.

When Haig was a boy extensive reform of the Army was carried out by Cardwell, reform which extended to its discipline. Flogging was abolished by the Army Act of 1881, only three years before Haig entered Sandhurst. It was however replaced by Field Punishment No. 1 (where an offender was shackled and secured to a fixed object, known as "crucifixion") and Field Punishment No.2 (where an offender was shackled but not secured to a fixed object). Moreover, the death penalty for serious offences was retained. What constituted a serious offence, how it was to be tried and how it was to be punished were all defined in the Army Act of 1881, which was re-enacted annually up to and during the Great War. In the late nineteenth century British Army (a small, all-regular colonial police force) the death penalty was in fact only inflicted for murder. During the Boer war only four men were executed, one for desertion and three (two of whom were Australian officers) for murder. During the Great War the death penalty could be inflicted for offences such as treachery, desertion, cowardice, mutiny, murder, striking or violence, disobedience, sleeping on post, quitting post and casting away arms. It was in fact inflicted for all these named offences except treachery.

During the Great War the Army was not a law unto itself dispensing summary justice. It continued to be governed by the Army Act, which Parliament continued to pass annually. It is unjust and illogical to condemn the Army for the court-martial and execution of soldiers for desertion, cowardice etc. when the Army was merely implementing the provisions of the Army Act. If condemnation is in order, then it should be directed at Parliament. It should be noted however that during the Great War, Parliament was not supine and the annual passage of the Army Act was no mere formality. It was always accompanied by trenchant debate, as was the passage of related legislation. Because of these debates, which reflected increased knowledge and changed attitudes over the course of time, clarifications and amendments were made both to the letter and to the interpretation of military law during the war. To give two examples, one of a clarification and one of an amendment. During the debate on the Consolidated Fund Bill (14 March, 1918), Macpherson, the Under Secretary for War, quoted from a letter from Haig clarifying the position regarding shell-shock:

> "When a man has been sentenced to death if at any time any doubt has been raised as to his responsibility for his actions, or if the suggestion had been advanced that he has suffered from neurasthenia or shell-shock, orders are issued for him to be examined by a medical board which expresses an opinion as to his sanity, and as to whether he should be held responsible for his actions. One of the members of this board is always a medical officer of neurological experience. The sentence of death is not carried out in the case of such a man unless the medical board expresses the positive opinion that he is to be held responsible for his actions".

A month later, on 17 April, 1918, during the Committee stage of the Army (Annual) Bill, Macpherson announced that henceforth those sentenced to death would be informed of the sentence prior to confirmation, rather than after confirmation as hitherto.

Although the final decision was his, Haig did not of course confirm or commute death sentences in a vacuum. Before the proceedings reached Haig's desk, the man's unit and formation commanders were all required to state their views about his character, the nature of his crime and the state of discipline in his unit or formation (and thus the necessity for an example to be made). Naturally, the preservation of discipline was the primary consideration in a fighting force engaged on active operations. A good character would of course provide a much better chance of a reprieve than a bad character but a good character was no guarantee, especially if the crime was blatant or discipline in the man's unit or formation was poor or deteriorating. And many of those executed were not of good character. Sometimes their unit and formation commanders said so in no uncertain terms. As Babington writes:

"One can imagine that when Haig was deciding whether or not to confirm a death sentence he was considerably influenced by the opinions regarding the condemned man's capabilities as a soldier which had been put forward by his colonel and his brigadier, the two reporting officers in the best position to ascertain the true facts. These comments were sometimes dispassionate and sometimes they were immoderate; sometimes they were even savage"[9]

The fact that discipline in the Russian, Italian, French and German Armies collapsed during the Great War whereas discipline in the British Army did not suggests that the latter was probably about right: not too soft, not too harsh. Of the armies during the Great War, the Russian Army was undoubtedly the most brutal. In the Italian Army an iron discipline reigned: smoking on duty was punishable by death. According to Prof. Brian Sullivan, of the 4,000 death sentences passed by Italian courts-martial during the war, 750 (18.75%) were carried out.[10] It would seem that the British Army inflicted the death penalty more often than the French and German Armies. It appears that during the war the French Army executed only 133 men while the German Army executed only 48 men. I say appears because we cannot exclude the possibility that the French and German Armies were less adept at compiling and preserving accurate statistics or deliberately falsified their statistics, excluding many summary executions. Professor Hew Strachan reminds us that in the British Army mutinies were rare and that, although discipline was dented in the spring of 1918, it did not collapse. He suggests that punishment was a larger factor in sustaining the British Army "than the conventional wisdom allows". He notes that the German Army's discipline was much harsher in the Second World War than it had been in the Great War (15,000 executions instead of 48) and that, unlike in the Great War, in the Second World War the German Army did not collapse in a welter of desertions but fought on till the bitter end.[11] During the Great War the American Army was noted for its softness: deserters were classified and treated as stragglers.[12] It is most unlikely that this softness would have been possible if the American Army had been as heavily engaged as other Armies or that it would have continued if the war had lasted. Interestingly, the American Army's softness did not extend to murder or rape and several men were executed for those offences.

Indian soldiers were tried and punished under the Indian Army Act. However, there was no appreciable difference between its disciplinary provisions and those of the British Army Act. Many Indian soldiers were executed during the war. Although the Canadian, South African and New Zealand governments were content for their soldiers to be tried and punished under the British Army Act, the Australian government was not. Australian soldiers were therefore tried and punished under the Australian Defence Act, which only allowed the death penalty for mutiny, desertion to or treacherous dealings with the enemy. No Australian soldiers were executed during the war. Haig (and others acting on his behalf) made strong representations for powers to inflict the death penalty upon Australian soldiers, thus bringing Australian forces in line with British, Canadian, New Zealand and South African forces. The sanction was continually denied to him by the Australian government.

In July 1916 the Australian government declined a proposal from the War Office that its forces overseas should be subjected to the disciplinary provisions of the Army Act. In December 1916 Haig reported to the War Office that the desertion rate in Australian divisions in France was "assuming alarming proportions" and urged that the introduction by Australia of the death penalty for desertion was "a matter of grave urgency". The Army Council informed the Australian government in February 1917 that the application of the Army Act to the Australian Expeditionary Force in France and Belgium had now become a necessity for the discipline of the BEF as a whole. The request was again refused. In the summer of 1917 Haig complained that the increasing ill-discipline of the Australians might well infect the other troops under his command. If that occurred, he said, he could not accept responsibility for the serious consequences which might ensue. He undertook, however, that if the death penalty was sanctioned by the Australian government it would be used "very sparingly" and only in cases of the most deliberate desertion where an example was badly needed. Again, the Australian government said no.[13]

The unco-operative and divisive attitude of the Australian government was maintained despite the appalling disciplinary record of Australian soldiers and the trenchant views of Australian senior officers. It is not surprising that junior Australian officers occasionally took the law into their own hands.

In the field offenders were tried by officers from neighbouring units and executed by soldiers from their own units. In other words, they were judged and punished by their peers: men who had faced the same dangers and who had experienced the same hardships.

A death sentence had to be unanimous: it could not be passed without the concurrence of all the officers making up the court-martial panel. A death sentence was not final: it could not be carried out without the approval of the Commander-in-Chief. The fact that almost 90% of death sentences were commuted demonstrates that a death sentence was very far from being final. Although there was no appeals procedure (not until 1951 in fact), every death sentence had to be referred up the chain of command for scrutiny and approval. The proceedings were passed to Brigade, then to Division, then to Corps, then to Army and finally to GHQ. At GHQ, after being scrutinized for legal irregularities by the Judge Advocate General, the proceedings were passed to the Commander-in-Chief. It was the Commander-in-Chief's responsibility to confirm, mitigate, remit or commute the sentence, taking into account every factor: any recommendation for mercy; any suspended sentence from a previous court-martial; evidence of the accused's character; evidence of the accused's past conduct; medical evidence; the comments of Brigade, Division, Corps and Army commanders; and the ruling of the Judge Advocate General. The surviving proceedings provide no evidence that the chain of command was circumvented or that those in the chain of command discharged their responsibilities frivolously or incompetently.

Our view of what happened is inevitably conditioned by the nature of the surviving documentary evidence. Because the files of those courts-martial where a death sentence was confirmed are the only ones that have survived, the only cases which we can study are those where mercy was not shown. If the files of those courts-martial where a death sentence was commuted had survived as well, we would be able to study every case: the vast majority of cases where mercy was shown as well as the small minority of cases where mercy was not shown. Many of the files which do survive are incomplete. However, incomplete documentation 80 years and more after the event is unsurprising and does not prove that correct procedures were not followed at the time.

After Haig's death and in the heyday of anti-war and pacifist feeling between the wars, British military discipline was greatly liberalized. In April 1928 the death penalty for most military offences was abolished by Baldwin's Conservative government. MacDonald's Labour government went even further. In April 1930 the death penalty for desertion, cowardice and leaving a guard or post without orders was abolished also, leaving just mutiny and treachery punishable by death besides murder.

The abolition of the death penalty for desertion, cowardice and leaving a guard or post without orders was contrary to the wishes of the Army Council and, as far as desertion was concerned, contrary also to the wishes of the Secretary of State for War. Abolition was publicly opposed by two of Haig's Army commanders: Allenby and Plumer. Speaking in the House of Lords on 15 April, 1930, Allenby (one of the finest generals of the Great War) said:

> "When [the recruit] joins he is well aware of the fact that certain offences in war are liable to the penalty of death. That does not trouble him at all; it causes no alarm to him, because he is young and he does not contemplate the possibility of his committing any of those crimes which would render him liable to that punishment. But the severity of the penalty indicates the enormity of the offence, and it creates a moral atmosphere which causes him to abhor that crime and anything that would affect his honour and duty as a soldier. The moral influence thus created would, I think, be very much lessened if the penalty of death were abolished".

Allenby also said:

> "I say most emphatically that in my opinion penal servitude is not a deterrent. It means safety. The only deterrent for the man who will wilfully behave in such a way as to endanger the lives of his own comrades in order to avoid the risk to his own life is the knowledge that, while his comrades may possibly incur death at the hands of the enemy, which will be a glorious and honourable death, he, if convicted of one of these offences by a Court-Martial and executed, will die a death which is dishonourable and shameful".

Plumer (not only one of the finest but also one of the most humane generals of the Great War) said:

"I can tell your Lordships from personal experience that there is no more painful duty a commander has to carry out, none which he would more gladly avoid, than signing the death warrant for the execution of one of his own men . . . If the Bill stands as it is now, I am quite confident that in the future far distant as that future may be, the effect will be to prejudice the morale and also the high standard of discipline which hitherto has been a proud tradition of the British Army".[14]

There is every reason to believe that, if he had been alive, Haig would have expressed himself in exactly the same terms as his fellow Field Marshals. Their fears proved well founded.

During the Second World War, apart from murder, the death penalty only existed for mutiny and treachery: 3 men were executed for mutiny, 1 for treachery and 36 for murder.[15] During the Second World War desertion was a very serious drain on manpower – very nearly 100,000 soldiers deserted[16] – and in 1942 Auchinleck, one of the most humane as well as one of the finest generals of that war, recommended the reintroduction of the death penalty to deter it. The Executive Committee of the Army Council unanimously endorsed the recommendation but it was not pursued because of political considerations. A comparison between the British Army's experience in the Great War and its experience in the Second World War tends to confirm the commonsense belief that men are less likely to misbehave in the presence of a deterrent than in the absence of a deterrent. During the Second World War prison was no deterrent. Indeed, the prospect of seeing out the war in the comparative comfort and safety of prison was not unappealing to many men, especially those at the sharp end.

I want now to discuss the most widely read books about this subject: *Shot at Dawn* and *For the Sake of Example*.

The statement at the beginning of *Shot at Dawn* that those executed "did not receive even the rudiments of a just hearing"[17] perfectly illustrates its approach to the subject. While undeniably the product of much research, the book is not authoritative. *Shot at Dawn* has a gaping hole at its centre. Sykes and Putkowski did not consult the surviving courts-martial proceedings from the Great War – for the simple reason that they were not publicly available at the time. In fact, the surviving courts-martial proceedings from the Great War were released to the Public Record Office beginning in January 1990 and ending in January 1994. Unable to consult the proceedings, Sykes and Putkowski had to use other sources: a list of those executed (WO93), medal rolls (WO329) and war diaries (WO95) in the Public Record Office; the basic details given by Babington in his book; and memoirs of the war, most of them extremely unreliable.

Babington had been allowed to examine the surviving courts-martial proceedings and publish the basic details of many cases, providing that the identity of the men and the identity of their units were withheld. Babington adopts a scholarly approach; prefers primary to secondary evidence; and does not jump to conclusions. He concedes that senior officers did their duty as they perceived it; that courts-martial were not manipulated for improper purposes; and that the death penalty was seen by senior officers as "indispensable to the fighting efficiency of the Army".[18] Babington draws attention to the setting in which courts-martial took place:

"When a soldier deserted on active service he left a gap in the ranks, to the prejudice of all his more-dutiful comrades. When he committed an act of cowardice in the face of the enemy he might have been jeopardising the safety of the men around him; and panic on the battlefield can spread with the speed of light, affecting even those who until then have been entirely resolute".[19]

He also draws attention to the fact that:

"the weaker brethren were only an infinitesimally small proportion of the men at the front. There were hundreds of thousands of others on the battlefields . . . who overcame their fear, their misery, and their personal tribulations and carried on with resolution in the performance of their duty".[20]

However, Babington is almost as critical of British military justice during the Great War as Sykes and Putkowski. While *For the Sake of Example* is a more authoritative and balanced book than *Shot at Dawn*, it strongly reflects the fact that Babington is a judge. Inevitably, Babington judges British military justice in the Great War by the standards of British civil justice in the 1970s and 80s.

Sykes and Putkowski have the dubious honour of publishing for the first time the names of those who had been executed. The publication of the names produced considerable distress on the part of the relatives of those executed. This was both predictable and understandable. During the first part of the war relatives had usually been told the sordid truth by the authorities and had thereafter kept it a secret within the family. During the last part of the war relatives had usually been told white lies by the authorities and had thereafter lived in blissful ignorance of the sordid truth. It was undoubtedly a sin against open government, which is all the rage these days, for the authorities to have been less than frank with relatives but it was done for the best of reasons and is to their credit I think. It is also to the credit of the authorities that the relatives of those executed received pensions; and that those executed were buried with their comrades and their graves are indistinguishable from those of their comrades.

Shot at Dawn contains many mistakes: some minor, some major. To give just two examples. Sykes and Putkowski say that Sapper Oyns of the Royal Engineers was executed for desertion.[21] He was in fact executed for the murder of CSM McCain. Sykes and Putkowski refer to the execution of five men from the Worcestershire Regiment in July 1915 as "the biggest execution the British Army would ever experience".[22] The treatment of the episode in *Shot at Dawn* implies that the authorities had taken leave of their senses and were in the grip of a blood lust. Perhaps we should speak of "The Worcester Five". The facts, however, are not as stated by Sykes and Putkowski. It is true that five men of the Worcestershire Regiment were executed in July 1915: Corporal Ives, Privates Hartells, Fellows, Robinson and Thompson. However, there was no connection between the five except that they were all in the same battalion (the 3rd): one deserted in September 1914, two in June 1915 and two in July 1915. Ives, the first to desert and the first to be tried, was shot on 22 July. The other four were shot on 26 July; they were shot separately and not together. *Shot at Dawn* insists, despite overwhelming evidence to the contrary, that all five were shot on the same day and together. There was no collusion between the five. Thompson and Robinson deserted together. Hartells and Fellows *may* have deserted together. Ives had deserted after only a month in France; he was arrested 9 months later in civilian clothes.

Rather surprisingly, *For the Sake of Example* is more critical of Haig than *Shot at Dawn*. True, *Shot at Dawn* states that:

"the judgement of Sir Douglas Haig was defective when he decided to have certain men executed".

However, it goes on to state:

"The suggestion that the commander-in-chief was solely responsible for the unfortunate demise of these men would be quite incorrect. Sir Douglas Haig, much maligned by previous authors for every conceivable disaster, was the final arbiter in a lengthy and complex legal military system".[23]

Taking his cue from Sir Basil Liddell Hart's *History of the First World War*, Babington writes of Haig's "utter isolation from the realities of the battlefield".[24] In fact, Haig did not inhabit an ivory tower. He did not spend all his time at his desk but got out and about as much as he could. Moreover, he employed liaison officers to be his eyes and ears at the sharp end. One of these, Charles Armitage, rejected allegations that Haig was out of touch and uncaring:

> "Haig is still often portrayed as being a hard man who had no true feelings for the men who served him in the front line. I can testify that this is a wicked slander which has never been substantiated; the exact opposite is the truth".[25]

Some of the most enlightening and informed comments on executions during the Great War are to be found in *The Redcaps* by Dr. Gary Sheffield of the Royal Military Academy Sandhurst, *The British Soldier on the Somme* by Peter Liddle of Leeds University and *On the Fringe of Hell* by Lieutenant-Colonel Christopher Pugsley. Sheffield judges that British military discipline was firm but not brutal. He emphasizes that the procedure whereby courts-martial were convened and sentences referred up the chain of command for confirmation or commutation was strictly adhered to, even at the time of the Ludendorff offensive. Liddle contrasts the small number executed with the large number serving; emphasizes that most of the offences were so blatant that "scant defence could be put forward"; emphasizes that soldiers knew what was expected of them and the penalties for transgression; and declares that there is "virtually no evidence" in contemporary documents or memoirs that British soldiers considered the death penalty "outrageous".[26] Referring to the accounts of New Zealand executions in *Shot at Dawn*, Pugsley writes that "each account has a number of factual errors and it is evident that both authors do not understand the procedure and levels of command at which courts-martial were confirmed and sentences reviewed and suspended".[27]

I want now, finally, to address the question of pardons.

I believe that the granting of pardons would be a great mistake. History is history. What happened, happened. We may not like our history but we re-write it at our peril. I greatly admire *1984* – but I would prefer that it remained fiction. I believe the saying "Strong emotion makes for bad law" to be true. I do not object to emotion: I do however believe that legislators should not let their hearts rule their heads. Have our legislators got nothing better to do than worry about the fate of convicted criminals who died before most of us were born? It is said that public opinion supports the granting of pardons (public opinion is, of course, a funny thing: it is also said that public opinion supports the restoration of the death penalty – not that our legislators have taken any notice). If true, this would not be surprising. What the average member of the public knows about the British Army during the Great War he has learnt from films and television. *King and Country, Oh, What a Lovely War, The Monocled Mutineer* and *Blackadder Goes Forth* are remarkable pieces of work – but nobody who has studied the subject accepts them as accurate portrayals of the British Army during the Great War.

Those who were tried, found guilty and executed during the Great War were judged and treated according to the laws, values and customs of their time. It was a time when the British Army was engaged in mortal combat with a powerful and dangerous foe. It was a time when British soldiers knew their place and did what they were told – or else. It was a time when for most people in Britain life was "nasty, brutish and short". It was a time when the death penalty was almost universally accepted by the British people. It was a time when most British people believed that in a national emergency the Crown had the right to put its subjects into uniform to fight its enemies – and that once in uniform, a subject's life belonged to the Crown, to dispose of as it saw fit. It was a time when most British people believed that certain things were worth dying for and worth killing for – and that the prevention of a German-dominated Europe was such a one.

The job of the historian is to try to understand the past. It is not the job of the historian to sit in judgement on the past and second guess the actions of our forebears – although, frankly, many historians do it. Much that passes as history nowadays is in fact ahistorical: it aims to judge the past in light of the present and makes little or no attempt at understanding it. Indeed, it often wilfully misunderstands the past. I am profoundly opposed to the contemporary fashion for rewriting history in accordance with modern laws, values and customs. To modern eyes, history is full of injustices. But is it not arrogant for one age to stand in judgement on another? Are we so sure that our laws, values and customs are superior to those of the past, in this case the early twentieth century? Are we really more civilized than our grandfathers? Do we really have a greater understanding of human nature than they did? Today, we no longer inflict the death penalty, not even for cold-blooded murder. Punishment and deterrence are almost dirty words. Today, medical knowledge is much greater than it was during the Great War, especially with regard to psychiatry. Nowadays, much anti-social behaviour is excused on medical grounds. Can we – should we – impose current legal and medical practice on the past? And if we are to rewrite history, where do we start and where do we stop? I am reliably informed, for example, that Guy Fawkes was not interviewed in accordance with the PTA, let alone PACE.

Can we, 80 years after the end of the Great War, grant pardons when the Darling Committee on Courts-Martial in 1919, the Southborough Committee on Shell-Shock in 1922, the Lawson Committee on Army and Air Force Discipline in 1925 and the Oliver Committee on Army and Air Force Courts-Martial in 1938 all failed to substantiate miscarriages of justice during the Great War? All four Committees examined documents and questioned witnesses. Few of the documents and even fewer of the witnesses are still available to us.

As the Darling Committee was specifically charged with investigating the operation of courts-martial during the Great War, its Report is of special importance and merits close examination. Despite some criticisms and proposals for change, the Committee was on the whole complimentary:

> "The results of our investigations into a limited number of cases put before us as typical lead us to the conclusion that, having regard to all the circumstances, the work of courts-martial during the war has been well done. We are satisfied not only that the members of courts-martial intend to be absolutely fair to those who come before them, but also that the rank and file have confidence in their fairness".

The Committee concluded that Commanders-in-Chief had discharged their responsibilities admirably, that they should remain the final arbiters and that they should not be supplanted by a civilian body. The Committee also concluded that the death penalty had been, and remained, essential to the maintenance of discipline.

> "In regard to sentences, we consider that, subject to the right to petition for clemency, the decision ought to be left, as at present, to the military authorities, who alone are in a position to form a correct judgement as to what sentences the state of discipline in the army, or a particular force requires. Nor do we consider that any exception ought to be made in the case of death sentences. During the recent war not a single officer or soldier was executed under sentence of court-martial in the United Kingdom. Abroad a certain number of death sentences were carried out. In each case they were only carried out after personal consideration by, and upon orders of, the Commander-in-Chief, and after the Judge Advocate General, or his Deputy, had advised upon their legality. Moreover, when considering them, the Commander-in-Chief almost invariably had before him recommendations from the officers commanding the unit to which the accused belonged, the Brigade, the Division, the Corps, and the Army. As showing the care with which all considerations were weighed and the desire to show mercy whenever the interests of the Army as a whole, and of the nation, permitted, it may be

stated that no fewer than 89 per cent of death sentences pronounced were commuted by the Commander-in-Chief. We doubt very much whether any Court, necessarily not possessing the information which he possessed as to the discipline and morale of the army, would have ventured to exercise clemency to any such extent. The Commander-in-Chief, of course, commuted sentences in many cases where the Court of Criminal Appeal would have no legal grounds for interfering, and must therefore have dismissed an appeal. The reasons for punishing crime on conviction in the Civil Courts are the amendment of offenders, the deterrent effect of punishment and the satisfaction of the outraged sentiment of the people, who otherwise would be apt to take private vengeance after slight injury and no proof. For the punishing of military offences there is the further reason that, unless discipline in Armies be preserved, such forces are but a mob dangerous to all but the enemies of their country. Therefore the considerations sufficient for civil government are not enough for the ruling of the armed forces of the Crown. On active service, especially, other sanctions must be sought when justice is to be done".

The Committee concluded its Report with the words:

"In our opinion a Commander-in-Chief, who is entrusted with the safety of his Army, must not be fettered in his decision as to the point which so vitally affects the discipline of that Army. The essence of military punishments is that they should be exemplary and speedy. This is recognized by the preamble to the Mutiny Acts and the Army Acts which have been passed annually by Parliament for centuries. An exemplary punishment speedily carried out may prevent a mutiny from spreading or save an Army from defeat".

The subject of pardons is bedevilled by the question: blanket or selective? If a blanket pardon, everyone is pardoned whether deserving or not: cold-blooded murderers and blatant deserters as well as the shell-shocked. If a selective pardon, who is to judge which men are to be pardoned and which men are to be denied a pardon (and thus re-condemned) – and on what grounds? The records are very much a mixed bag: some are full and informative; some are incomplete and uninformative. Should those men whose cases cannot be properly judged because the records are incomplete and uninformative be denied a pardon for that reason or given a pardon for that reason?

The advocates of pardons cannot even agree among themselves. Babington opposes a blanket pardon and favours a selective pardon. Mackinlay favours a blanket pardon but would settle for a selective pardon; he has called for a pardon for 307 men. Sykes and Putkowski favour a blanket pardon: in 1989 they called for a pardon for 312 men; in 1992 they called for a pardon for 351 men.

The Bill proposed by Mackinlay made provision for either the granting of a general pardon or the establishment of a tribunal to review each case and to recommend pardons in those cases considered deserving. One aspect of the Bill may be noted: about a tenth of cases are excluded from consideration (although there is provision in the Bill for more, as yet unspecified, cases to be added later). The excluded cases relate to murder – although murderers were tried by court-martial and executed by firing squad just like deserters and the rest. The exclusion of cases of murder (at least initially) was intended to increase the Bill's chances: it was considered politic because of the inconvenient fact that until the 1960s murder was punishable by death under civil as well as military law. However, if Mackinlay wishes to be consistent, he cannot exclude cases of murder. Were all those executed for murder represented? Might not some have been suffering from shell-shock? Mackinlay clearly considers desertion and cowardice lesser crimes than murder. Yet during the Great War they were of equal seriousness in the eyes of the law. Indeed, in extreme circumstances desertion and cowardice could amount to mass murder.

Professor Peter Rowe of Liverpool University has highlighted the great difficulties that would face a tribunal.[28] Would the tribunal recommend a pardon where a medical problem was claimed and no medical evidence was sought? Would it recommend a pardon where there was no evidence that the accused was represented? Even if the accused *had* been medically examined and *had* been represented, it does not follow that he would have been acquitted (as several cases testify). Rowe has pointed out that a pardon goes to the conviction itself and not to the choice of sentences available to the court. A pardon would not say that the death penalty had been excessive: a pardon would say that the accused had been wrongly convicted of the crime for which he had been tried (a very different matter). He has also pointed out that the proceedings of courts-martial were subject to confirmation both as to finding and sentence; that the vast majority were not confirmed; and that bias or impropriety would have to be demonstrated on the part of the confirming officer with regard to the small minority that were confirmed. Lastly, he has pointed out that the death penalty still exists for five military offences (to do with mutiny and treachery) and that its existence has been reaffirmed regularly by Parliament. While this last point has been overtaken by events (the death penalty having recently been removed from the statute-book completely – a triumph of hope over experience), the fact is that for eighty years after the Great War the gravest military offences continued to be punishable by death.

How long would the tribunal take to do its work and how much would it cost? Pardons would please the relatives of the executed men, now judged to be innocent, although it is unlikely that they would be pleased enough to forgo compensation claims. On the other hand, the relatives of those who participated in the trials and executions, now judged to be murderers, would be displeased.

Let me close this discussion of pardons by endorsing the plea of Ian Curteis:

> "All war is hideous and grotesquely unfair. Millions died unjustly on both sides in World War I and sleep now in those lines of ordered, cared-for graves – in 'some corner of a foreign field that is forever England'".[29] The dust of those who died bravely and those whose deaths were shaming are irretrievably mixed. For God's sake, let them rest in peace.

I now want to make some concluding remarks. Haig's primary function as Commander-in-Chief of the BEF in France and Belgium was of course to defeat the enemy and win the war. This naturally occupied most of his attention and most of his time. Discipline consequently figures little in his diary and has figured little in accounts of his tenure as Commander-in-Chief. However, that discipline was essential to victory – and was seen by Haig to be such – is beyond doubt. The facts speak for themselves. It was no coincidence that discipline in the BEF was preserved intact and the BEF emerged victorious whilst discipline in the German Army collapsed and the German Army surrendered. As Commander-in-Chief of the BEF Haig was not only ultimately responsible for the conduct of operations on the Western Front but was also at the apex of British military justice in France and Belgium, wielding the power of life and death over those convicted of capital offences. To this historian, the remarkable fact is not that Haig refused to reprieve 258 men sentenced to death but that he reprieved nine times that number. The execution of 258 men during the 40 months of his command must be seen against the background of massive casualties on the Western Front, where seventy four times that number were killed on 1 July, 1916, alone. Two conclusions may fairly be drawn from this assessment of Haig and discipline during the Great War. Haig successfully maintained the discipline of the British Army on the Western Front. He did so by a judicious use of exemplary punishment.

Notes

1   "Hansard", 5th May, 1921.
2   *Statistics of the Military Effort of the British Empire during the Great War*, War Office, 1922, HMSO, pp. 643–670.
3   *Shot at Dawn*, Leo Cooper, 1992, pp. 19–20.
4   *The Right of the Line*, Hodder and Stoughton, 1985, pp. 527-528.
5   *For the Sake of Example*, Leo Cooper, 1983, p. 7.
6   Ibid, p. 81.
7   Haig diary, Wednesday 6th December, 1916: WO256/14.
8   *Psychiatry in the British Army in the Second World War*, Routledge & Kegan Paul, 1958, p. 273.
9   *For the Sake of Example*, Leo Cooper, 1992, p. 182.
10 *Time to Kill*, eds. Paul Addison and Angus Calder, Pimlico, 1997, p. 178.
11 Ibid, p. 375.
12 *The First World War*, Cyril Falls, Longmans, 1959, p. 335.
13 "*Official History of Australia in the War of 1914–1918*", C.E.W. Bean, Vol. V.
14 Parliamentary debates, (77) Lords (1929–1930), Army and Air Force (Annual) Bill: Committee stage.
15 "Hansard", 20th November, 1970.
16 *Discipline*, Brigadier A.B. McPherson, War Office, Nov. 1950: WO277/7, pp. 116–117.
17 *Shot at Dawn*, Leo Cooper, 1992, p. 6.
18 *For the Sake of Example*, Leo Cooper, 1983, p. 193.
19 Ibid, p. 57.
20 Ibid, p. 83.
21 *Shot at Dawn*, Leo Cooper, 1992, p. 234.
22 Ibid, p. 50.
23 Ibid, p. 9.
24 *For the Sake of Example*, Leo Cooper, 1983, p. 192.
25 *Haig as Military Commander*, General Sir James Marshall-Cornwall, Batsford, 1973, p. 293.
26 *The British Soldier on the Somme*, Strategic and Combat Studies Institute, Occasional Paper No. 23, 1996, p. 22.
27 *On the Fringe of Hell*, Hodder and Stoughton, 1991, p. 61–62.
28 R.U.S.I. Journal, August 1994, pp. 61–62.
29 *Daily Mail*, 12th October, 1995, Associated Newspapers.

Chapter 13

Douglas Haig, the Common Soldier, and the British Legion

By Niall Barr and Gary Sheffield[1].

It is a commonplace that as Commander-in-Chief of the BEF Douglas Haig was a remote figure, separated by considerable physical and psychological distance from the common soldier in the trenches. A recent biographer has argued that 'For too much of his career he [Haig] was far too removed from the command of men. The gulf between him and the common soldier was dangerously wide'. Moreover, Haig 'failed to notice' this chasm.[2] Yet this received wisdom sits uneasily with other evidence. Under the caption 'Our Man: With Mr. Punch's Grateful Compliments to Field-Marshal Sir Douglas Haig', a full page cartoon of November 1918 shows Haig, the very picture of a conquering hero, riding through a crowd of cheering Tommies.[3] Ten years later, when the train bearing Haig's body arrived in Edinburgh shortly after midnight on 3 February, 1928, 'the route [to St. Giles' Cathedral] was lined by silent crowds, far denser than had ever been seen even for a Royal visit'. During the four days that Haig lay in state, some 90–100,000 people filed passed his coffin.[4] What, then, was the nature of Haig's relationship with the common soldier?

Douglas Haig's views on the common soldier were typical of those of late Victorian officers of his generation. The second half of the nineteenth century saw the emergence of the ideal of the British officer as a Christian gentleman, and paternalistic concern for the well-being of the common soldier became a central part of the officer's code. Relations between the ranks were far from close, but they were characterized by mutual respect and even by affection. Other Ranks admired paternal, brave and competent officers.[5] The evidence suggests that not only did Douglas Haig the regimental officer share the paternalistic 'ideology'

OUR MAN.

WITH MR. PUNCH'S GRATEFUL COMPLIMENTS TO FIELD-MARSHAL SIR DOUGLAS HAIG.

held by his peers, but that it continued to be a major influence on him during his time as Commander-in Chief of the BEF in France and indeed after the war in his work with the British Legion.

Several pieces of evidence suggest that Haig was held in high regard by the men he had commanded as a regimental officer. On leaving his regiment in India in 1892 Haig's RSM 'wrung my hand and said that I was "the best sort he had ever had to do with"'.[6] In 1903 one of Haig's former troopers wrote an appreciative letter, conveying his 'deep respect for you'.[7] The most impressive piece of evidence of Haig's paternalism is found in the memoir of his soldier-servant, a regular cavalryman who joined Haig in 1900. If no man is a hero to his valet, then for Sergeant Secrett, Haig came very close to it. However, Secrett was an astute commentator; judging from their respective memoirs, he understood the Field Marshal rather better than did Lady Haig. Secrett's portrayal of Haig's attitudes to the common soldier is perfectly consistent with the social ideology of the late Victorian officer.

According to Secrett, Haig frowned on 'familiarity', yet '[w]hile preserving his dignity, he managed to convey to the Tommy the fact that he respected him'.[8] In part he did this by respecting the individual soldier's dignity, talking 'gently to Tommies as though he were talking to an equal who was somewhat a stranger to him, never familiar, never condescending, but always with great respect'.[9] Haig understood the 'soldier's heart. He knew perfectly well the difficulties and burdens borne by his men' and sympathized with them.[10] Haig respected and admired the wartime volunteers and conscripts who came to fill the ranks of the BEF, but he felt most at home with soldiers of the old pre-war professional army.[11] In this he was not unusual among his peers.[12] Haig, like other Regular officers, worried that wartime temporary officers were not able to handle their men. This emerged from Haig's account of a visit to an old friend, a fellow cavalryman, Major-General David Campbell, in 1917. Campbell was commanding a New Army formation, 21st Division, and Haig recorded (evidently with approval) that

> He says that old cavalry NCOs make the best subaltern officers. They are able to talk to their men and yet maintain discipline. In some cases the young 'civilian' officer does not talk at all to his men, or becomes too intimate and discipline suffers.[13]

Posterity has seen Haig as callous. The evidence suggests that this is unfair. According to Secrett, Haig was moved by the suffering of his men and strove to make the lives of individual soldiers a little easier.[14] Evidence from Haig's own writings supports this contention. In

January 1915, for instance, Haig wrote in a private letter of the terrible conditions being endured by 'the poor d—ls in the trenches'.[15] The paternal attitudes of Haig and his fellow senior officers were instrumental in creating a vast infrastructure of canteens, baths and the like that was aimed at enhancing the morale of the ordinary soldier. This was a significant factor in the maintenance of British army morale right up to the Armistice.

However, Haig's professionalism and conception of his duty overrode any personal feelings of squeamishness. This was true of his conduct of operations, and also of Haig's attitude to the death penalty for soldiers that he perceived had 'failed' in their duty: 'I am of the opinion that it is necessary to make an example to prevent cowardice in the face of the enemy as far as possible'.[16] Haig's views need to be placed into context: only 351 men were executed for all reasons, about 10% of those sentenced to death, out of an army of about 5 million. Again according to Secrett, Haig was far from stony-hearted about such executions[17] although he held conservative views on 'shell shock'. He seems to have viewed the imposition of the death penalty much as he viewed the commitment of men to a bloody battle: unpleasant, even distressing, but something that simply had to be done.

Haig also had his fair share of courage. One version has him personally rescuing a wounded Egyptian soldier from the Dervishes at the battle of Atbara in 1898.[18] During the First Battle of Ypres in 1914, when it appeared the British front had been broken, Haig mounted his horse and rode down the Menin Road. A machine gunner of 17th Division who wrote of the 'troops' respect' for Haig when he addressed them near Arras in 1917, highlighted the fact that the parade took place 'within shelling distance' of the front line.[19] On one occasion, the German surprise attack at Landrecies on 25 August, 1914, Haig does seem to have been rattled, although he was unwell at the time. Haig was thus paternal, courageous, and professional; the very things that soldiers of the Great War era expected their officers to be.

Perhaps the most controversial part of Secrett's portrait of Haig is his assertion that the Field Marshal 'had a positive genius for inspiring loyalty and affection on the part of the troops he commanded'.[20] By contrast, Charteris wrote that although he was respected, Haig failed to gain 'the personal affection' of the men of the BEF.[21] Where precisely did the truth lie? The difficulties in answering this question are compounded by the fact that post-war memoirs are liable to have been influenced by either the adulation of Haig within the British Legion, or the later sustained denigration of him in the media. Moreover, a former junior officer writing long after the war wrote that Haig did indeed become 'the hero of the British people' as a result of the victory of

1918.[22] Thus postwar anecdotal evidence, while not necessarily inaccurate, needs to be treated with caution.

As a preliminary, it is worth considering the question of 'command recognition': how reasonable is it to expect a soldier in a huge army to even know the names of generals, let alone have an opinion on them? Michael Howard has suggested that the average private on the Western Front would have known about Haig, 'if only from the press'.[23] One of Haig's recent biographers went further, suggesting that

> It was highly unlikely that Haig would be criticised by the average soldier during the war. The vast majority of them never set eyes on him: to them, he was a figure so remote in rank and personality as to be almost unimaginable. Soldiers have no time for detached thought about the Higher Command . . . Many would have been perplexed if asked to name him: Kitchener was a more familiar name and face.[24]

Certainly, it is fairly rare to find references to Haig (or indeed any generals) in the letters and diaries of wartime rankers, and rarer still to find criticism. This sparse entry from the diary of a private in 2/6 Manchesters is typical: 'Paraded with Coy & inspected by Sir D Haig & marched past him'.[25] An Australian infantryman, Private Jack Hutton, noted that his battalion, the 17th, was especially chosen to parade in front of Haig, and Hutton was clearly proud of this.[26] Such snippets of evidence suggests that soldiers neither worshipped nor hated Haig.

The circumstances of 1914–18 rendered it very difficult for Haig to impose his personality on his army. The BEF was too large and too dispersed for Haig to behave as a 'leader' in the style of Napoleon or Lee. A generation later Montgomery and Slim were to develop 'democratic' styles of leadership that differed greatly from Haig's approach, in part at least in response to their experiences of the First World War. This option was not one available to Haig. The BEF was much larger than the forces commanded by Haig's Second World War successors; and they had superior means of communication and transport at their disposal. In any case, Haig the inarticulate Victorian would almost certainly have regarded Montgomery's beret-with-two-badges-wearing, and 'gather round, pass out cigarettes' style of leadership, as vulgar. And it is far from certain that the common soldier of 1914–18 would have appreciated it; in that deferential age, working class soldiers expected their officers to dress and behave as gentlemen, which entailed a certain level of aloofness.

Secrett may have been right: that Haig did inspire affection in those common soldiers who met him. Charteris's view that the BEF 'admired' and 'trusted' Haig 'but they did not love him' is equally valid. In the margin of the Sandhurst Library's copy of Charteris's biography of Haig, an unknown hand, apparently that of a Western Front veteran, noted that Haig 'was known as Duggy [to the army]; but with no enthusiasm. He was too remote – but that was not his fault. The show was too big'.[27]

Haig's relationship with his soldiers had thus been been set long before the end of the war. However, while Haig was a relatively remote, unknown figure to British soldiers during the war, his work for ex-service men after the war created much stronger associations and perceptions of Haig amongst British veterans. Indeed it is not too much to say that a legend grew up around Haig's work for the British Legion which has informed views on the man ever since.

Following the pattern set by Sir George Arthur,[28] every subsequent biographer of Haig[29] has listed the founding of the British Legion as the greatest of Haig's post war achievements. John Terraine stated that:

> The first achievement, which only his reputation among the ex-soldiers could have accomplished, was to bring together the various ex-Service organisations; there were four of them in existence, with inevitably conflicting interests and policies. In June 1921 these were welded together in the British Legion.[30]

Terraine considered Haig's work with the Legion to be an 'important gloss' on Haig's character and also a refutation of the charge that 'he was ever callous or insensible to the sufferings of his men'.[31] Taking a very different line, Norman Dixon argued that Haig's founding of the Legion was a way of rehabilitating his image.[32] These arguments, which have crossed swords for many years, constitute almost all the mainstream attention given to Haig's post-war career. This is a particularly sterile debate given the fact that Haig was not the founder of the British Legion.

No one man could possibly have founded single-handedly a unified ex-service movement based upon the comradeship and experience of the Great War. Graham Wootton was the first historian to point this important fact out: 'The Legion has no founder, only founders. It is a monument to a number of men not one'.[33] The origins of the British Legion lie, not with Haig, but with the groups of veterans formed during the Great War as a response to grievances about their treatment as returned soldiers.[34] The National Association of Discharged Sailors and Soldiers [Association], founded in Blackburn in 1917 was the first organization *of* ex-service men *for* ex-service men. Veterans came together to protest about their treatment and to help one another deal with the hardships of disablement and unemployment. The National Federation of Discharged and Demobilised Sailors and Soldiers [Federation], formed in January 1917, soon became the most vigorous and strident organization and the conservative Comrades of the Great War [Comrades] came into existence as a direct response to its radicalism.[35] The Association, Federation and to a lesser extent the Comrades, owed their existence to the conditions which ordinary veterans experienced during and after the war, and their main vision of justice from the government, self-help and a sustaining comradeship, eventually found expression in the Principles and Policy of the British Legion. Such organizations could not have been created out of nothing even by a man of Haig's influence and prestige.

Haig did have an important part in founding the Officers' Association, but this was not a membership organization, nor, ironically, did it fully submerge its identity when the main groups came together in 1921 to form the British Legion; the Royal Charter guaranteeing the separate existence of the OA came into effect on 30 June, 1921 – one day before the formal establishment of the British Legion. Haig was also not the first prominent soldier to encourage unity between the antagonistic ex-service organizations. A conference between the main groups under the chairmanship of General Sir Horace Smith-Dorrien was organized in June 1918 but this attempt foundered on the bitter political divisions which existed between the organizations. Later in 1918, a War Office committee, chaired by General Sir Ian Hamilton, explored the amalgamation of the rival organizations by making them responsible for the administration of the profits from the Expeditionary Forces canteen funds. Haig, through the representation of his military secretary, Major Ruggles-Brise, did have an influence on these discussions. Although the proposed British Empire Services League bore a remarkable resemblance to the British Legion as it was finally constituted, the ex-service groups were united in their distrust of any government-sponsored body which might attempt to 'gas' (sic) ex-service protest over pensions.[36]

Ultimately, the conditions for unity were brought about by the failure of the Federation's attempt to carve a distinctive role for ex-service men in politics at the 1918 General Election,[37] waning public interest in the ex-service movement, Government reform of the pensions system which removed most (but by no means all) glaring injustices,[38] and the realization of all the groups that if they were to survive – and deal with the considerable distress amongst veterans – they would have to work together.[39] Haig's part in this was to preach the cause of unity to numerous gatherings of ex-service men during

1920, but as Wootton has pointed out, he was, for the most part, preaching to the converted.[40]

Unity between the existing organizations was finally brought about by much hard work and a series of hotly argued Unity Conferences which began on 7 August, 1920. Haig took no part in these long and complicated but decisive proceedings although his firm views on the need for unity were an important influence on the discussions. The British Legion then, was not founded by any one man,[41] and although Haig's influence was important it was not decisive.

Yet Haig never claimed to have founded the Legion. He knew the process which had led to its birth and the men who had taken the lead in its creation.[42] In a 1927 speech, he acknowledged the efforts of the leaders of the earlier organizations, many of whom later became important figures within the Legion:

> When the inner history of those days comes to be written from the im-
> partial standpoint, and with the fuller knowledge of future years, full
> credit will be given to the leaders of those earlier organizations who had
> the wisdom, foresight and true patriotism to sink all personal aims and
> differences in order that the Legion might be established.[43]

This evidence should finally lay to rest the myth that Haig founded the Legion and it is unfortunate that, even many years later, the real architects of the British Legion remain unacknowledged.

Once the Legion had been formed Haig did work hard for its cause and, with his great prestige as the victorious commander of the BEF and as a known friend of ex-service men, the Field-Marshal had a much greater impact on the character of the British Legion after its formation. However, Haig, as National President, did not become directly involved in the detailed administration of the many areas of Legion activity. Practical relief work to help disabled or unemployed ex-service men was the cornerstone of Legion activity, and this was accomplished almost exclusively by the grass-roots membership working in the Legion's branches,[44] supported by a small paid staff at National Headquarters. Earl Haig's correspondence concerning the Legion is, unsurprisingly, taciturn, consisting mainly of comments about the wider direction of the movement. In fact, the bulk of the rather sparse correspondence consists of letters from Colonel G.R. Crosfield (the Legion's Vice Chairman) to Earl Haig, with much of Haig's writing limited to comments written in the margins of Crosfield's letters.[45] It is also clear from these letters that Crosfield wrote Haig's Legion speeches with minor modifications made by Haig himself. This was Haig's main role within the Legion, a position he filled admirably; to create interest and enthusiasm for ex-service issues – both for the Legion and the general public. Haig made countless key-note speeches, addressed large meetings, inspected Legion parades and reviews and generally helped to keep the Legion in the fore-front of the public mind. Haig was extremely popular within the Legion, and admired by the general public, because he was one of the few high-ranking officers who took a truly active and personal interest in the ex-service movement.

Haig's undoubted prestige meant that his work for the Legion, and his views on ex-service matters were taken seriously by the public *and* the government. Yet Haig's prestige creates real difficulties in any examination of veterans' perceptions of their leader. An article in the first issue of the British Legion Journal entitled 'Personalities in the Movement' explains the dearth of stated rank and file views on Haig:

> No word of mine can embellish the record of Earl Haig. His photograph in this issue speaks for itself. It has written all over it the quality which Napoleon described as being all things the most essential in a commander of armies, namely *character*. The British character of dogged honesty of purpose won the war: Haig is the incarnation of it – and that is all that need be said.[46]

It was generally accepted within the Legion that Haig was above criticism or comment. As commander of the British Armies in France, and now as President of the British Legion, his position was unchallengeable. A good example of this was the annual election for President. While Haig did stand for election in 1921 (in his absence), he beat the only other candidate, Captain Colin Coote, by a large majority, and in every other year, Haig was elected unopposed. Given the nature of the hierarchy within the Legion and society as a whole, ordinary Legion members would not presume to make public statements about their feelings concerning their President. In an organization which stressed the virtues of patriotism, duty and loyalty, criticism of the President was unthinkable. Legion members gave Haig their unquestioning loyalty just as they had done as soldiers during the war.

Such views were certainly not held by all veterans. The Labour and trade union movement, which included many ex-service men, developed a deep suspicion of Haig and the Legion during the twenties. Indeed many left-wing ex-service men believed that Legion members were being held together not for comradeship and mutual help but to act as a para-military force which would be activated in any strike or left wing disturbance. These beliefs found voice in the nickname 'Haig's White Guard' (a reference to the White Russian Armies during the

Russian Civil War), a phrase first coined by *The Daily Herald* in 1924.[47] Haig's use of military metaphors and images of veterans rallying together against 'subversive tendencies ... at work in our midst, ... unstable intellectuals and the out-pourings of street agitators'[48] and his exhortation that Legion members should offer 'unwavering resistance to the Bolshies'[49] can only have exacerbated the problem.

None of these facts should obscure Haig's deep personal sense of duty and paternalism for his men which motivated his work for the Legion. Indeed, Haig was almost unique as a military commander who subsequently worked hard on behalf of the men who had fought under him. Veterans' movements in France and Germany were bitterly divided by politics and many other issues and acted, particularly in Germany, as catalysts for social unrest and political violence.[50] Haig's prominent part in the foundation and growth of the British Legion as a 'steadying influence' in British life, and a permanent institution which cared for veterans and fought for their rights within the existing political and social system, can be seen a major personal achievement.

With Haig's death in January 1928, it was said that 'the Legion had lost a President, but gained a Patron Saint'.[51] Just as Haig had been described in 1921 as the incarnation of British values, so after his death he became 'a personal symbol of the Legion's essential qualities'.[52] The British Legion became the staunchest defender of Haig's reputation and also created a fertile myth surrounding Haig, according him attributes and powers more appropriate to a 'patron saint' than to a man.

Surprisingly, the Legion itself created and developed the myth that Haig was its founder. George Crosfield, when Legion Chairman, paid tribute to Haig just after his death and initiated this process. He argued that:

> Lord Haig has been rightly called the Founder of the British Legion, for, although he did not initiate the steps which the Association, Comrades and Federation took to come together, it was his far sighted action which made those steps necessary.[53]

By 1934, this questionable argument had been transformed into a Legion article of faith. The Legion Annual Report of that year stated that the creation of the Legion:

> resulted from the efforts of the late Field-Marshal Earl Haig who ... set his heart on bringing together the several Associations that had sprung into being during and as a result of the War, having for their object the amelioration of the lot of returned service men and women of all ranks

and the care of the widows, orphans and other dependants of the fallen. Of these there exist some millions who have good cause to be grateful to Earl Haig and those associated with him for the beneficent work then set in motion.[54]

Haig, who had been a powerful influence within the Legion while alive, had been transformed into a colossus in death.

Legion myth-making about Haig sometimes verged on the ridiculous. The 1928 Battlefields Pilgrimage Souvenir book was a record of the Legion sponsored visit of 10,000 widows, orphans, relatives and Legion members who visited the old battlefields of the Western Front – an event which was to have been led by Haig. On the frontispiece there was a remarkable piece of doggerel by J.F. McMilan:

"Great is our loss, old comrades, yet he taught us to understand
Our stay in the ranks of the living is ruled by the Higher Command;
For Haig, our belov'd Field Marshal has answered the final call,
With the Deathless Army he takes his place, and we mourn them, one
    and all.

He never stooped nor faltered, but with a courage staunch and true,
He gave us strength to 'Carry on' and see those dark days through.
He could read our hearts like an open book, and with pride we still recall,
How we served with Haig in those grim War days, when backs were to
    the wall.

He was known as 'Haig, Field Marshal', but up in the old Front line,
When he passed that way, you could hear men say, 'Why, he's a pal o'
    mine.'
We have lost our pal, our hearts are sad, and things don't seem the same,
Yet memory lives for ever, and he's calling 'Play the Game!'

'Work for the Night is coming, I have blazoned the path to tread,
Look after your broken comrades, honour your glorious dead,
Carry your burthens bravely, though they may be drear and long,
From the Shadows I am watching – Carry on, boys, carry on'."

This image of Haig was pure fantasy. As noted earlier, most soldiers at the front line did not know Haig – let alone consider him a comrade. In this respect, the Legion was using hindsight; Haig had been a 'pal' to ex-service men after the war and the deep regard which many ex-service men felt for Haig and his work on behalf of veterans was translated back to the trenches with the rosy glow of old soldiers' memories.

Clearly, Haig was seen in the late twenties as a very important part of the Legion 'spirit'. To have pride in the British Legion was to have pride in British achievements and feats of arms during the Great War – and to have pride in the Legion's 'founder'. As far as Legion members had been concerned, while alive Haig had been beyond criticism, and in death he had been transformed into an important symbol of the Legion, quite literally a patron saint. Thus, when the re-appraisal of the Great War began with the 'War Book Boom' of 1929–30, the Legion myth of Haig was soon challenged. When the Legion, and particularly its leaders, some of whom had known Haig personally, felt that Haig's memory was being attacked they responded with a vigorous and indignant defence of their first President.

The worst storm over Haig's reputation broke in 1934, with the publication of Lloyd George's *War Memoirs*. These not only attacked Haig, but also General Sir Frederick Maurice,[55] who had become the Legion President in 1932. When the Memoirs were first published, the Legion Journal actually carried adverts for the two volume work, and then quickly withdrew them when the controversy grew over Lloyd George's accusations over Haig's conduct of the war on the Western Front. The worst accusation (from the Legion point of view) was that instead of admitting that the Passchendaele campaign was 'a complete failure', Haig had perservered 'stubbornly with his attacks'.[56] Although most of Lloyd George's allegations overstepped the bounds of truth, his views became popular and the basis for many of the modern opinions about Haig and his armies.

Legion Branches composed strong resolutions refuting Lloyd George's claims. This example was only one of many which Legion branches, Counties and Areas had composed:

> That this branch of the British Legion deplores the recent attacks upon Earl Haig in Mr Lloyd George's Memoirs and places on record our unshaken faith in our beloved leader both in war and peace.[57]

As such a resolution demonstrates, ordinary Legion members were defending a man whom they had not known during wartime, but whom they had become acquainted with during the post-war years. Most Legion members were not really qualified to challenge Lloyd George's assertions but the main defence came from the numerous speeches made by Legion leaders who had actually worked with Haig in the British Legion. To attack Haig was to attack them, and in defending

Haig they were defending themselves – a fact which was particularly true of Maurice. Legion leaders argued that

> We saw him spend himself in the service of his comrades and shorten his life by that service, and we know that the statement that he sacrificed the lives of his men through vanity and because he was too obstinate to admit that he was wrong is a dastardly lie.[58]

The Legion leaders were justifying their view based on what they knew of Haig as the veterans' friend, not on Haig the commander. Indeed, it would appear that much of the biographers' 'version' of Haig and the British Legion actually draws its inspiration from the Legion's indignant defence of 'their' Haig.

The public face of the Legion was stiff in its condemnation of Lloyd George. However, privately, not all Legion members felt the same. As one of Haig's few surviving contemporaries of similar standing and rank, General Sir Ian Hamilton took a very different stance from the other Legion Leaders. When asked to move a resolution at the Metropolitan Area Conference, protesting against Lloyd George's accusations, Hamilton refused saying:

> although I deeply resent as much as any man in the Kingdom Lloyd George's false statement that Haig sacrificed lives owing to his personal vanity, that does not affect my other belief, namely, that Passchendaele was the most damnable battle in history and should never have been fought.[59]

Hamilton had worked with Haig, and experienced high command. His view was thus better informed and did not seek to connect Haig's wartime leadership with his work for the Legion. It is enough to say that this view was not popular within the Legion as a whole.

General Sir Frederick Maurice, who had the most to gain by defending Haig, connected Lloyd George's attacks with a wider issue; the British perception of the Great War:

> He deplored these attacks, not only because they were untrue and unworthy in that respect of their great Founder – but also because they gave the younger generation an impression that England's part in the war was nothing but a grisly failure ... In point of fact, at the end of war, Great Britain had the finest Army in existence in the field, the finest Air Force, and throughout the war they had the finest Navy ... That fact should give them confidence in themselves and make them bold to lead in the right.[60]

Maurice's explicit connection between the attacks on Haig and British performance in the Great War was accepted by most Legion members. They could not see Haig criticized without feeling attacked themselves because it cut to the core of their sense of identity as members of a victorious army which had made enormous sacrifices, surmounted disaster and won.

Field-Marshal Earl Haig had become the essential symbol which represented these beliefs for Legion members. One of the Legion's main functions was seen as passing on their beliefs, principles and knowledge of the horrors of war to the next generation. The Legion wanted Haig's image – as a great leader in war and peace – fixed in stone for future generations[61]. This would honour Haig but would also pass on their view of the Great War as a glorious, dangerous sacrifice in which the soldiers had saved the country. Changing perceptions of the Great War were, by the thirties, beginning to challenge the Legion's views both in its choice of symbols and substance. During Haig's life, the Legion's view of their President was the accepted version. Today, this view is obscure and held only by a minority of people even within the British Legion. And yet we should realize how important an influence the Legion's view of Haig has been on historiography and indeed in shaping our own attitudes towards the enigma that is Douglas Haig.

Notes

1   Gary Sheffield would like to thank Dr. Stephen Badsey and Dr. Jeremy Crang for providing him with valuable references.

2   Gerard J. De Groot, *Douglas Haig, 1861–1928* (London: Unwin-Hyman, 1988) pp.132, 164.

3   Punch, 27 Nov, 1918, p.357.

4   C.L. Warr, *The Glimmering Landscape* (London: Hodder and Stoughton, 1960) pp. 171–2.

5   See G.D. Sheffield, *Leadership in the Trenches: Officer-Man Relations, Morale and Discipline in the British Army in the Era of the Great War* (London: Macmillan, forthcoming).

6   Duff Cooper, *Haig I*, (London: Faber and Faber, 1935) p.37 (quoting Haig's diary).

7   Philip Warner, *Field Marshal Earl Haig* (London: Bodley Head, 1991) p.85

8   Sergeant T. Secrett, M.M. *Twenty-Five Years with Earl Haig* (London: Jarrolds, 1929) p.66.

9   Secrett, pp.152–3. Secrett's opinion contrasts somewhat with Charteris's oft-quoted view of Haig's formal and inarticulate conversations with Other Ranks. Brigadier-General John. Charteris, *Field-Marshal Earl Haig* (London: Cassell, 1929) pp.387–88.

10   Secrett, p.116.

11   Secrett, pp.116–17, 188.

12   For the views of Lt. Gen. Haking in 1916, see J.C. Dunn, *The War the Infantry Knew*, (London: new edition, Jane's, 1987) p.185.

13   Haig diary, 16 May, 1917, WO 256/18, PRO.

14   Secrett, pp.14, 33, 64.

15   Haig to brother, 12 Jan, 1915, quoted in Warner, p.12.

16   Quoted in Desmond Morton, *When Your Number's Up: The Canadian Soldier in the First World War* (Toronto, Random House, 1993) p.250.

17   Secrett, p.105–6.

18   The Countess Haig, *The Man I Knew* (Edinburgh and London, Moray Press, 1936) pp.320–1 followed by Warner, p.50.

19   In C.E. Crutchley (ed.) *Machine Gunner 1914–1918* (London: Purnell, 1973) p.90.

20   Secrett, p.114.

21   Charteris, p.387.

22   P.G. Heath, unpublished memoir p.405, L[iddle] C[ollection], University of Leeds. Heath was by no means an admirer of Haig.

23   Michael Howard, 'Leadership in the British Army in the Second World War', in G.D. Sheffield (ed.) *Leadership and Command: The Anglo-American Military Experience since 1861* (London: Brassey's, 1997) pp. 119–20.

24 Warner, pp.4–5.

25 Pte O.G. Billingham diary 29 Oct 1917, LC.

26 Pte. J.T. Hutton, diary, 26, 29 August, 1917, ML MSS 1138, Mitchell Library, Sydney.

27 Charteris, p.387, marginal note in copy in RMAS library.

28 Sir George Arthur, *Lord Haig* (London: William Heinemann) 1928.

29 including Charteris; Secrett, De Groot, p.403; E.K.G. Sixsmith, *Douglas Haig* (London: Weidenfeld and Nicolson) pp. 183–184.

30 John Terraine, *Douglas Haig: The Educated Soldier* (London: Hutchinson, 1963) p.484.

31 ibid.

32 Norman F. Dixon, *On the Psychology of Military Incompetence* (London: Jonathan Cape, 1976) p.387.

33 Graham Wootton, *The Official History of the British Legion* (London: MacDonald and Evans, 1956) p.107.

34 See Graham Wootton, *The Politics of Influence: British Ex-Servicemen, Cabinet Decisions and Cultural Change 1917–57* (London: Routledge and Kegan Paul, 1963); Charles C. Kimball, 'The Ex-Service Movement in England and Wales, 1916–1930', unpublished Ph.D. Thesis, Stanford University, 1990, and Niall Barr, 'Service Not Self: The British Legion 1921–1939', unpublished Ph.D thesis, University of St Andrews, 1994.

35 Wootton, Official History, p.3.

36 For details on the B.E.S.L, see Liddell Hart Centre for Military Archives, King's College London [LHCMA], General Sir Ian Hamilton's papers IH29/37/5.

37 Stephen. R. Ward, 'The British Veterans Ticket of 1918', *Journal of British Studies*, Vol VIII, No.1, (Nov.1968).

38 The system of Final Awards and Seven Years Time Limit introduced in the 1921 Pensions Warrant did stabilize pensions administration, but later also caused many grievances and campaigning for their repeal occupied the Legion for much of the twenties and thirties. See Barr, chapter 5.

39 See Wootton, *Official History*, p.12–16, Kimball, pp.117–118.

40 Wootton, *Official History*, pp. 21–22.

41 Thomas Lister, as the skilled Chairman of the Unity Conferences and the first Legion Chairman might well have the best claim to be the true architect of the Legion.

42 Thomas F. Lister (Federation), James Howell (Association), Col. George R. Crosfield (Comrades) and General Sir Frederick Maurice (Officers' Association), to name only the most important.

43 Haig Papers, N[ational] L[ibrary] S[cotland], speech at Galashiels 1927, no.235c.

44 In 1927, the last full year before Haig's death, the British Legion had

2,939 working branches with 202,834 paying members, see Barr, pp.252–253.

45 Haig Papers, NLS, Acc3155., no 227d-j.

46 *British Legion Journal*, July 1921.

47 Wootton, *Official History*, p.66.

48 British Legion Scotland Headquarters, Haig's Presidential Address, British Legion Scotland Annual Conference 1926.

49 British Legion Headquarters [BLHQ], Verbatim Report of the British Legion Annual Conference 1923, Haig's Presidential Address.

50 Antoine Prost, *In the Wake of War: Les Ancien Combattants and French Society 1914–1939* (Oxford: Berg, 1992); James M. Diehl, *Paramilitary Politics in Weimar Germany* (Bloomington, Indiana University Press,1977).

51 Thomas Lister, quoted in *BLJ* March 1928.

52 Wootton, *Official History*, p. 110.

53 *BLJ* March 1928.

54 BLHQ, Annual Report, 1934.

55 Maurice, of the Maurice letter fame, and thus a prime target for Lloyd George, who wrote a blistering attack on Maurice in the Daily Telegraph Wednesday, 22 July, 1936.

56 David Lloyd George, *War Memoirs*, Vol.II, (London: Odhams Press, 1936) p.1311.

57 *BLJ* December 1934, p.228.

58 Sir J.B.B. Cohen, *Count Your Blessings* (London: Heinemann, 1965) p.93.

59 LHCMA, Hamilton to Admiral Sir Henry Bruce, 25, Feb 1935, IH29/20.

60 BLHQ, General Sir F. Maurice's Presidential Address, BL Annual Conference 1935. It would appear that what is now accepted as 'revisionism' of the Great War by military historians is in fact, the 'traditional' view held by veterans after the war.

61 Niall Barr is currently preparing an article on the controversy surrounding the statue erected to Haig in Whitehall in 1937.

Chapter 14

Haig and Religion.

Nigel Cave

Haig and Religion? Haig and Morality? Haig and Duty? Haig and Obstinacy? Haig and Implacability? I suspect that it will be impossible to write a convincing personal biography of the man, given the seemingly contradictory evidence, and given that Haig was such an intensely private, yet equally public, man. *Mores* have changed, making it more and more difficult to empathize with a bygone age; as we move into the era of individualism and counselling, where there is no such thing as an Act of God, and everything done by anyone in the Establishment has to be treated with the uttermost of suspicion.

To talk of any man and his religion is difficult, especially if the person concerned does not write (much) about it and does not wear his faith on his sleeve. At the best of times it is a risky business to peer through the window into a man's soul. It is complicated still further in a contemporary world which numerous pundits, in their characteristically parochial way, assure us is post-Christian. The bonus side is that there are not too many out there that know any better!

Religion in the Edwardian era had a seemingly assured position. It permeated all sectors of society and had an active and vibrant part to play in the lives of the majority of the people. This does not mean, of course, that this was exclusive to the two branches of Christianity by law established – that is the Church of England and the Church of Scotland. Methodism and Non-Conformism had very strong roots in the industrial areas of north east and north west England; amongst the miners and in the north of Wales; amongst the tin workers, the fishermen and the rural workers of the south west, and in particular in Cornwall. The Roman Catholic Church was particularly strong in Liverpool, parts of London, in Glasgow, Cardiff and Newport – where so many of the Irish immigrants from the mid nineteenth century onwards had settled. Despite the variations of Christian creed, the tensions between them had considerably dissipated, although suspicions remained. In general, the British were quite tolerant in such matters, with some notable local exceptions. Certainly the tolerance was considerably greater than that to be found in many of the nations of the continent.

In France the radical government of Waldeck Rousseau had expelled the Roman Catholic religious orders as recently as 1905 – indeed so many of them took refuge in Britain that the normal language of mealtime conversation at Archbishop's House in Westminster was French.[1] The division between Freethinkers and Catholics split all levels of society, certainly not least the French Army. A telling symbol of this split is the arrangement of war memorials in France. In village centres there are to be found lists of the dead killed in the Great War, accompanied by a statue of a soldier in heroic pose or a symbol of the French state. Inside the local church is usually found an identical list, accompanied by Christian symbols. It is difficult to think of a war memorial in Great Britain, by contrast, which does not have some form of Christian symbol upon it.

Catholicism had an intolerant stranglehold in Spain, but on the other hand was under institutional threat from the revolutionary government in Portugal. Utraquists still faced persecution, generally of a not very subtle type, in Bohemia. Anti-semitism was rife throughout Europe, perhaps nowhere worse than in Vienna; and it existed at the very least as a bias in Britain.

Religion was still very much seen by a number of governments as an indirect means of social control. It is worth noting that the Austro-Hungarian government could still use its power of veto in the Papal election of 1903 to halt the progress of a cardinal of whom they disapproved; the result of this conclave was the election of Pope St Pius X, who took immediate steps to have the right removed.[2]

Religion was important to the British Army as an integral part of the glue that held it together. Chaplains were on the establishment from the earliest times of what we would recognize as the professional army. In 1662 the Articles of War stated that the chaplain was to read the prayers of the Church of England every day and to preach as often as he saw fit. Every officer or soldier absent from prayers was to lose a day's pay![3] The value of allowing religious observance of other denominations also came about early – in 1795 an officer of the Royal South Down Militia was court-martialled and reprimanded for not allowing his soldiers to attend mass, and this over thirty years before Catholic Emancipation.[4]

The key notion that fired so many men, and in particular men of the middle classes, to service in this period was that of duty – duty to God, King and Empire. Doubtless such arguably admirable convictions were a useful cover in some cases for rather baser motives, such as profit, adventure and a desire to dominate; for most religion had an importance – or perhaps it could be better stated that religion was seldom quite without importance. The era was dominated by the perception of the need to serve and to do one's duty. A casual glance at the memorial tablets in innumerable parish churches and the walls of the chapels of public schools brings this home strongly and, occasionally, quite eloquently. To understand Haig and his approach to religion it is essential that its contemporary importance is understood.

It is something of a mystery to me that historians – military or otherwise – have no problem assimilating this when it comes to a study of Cromwell's New Model Army or to Gustavus Aldolphus's Swedes in the Thirty Years' War – but find it imaginatively impossible when it comes to the Great War. Even more noticeable is the dichotomy in critical approach towards the fully acknowledged influence of religion on Oliver Cromwell[5] and the generally critical view of the effect that religion had on Haig.

This topic requires examination from two viewpoints, though they are by no means mutually exclusive – the importance which Haig attached to religion as Commander in Chief of the British Expeditionary Force between 1915 and 1919 and the importance of religion to Haig personally.

RELIGION, THE BEF AND HAIG

It is important to remember that the concept of muscular Christianity had been one of the driving principles behind educational development for much of the nineteenth century. A whole cluster of public schools had been founded upon Christian principles which underlined the importance, above all, of duty – duty to God and a God who quite obviously – if he was not an Englishman – smiled kindly on Britain and its great Empire. Schools from as far afield as Glenalmond in Scotland (Gladstone was one of its founders) and Lancing in Sussex were firmly based on the guiding principle of duty to a combination of God and Empire. Arnold's impact on Rugby was felt throughout these establishments, not least on Clifton, Haig's own school, which was founded by one of Arnold's housemasters.[6] This attitude also worked its way socially downwards – through Church schools, Sunday schools and the like.

Almost immediately upon taking over command of the BEF Haig summoned Bishop Gwynne, the Deputy Chaplain General with responsibility for chaplains and troops in France, to see him. At this meeting he was told that he regarded Gwynne's job as one of the most important under his command. 'A good chaplain is as valuable as a good general. ... We are fighting for Christ and the freedom of mankind.' He was so impressed by Bishop Gwynne's sermon on Christmas Day 1915 that he had the sermon printed and circulated amongst the troops.[7] He followed this up by speaking to him after dinner on 13 January, 1916.

'I spoke to him regarding the importance of sending messages to all the clergy to preach about the great object of the War, viz, the freeing of mankind from German tyranny. Many are too narrow in their views. They must be enthusiasts to do any good.'[8]

In May 1916 he took the opportunity of a lunch party that included a number of clerics, including the Archbishop of Canterbury, to expand upon this view. The Archbishop asked a question which led to Haig saying that,

'. . . I had only two wishes to express, and I had already expressed them to Bishop Gwynne and these are:
    Firstly: that the Chaplains should preach to the troops about the objects of Great Britain in carrying on this war. We have no selfish motive, but are fighting for the good of humanity.
    Secondly: the Chaplains of the Church of England must cease quarrelling amongst themselves. In the Field we cannot tolerate any narrow sectarian ideas. We must all be united whether we are clerics or ordinary troops. The Archbishop thought his people were united now, but "possibly some six months ago some were troublesome".'[9]

Haig saw the purpose of religion, and therefore the duty of the chaplains, to reinforce this view of the justice of the cause, and that was to be done by a unanimous voice. Further, the responsibility of the ministers of religion was to act as a unifying force, to underline the duty of each and every one within the Empire. On 22 July, 1917, Cosmo Lang, then Archbishop of York, spoke to Haig privately,

'about the necessity of opening the doors of the Church of England wider. I agreed and said we ought to aim at organising a great Imperial Church to which all honest citizens of the Empire could belong. In my opinion, Church and State must advance together, and hold together against those forces of revolution which threaten to destroy the State.'[10]

Almost immediately after he relinquished command and returned to England he came back to this theme in an audience he had with George V.

> 'I urged the King to press for the formation of a great-minded Imperial Church, to embrace all our Churches, except the Roman Catholics. This would be the means of binding the Empire together. In my opinion the Archbishop of Canterbury had missed his opportunity during the war, and not a moment's time should be lost now in getting to work and organising an imperial body of control, consisting of bishops, moderators, etc. . . . Empires of the past had disappeared because there was no church or religion to bind them together. The British Empire will assuredly share that fate at no distant date unless an Imperial Church is speedily created to unite us all in the service of God.'[11]

Haig was not alone among his Army Commanders in noting the significance for morale of the chaplains. Dean Inge noted in his diary in 1934 that Lord Plumer had expressed the opinion that of all men Bishop Gwynne did the most to win the war.[12]

The role of chaplains in 1914 was far from clear. For the Roman Catholics there was no great difficulty as it is a sacramental church which required the ministration of the priest in the front line – and certainly as far forward as the Aid Post. The Church of England and other Protestant churches found things rather more difficult. F.R. Barry commented on chaplains' treatment in the early days of the war,

> 'When the padre first went out with the BEF, the army had little idea what to do with them. In battle they were left behind at the base and were not allowed to go up to the fighting front. What on earth, it was asked, could they do up there? A colonel would say, 'No work for you today, padre', meaning by that, no corpses for burial. The chaplains' job was to take church parades, on such rare occasions as they were practicable, to run entertainments, to help in censoring letters, and in general to act as welfare officers, thereby helping to keep up morale. But was that what they had been ordained to do?'[13]

In the fullness of time the administrative order hindering the chaplains' going into the Front Line was changed, something about which Haig was very enthusiastic when the matter came up in discussion with Randall Davidson.

It is quite clear that Haig was no bigot when it came to the differing denominations of Chaplains; only (to his mind) trivial disagreements obstructing 'the great cause' earned his ire. On 30 March, 1916, he noted in his diary,

'I saw three parsons of different persuasions standing together, – a Roman Catholic, a Wesleyan and another; all most friendly! On the other hand the clergy of the Church of England are squabbling terribly amongst themselves over High Church and Low Church methods. It seems to me most disgraceful at a time like the present, that the National Church should be divided against itself, instead of giving us a noble example of unity and good fellowship.'[14]

He met the leader of the English and Welsh Roman Catholics at his headquarters on 21 October, 1917.

'His Eminence Cardinal Bourne from Westminster, accompanied by the Rev B Rawlinson (assistant to the Principal Chaplain for the Roman Catholics) came to dinner. The Cardinal is neither eminent in appearance nor in conversation, but I expect means well. On the other hand, Rawlinson is a most agreeable fellow and seems to have all the qualities of an efficient Jesuit Father.'[15]

However, the obstructionism of the Roman Catholic authorities could try his patience.

On 4 August, 1918, there was a Special Service of Thanksgiving in Montreuil, in the École Militaire where the GHQ offices were established. Haig commented in his diary,

'A hollow square was formed of British Officers and clerks of GHQ as well as of the Battalions forming the Guards (the Guernsey Militia), WAAC and a large number of French officers and a few Americans.

The service was carried out by the Rev George Duncan (Church of Scotland) and the Rev Bateman Champain (Church of England). The Roman Catholic priests were not allowed to take part in the ceremony, but many RC officers attended. The attitude of the RC clergy over this service should open our eyes to what the RC religion in our empire really is. They must be RC first, and English afterwards, if their Church discipline permits.'[16]

Haig saw institutional religion as one of the best means of binding the Empire together and as a defence against social revolution – in that sense it must be as all-encompassing as possible. He only had the vision to see it from this narrow and institutional viewpoint – the Church by law established. On the other hand, his view of the role of the churches (as opposed to individual spiritual life) would be far from extra-ordinary, and would be held by large numbers of influential people as well as a significant element of Broad Church clerics in the Church of England.

The churches actually shared something of this vision, but for rather different reasons. A symposium under the chairmanship of Bishop ES Talbot brought together eleven churches, and even the Roman Catholics were represented by a non-voting delegate.[17] The results of their discussions were published under the title, *The Army and Religion*. Its deliberations on the experience of religion during the war did not make altogether happy reading, but its conclusions were positive. Thus, like Haig, the report argued that the Churches must draw together to promote the Kingdom of God – the YMCA and the SCM had set an example. Pledges to serve Christ and his Kingdom had been signed by no fewer than 350,000: men will serve sacrificially for war; why not for peace? '"The long battle of defence and retreat is over, the moment for a great common advance has begun." So the Committee added its influence to the movements which supported church reform, ecumenism, social concern, the League of Nations and liberal theology.'[18] This is not perhaps what Haig had in mind – no mention of Imperial ideals here.

HAIG'S PERSONAL RELIGION.

Haig's religious beliefs have become a relatively recent addition to the historiography of the man. The controversy can be said to centre on two views of Haig's religious beliefs and convictions. The first may be summarized as arguing that religion was a vital support, not available from any other source, for Haig, entrusted as he was with the direction of the greatest overseas enterprise the British people had engaged upon. Alternatively some have argued to the effect that Haig used the will of God and the inscrutability of His ways as an excuse for failed campaigns; and that his turning to religion on reaching supreme command was a matter of convenience. His dependence on God, it seems, was a reason not to look to alternative methods of achieving victory, for example, to attrition; and that religion became an obstacle to Haig's development as a commander. Indeed, some of those who would question the strength and sincerity of Haig's religious convictions also point to his apparent interest in spiritualism.

Lloyd George makes no mention of Haig's religion in his *War Memoirs*. Winston Churchill does not refer to its influence in the *World Crisis*. Charteris made several references to Duncan as Haig's Chaplain, but did not dwell on Haig's religious beliefs.[19] He was rather more forthcoming in his later book, *At GHQ*. On 29 April, 1917, Charteris describes what he called a 'regular Scottish Sunday'.

'The sermon was to the effect that we all had to believe that God is working for a definite purpose; all very cheering if you are certain that that purpose is our victory. But it is difficult to see why a German preacher could not preach just such a sermon to Hindenburg and Ludendorff. All the same, DH seems to derive an extraordinary amount of *moral strength* [my emphasis] from these sermons. We discussed it after lunch, for all the world as one used to do as a boy in Scotland. Then DH suddenly switched off to a paper which he is preparing for the War Cabinet at home, and was back in 1917 and at war.'[20]

Charteris goes on to describe the importance of religion to Haig at the time, possibly of his lowest ebb, before the strike back against the German in 1918. Charteris, writing on 18th June, 1918, noted that Wilson had said (on 17th June) that the government did not intend to replace Haig 'at present'; he thought the situation was impossible for a Commander-in-Chief.

'Curiously enough, DH does not let it worry him too much. He has become almost fatalistic in his outlook on life, and very deeply religious. He seems to acquire great comfort from the Sunday services at the kirk, and is, I think, quite convinced that he has the especial favour of Providence. I hope that he is right. Providence in Heaven and princes on earth are valuable allies!'[21]

The first detailed examination of the matter comes up in Duff Cooper's, *Haig*, published in 1935; he had the first free access to the Field-Marshal's diaries. When he comes to the chapter dealing with Haig's first days as Commander in Chief, Duff Cooper had this comment to make,

'He knew that upon his conduct now depended the future of the Empire that he had served all his life. And in this period of supreme trial, which was to prove longer than all expectation, he was supported from first to last by his deep religious belief.

The faith in which he had been brought up, and which had hitherto played no great part in a full and fortunate existence, now entered into the very fibre of his being and remained with him *to the end* [my italics].'[22]

As though seeing the ammunition that religion might give Haig's detractors, Cooper goes on to point out how many others of the great commanders were also men of faith, quoting a letter from Lord Bertie to Haig about a possible new French Commander-in-Chief,

> Foch is objected to because he has a Jesuit brother, Petain because he was brought up by the Dominicans and Castlenau still more because he goes to Mass.[23]

To these may be added Horne, well-known for his very devout faith – indeed, when he could, he went to church twice on Sundays; Plumer was a devout man and considered Bishop Gwynne one of his best friends whilst, in the Second World War, Montgomery was both religious and highly rated religion's importance to the army.[24]

Disappointed with Duff Cooper's work, Countess Haig published her own memoir, *The Man I Knew*, in 1936. This is a very interesting book, perhaps rather neglected in more recent years when so much attention has been paid to the direction of the war. The introduction itself is worthy of considerable comment. There the Countess tells us that Haig instructed her to destroy the diaries written before the Great War when she was packing up Government House in Aldershot, on the grounds that they were worthless. He was not aware that this 'drastic order' had not been carried out, and in fact never mentioned the subject again. What follows here is revealing about the intensely private man that Douglas Haig was, for Dorothy Haig goes on to say,

> '. . . it is interesting to note that the putting together of these early diaries gave the greatest comfort to me after Douglas had passed away, for they gave me details of his life before I knew him. All who knew Douglas will know of his extraordinary reserve (true to Scots type), and he had told me very little of what he had done before I married him.'[25]

The fact that his wife knew so little about his early years underlines the difficulty of talking definitively of the depths, nature and importance of his religious faith. However it is notable that all of the significant women in his life showed an interest in religion. His mother was extremely devout; his sister, Henrietta, had a rather eccentric approach and was a dabbler in spiritualism – Haig was very fond of her, but seems to have put up with her fancies and eccentricities, and certainly did not adopt them; whilst his wife seems to have been conventionally religious, but in those days that meant significantly more than it does today, in terms of biblical knowledge, *mores* and approach to life.

His early years were dominated by his mother, who had her own, very definite, agenda for her children. They had to pray daily in her presence; whilst he was at school Haig had 'to send his weekly biblical texts, accompanied by his comments, to his mother'. All her letters to him made some reference to God, most frequently reminding him of 'the All-seeing, loving Eye ever upon you my dear boy'.[26] Whether it was an earnest desire to please his mother or not, there is no doubt of the pleasure that Haig's prowess in Scripture at school would have brought her.

One area of controversy has been in the matter of Haig's curiosity in Spiritualism. It was an area that truly fascinated Haig's sister, Henrietta. De Groot feels that Haig entered into this with more than just fraternal devotion, feeling that the number of visits that he made were more than just idle curiosity. '. . . The sessions he enjoyed most were those in which he was given a glimpse of his own future. They were undoubtedly attractive because they invariably revealed glorious successes.'[27] But it seems apparent that these messages had no impact on Haig, nor did he continue to make any note of them after 24 November, 1908. Although Henrietta still communicated some of the contents to him, there is no reference to them at all in his vast war diary or, indeed, in any other document.[28]

My earlier comments show that Haig was not particularly moved by denominational considerations. He could be critical of the church – his diary at Oxford, for example, talks of an argument late into the night in which he commented on preferment in the Church of England. 'Something does seem to be wrong in younger sons entering the Church because there is a living in the family and not because they have any inclination to it . . .'[29] He did attend religious services quite regularly, it would appear; but the times when he did go it was as likely as not to a Church of England service, if only because of the nature of the church parade in the station where he was located. On arrival in France he still continued this procedure, attending services but not finding any great inspiration from them. This is not to say that he did not admire individual chaplains – for example Harry Blackburne, an early winner of the MC, and a most effective worker, had his transfer to the Cavalry Corps from 3rd Brigade cancelled by Haig in June 1915.[30]

The controversy about Haig's religious beliefs and its influence upon him starts after his appointment as Commander in Chief. The diary entry for 2 January, 1916, has often been quoted, but it will not hurt to repeat it here.

'I attended the Scotch Church at 9.35 am. Service was held in a school up a stair. A most earnest young Scotch man, George Duncan, conducted the service. He told us that in our prayers we should be as natural as possible and tell the Almighty exactly what we feel we want. The nation is now learning to pray and that nothing can withstand the prayers of a great united people. The congregation was greatly impressed and one could have heard a pin drop during the service. So different to the coughing and restlessness which goes on in Church in peace time.'[31]

This extract follows on from a letter to Lady Haig on 27th December, a week or so after he took on the burden of Commander in Chief, 'As you know, while doing my utmost, I feel one's best can go but a short way without help from ABOVE. . . .'[32]

What does this tell us about Haig's approach to his faith at this stage? It seems to me that he is falling back, in times of great uncertainty, to the injunctions that his mother so frequently urged upon him. For example, she wrote to him about going to University, and concluded her remarks,

'. . . seek to be directed – and you may rest assured God will shew you – and my dear boy isn't it delightful to feel that you will be wisely directed and that you may rest passive in the matter . . . I trust that you will ask for guidance as the matter concerns much of your future happiness in life and we know nothing can prosper without God.'[33]

These passages should have caused historians to stop and consider the nature of Haig's religious upbringing before going on to postulate on its influence in his conduct as Commander in Chief. None of them have considered this aspect. The danger of this is that the depth of religious conviction of this era has been either ignored or dismissed. Haig had been brought up as a member of the Church of Scotland, a Church whose theology is firmly based in the writings and teachings of John Calvin, probably the greatest of all the sixteenth century reformers. The basic tenet of Calvinism is the concept of Justification by Faith alone and the logical consequence of that, the doctrine of predestination. The preferred church service is built around the sermon – the usual custom of the time in the Church of England as well – and every member of the congregation would be well versed in the bible, particularly in the Old Testament. The Church of Scotland did not have a priestly oriented hierarchy – indeed probably the most important members of the Kirk were the Elders. The minister's sermon would then be a matter of discussion and debate afterwards – in other words, everyone would be listening attentively to what he had to say. It was not unusual for these sermons to go on for considerable lengths of time.

John, one of Haig's brothers, recalls a church service when they were at Dr Bryce's school in Edinburgh – he was then coming on to nine years old. There they were taken to the Free Kirk every Sunday to listen to Dr Moody,

> 'He had a long rostrum which served as a pulpit, on which he walked about. He preached the dullest sermons, usually for over an hour. We much resented having to put the whole of our weekly allowance (3d.) into the collection plate, for the benefit of the Free Kirk.'[34]

It is not too surprising that Haig appreciated Duncan's sermons, the whole service not lasting much more than half an hour. What he did do was to carry on a well-established habit of recording in his diary the principle elements of the sermon.

Denis Winter, unsurprisingly, is one of those who sees unsettling conclusions to be drawn from the effect of religious convictions on Haig's judgement.

> 'Before the war he seldom went to church, preferring to spend the Sabbath upon a golf course.[35] War changed this habit of mind, but during his command of first a corps and then an army, Haig makes few references in his diary to Providence or religious matters of any sort.'

To interrupt the flow here, this is not strictly true – it depends on what is meant by 'few'. There are examples, such as the occasion when Haig visited a rather downhearted Gough whilst Loos was still in progress.

> 'I reminded Gough that we shall win 'Not by might, nor by power, but by *my spirit*, saith the Lord of Hosts.'[36]

Winter continues,

> As soon as he became Commander in Chief, however, a religious dimension appears. God, to be sure, was never mentioned by name, and Haig's denomination seems almost to have been chosen as a result of a particular preacher's good looks, youthful energy and simple sermons, but [from] December 1915 Haig's writings make frequent references to a Providence, not the less re-assuring for its devotion to FSR and its corresponding approval of most of Haig's military decisions.[37]

There we have it, Haig is a closet homosexual who likes young men and can only understand simple sermons, which obviously means that all the years that Duncan had been toiling away at numerous universities collecting various prizes en route was obviously a waste of time. Dr DeGroot would obviously disagree about Duncan, at least, as he describes him as looking, 'more like a young, suitably eccentric university professor than a potential Messiah'.[38]

The point of Mr Winter's remarks is to be found in his conclusion to this passage. 'It was an unhealthy development in a man already tending towards delusions of infallibility. . . .' And then supports this with (carefully) selected extracts from Haig's diary.[39]

It seems a suitable point to state that the evidence suggests that this 'religious dimension' was not a wartime expedient or prop, to be discarded once conflict was over. Haig retained his commitment to the Church after the war, becoming an Elder at the church in Pont Street in London and in his home parish near Bemersyde.[40] His son recounted that, 'On Sundays we sometimes went on foot two miles each way to Mertoun Church, where he was an Elder'.[41]

The most public display of Haig's commitment to his religion in the post-war period was over the controversial matter of Prayer Book revision. When the issue came up before the Lords he was in Scotland, but he considered it to be his duty to be present and therefore travelled to London and sat throughout both days of the debate in order to hear the arguments. He voted in favour of the Revised Book, 'although this was not the view of a single Scottish or United Presbyterian member of the House of Commons'[42] – and, mark you, this was the Prayer Book of the Church of England that was under debate. In other words, Haig was willing to move away from the *status quo* if he felt that it was both in the interest of the Church and of the nation.

Haig's existence at GHQ enabled him to attend services at Montreuil regularly. He liked the preacher, and Duncan found himself transferred to Montreuil as the Church of Scotland chaplain there. Haig attended services as regularly as he could, part of a Sunday routine which enabled him to go to the church first and then to carry on and visit the offices of GHQ before returning to Château Beaurepaire for lunch, to which Duncan was regularly invited and thereby a witness to a number of very important discussions. When Haig was at one of his advanced GHQs Duncan would be invited to follow on. When Duncan was concerned to go to a more active posting, Haig told him, 'If you are of service to me I hope that you will be satisfied' but did encourage him to feel free to minister to troops in the forward area during the week. Obviously this desire to be more active had gone up the chain of command, because Dr Simms, responsible for all non-Church of England chaplains, wrote to him on 4 August, 1917, a very hurried letter,

'I look on you as a gift of God to our great Chief. Do you not think that that is duty grand enough for any chaplain, to stay and strengthen and uphold his hands in this titanic struggle? Who needs it more, who deserves it better, what more splendid work, God knowing and man helping could any chaplain at this crisis in our fortunes put his hand to?'[43]

Duncan certainly felt that he got to know the man well, as is shown quite clearly in his rather under-rated but important book, *Douglas Haig As I Knew Him*, published posthumously in 1965. This work has been supplemented by the recent publication by the Army Records Society of his wartime papers, edited by Gerard DeGroot, in *Military Miscellany I*.

As we have seen, at least one historian thinks that Duncan was something of an *eminence grise*, who enabled Haig to shirk from responsibility for his actions – and the consequences of them – and see in everything the will of God. Indeed he is almost portrayed as being an unwitting and unthinking tool of Divine Providence. This, though, is to misread the theology of the Church. This might be summarized as follows. All our actions, endeavours and aspirations are as dust if they are not Divinely inspired. However, this does not mean that we can adopt passivism – an approach that led to a movement fashionable in the court in the mid-years of Louis XIV and known as Quietism, which the Catholic Church condemned as heretical. Indeed, if that was the message being preached in Scotland, it does not explain convincingly the extraordinary creative powers of that nation. The imperative of Calvinism was rather the opposite – the God given gifts of the individual were to be used to their fullest extent – it was sinful, indeed, not to seek to use all those powers and abilities with which God had seen fit to endow the individual. Since God alone could only know who was predestined, there had to be external signs if one could feel even the possibility of being one of the Elect. One of these signs was earthly success in one's endeavours.

Haig was not being particularly self-effacing, or even ingenuous, when he frequently described success to a Higher Power, or put himself in that Power's hands. Indeed he made it plain time after time after time that he regarded success as God's judgement on the moral stature of the cause of the Entente powers and of the commitment, tenacity and bravery of his soldiers.

Thus, although he famously wrote on 11 November, 1918,

'We heard this morning that the Kaiser is in Holland. If the war had gone against us, no doubt our king would have had to go, and probably our Army would have become insubordinate like the German Army. Cf John

Bunyan's remark on seeing a man on his way to be hanged, "But for the Grace of God, John Bunyan would have been in that man's place!"'[44]

he more often than not insisted on praising the men under his command. An example of this was recorded by Duncan himself, referring to meeting Haig on 13 November, 1918,

> 'When I attempted to express congratulations his immediate reaction was: 'Oh! You mustn't congratulate me; we have all been in this together, all trying in our different ways to do our part.' After a time he added, pointing to a piper [there was a Pipe-Major nearby, to whom Haig had been talking]: 'Come and speak to this fine fellow over here. He came out in 1914; and in the early days was through some of the worst of it. It is fellows like him who deserve congratulations'.[45]

The problem we face at the turn of the twentieth century is that our cynical and worldly generation cannot possibly accept this at face value. All motives have to be from some base level – coarse ambition, a thirst for power, a desire to manipulate, a wish to leave one's mark. No one can deny that Haig felt firmly convinced that he was the right man to do the job; nor can anyone deny that his faith was an enormous comfort to him when he was carrying the burden that would most certainly have crushed a lesser man. He faced a seemingly never ending load of responsibility from the outbreak of the war to its end – Corps Commander, Army Commander and then Commander-in-Chief for just short of three years, a record of high command unsurpassed by anyone on the Western Front.

Examples of this in his writing, particularly to his wife, but also in his diary, are numerous. To take an instance, he wrote in a letter to Dorothy,

> 'I note what you write that 'for this coming offensive ask for God's help'. Now you must know that I feel that every step in my plan has been taken with the Divine help – and I ask daily for aid, not merely in making the plan, but in carrying it out, and this I hope I shall continue to do until the end of all things which concerns me on earth. I think it is this Divine help which gives me tranquillity of mind and enables me to carry on without feeling the strain of responsibility to be too excessive. I try to do no more than "do my best and trust to God", because of the reasons I give above. Very many thanks for telling me your views on this side of my work, because it has given me the chance of putting my ideas on paper. For otherwise I would not have written them, as you know I don't talk much about religion.'[46]

This extract underlines the view that Haig's religious outlook almost certainly helped him to maintain that placidity which served him well under the strain of the war. He is noted as not raising his voice, of remaining unemotional under stress (although both Currie and Monash noted his tearfulness when referring to the work of the Canadians and Australians at crucial points in 1918) and of maintaining an overwhelmingly powerful attitude of what the ancients would call *gravitas*. Whatever other criticisms he might have had about him, Churchill could comment,

> '... no other subject of the King could have endured the ordeal which was his lot with the phlegm, the temper and the fortitude of Sir Douglas Haig.'[47]

Religion was undoubtedly a comfort and consolation for many of the fighting men; whilst for numerous others it was seen as hypocritical and partisan. Haig's approach was mirrored in the view of others. Major W (Billy) Congreve VC DSO MC is one of the better known and outstanding junior officers of the war. He could write, quite unselfconsciously, in a letter to his mother,

> '... it's just too *wonderful* how God seems to help and help and always help me – it's so vividly real, this help, that it almost startles me. Do you know the feeling? In everything He helps, and now I believe that there is nothing too great for Him to do for one'.

Elsewhere he wrote,

> 'I remember in that little book [The Practice of the Presence of God] Uncle George gave me, and which I always carry, came the words, "I cannot do this unless Thou enablest me," and often and often have I said those words to God, knowing their truth, and knowing too that His help *would* always come – and it ALWAYS has. So one could never feel *proud* of whatever one did, could one?'[48]

What is noticeable about this is that Congreve's spirituality, here based on an Anglo-Catholic approach, comes from a completely different part of the British Christian spiritual spectrum from Haig's. Yet the conclusion to which he comes is strikingly similar.

John Charteris, a son of the Manse and therefore fully exposed to religion, and that of the Church of Scotland in particular, wrote to Liddell Hart in October 1935 after the latter had reviewed Duff Cooper's, *Haig*.

'He rarely erred but like all human beings he erred at times. I sometimes think that it was recognition of these errors, still unaccountable to him, that led him into his deep religious tendency which arose late in life and afforded to him the explanation of the otherwise unexplainable.'[49]

When it comes to religion, and the influence that it had upon Haig in both his public and internal expression, it is probably best to leave it to one who knew his spiritual life best – in so far as anyone could be said to know it – and that is George Duncan (and it is worth noting that his commentary upon Haig came after the publication of Blake's *Private Papers*). Even he did not always understand him as is shown by an incident on 15 July, 1917.

'I asked if I might speak with him for 2 minutes. So on our way back from the garden to the Château I asked if he couldn't stay behind some Sunday for Communion. I'm afraid I took him unawares for his natural shyness overtook him & he could just mumble, 'No; no I don't think so' and when, with perhaps an appearance of pressing him (though I only meant to convey the impression that it would be a great pleasure for me to see him there), 'You know, sir', I said, 'You treat me in such a way that I speak to you as I would an ordinary Tommy.' He replied, 'Yes, but you know that I must be the judge of that.' By then we were well off the stairs of his château. He seemed disinclined to continue the discussion and simply shook hands again & said goodbye and disappeared into his room.'[50]

Duncan seems to me to read Haig well. He makes a comparison with Lincoln, of whom it was said that his theology was 'limited to an intense belief in a vast and over-ruling Providence. And this Providence, darkly spoken of, was certainly conceived by him as intimately and kindly related to his whole life.' Thus Lincoln spoke during the presidential elections.

'"I see the storm coming, and I know that His hand is in it. If He has a place and work for me, and I think He has, I believe I am ready. I am nothing, but truth is everything." Lincoln's thoughts might well have been Haig's though. . . .'

And here Duncan perceptively adds,

'. . . Haig would probably have kept his thoughts to himself.'

Duncan goes on to say,

'With some men, no doubt, belief in a divine "call" leads easily to fanaticism. But Haig was no fanatic. There was about him a mental balance which was associated not a little with his stern sense of duty; and like other devout men down the ages he heard in the call of duty the voice of God.'

He was a man who saw the need for action in the situation that faced them and,

'then in a spirit of obedience and faith in God, find themselves braced to meet it with courage and resolution, and in so doing draw strength from unseen sources.'[51]

Duncan concludes his book with this comment,

Well indeed it was for the British nation that in one of the most critical periods in its history it had ready at its call as the leader of its armies a man with the military gifts, the sublime faith, and the unconquerable soul of Douglas Haig.[52]

Notes

1   Conversation with Mgr A Howe, Ely Place, London on 3 January, 1999. Bourne did, in any case, his training for the priesthood at St Sulpice in France.

2   Donal Attwater, *A Dictionary of the Popes* (The Catholic Book Club, London, 1939), 315.

3   Sir John Smyth, VC, *In This Sign Conquer* (Mowbrays, London, 1968), 26.

4   Tom Johnstone and James Hagerty, *The Cross on the Sword* (Geoffrey Chapman, London, 1996), 2.

5   See, for example, Cromwell's entry in Trevor N. Dupuy, Curt Johnson and David L. Bongard, *The Harper Encyclopaedia of Military Biography* (HarperCollins, New York, 1992), 199–200.

6   For a somewhat controversial view of pre-war public schools, see Peter Parker, *The Old Lie: The Great War and the Public School Ethos* (Constable, London, 1987).

7   Alan Wilkinson, *The Church of England and the First World War* (SPCK, London), 1978, 127, quoting from H.C. Jackson, *Pastor on the Nile*.

8   Robert Blake, ed., *The Private Papers of Douglas Haig*, (Eyre and Spottiswoode, London, 1952), 124.

9   Ibid., 143.

10 Ibid., 246.

11 Quoted in Duff Cooper, *Haig*, (Faber and Faber, London, 1935), 414.

12 Wilkinson, *The Church of England and the First World War*, 127.

13 Quoted in Wilkinson, *op.cit.*, 128. Arguably, and in the context, these were legitimate activities for ordained men. It says something about the lack of imagination at work here, for by doing such materially useful functions, the responsibility of no one else, the chaplain would also have the chance to exert a spiritual and moral influence. From such work could the likes of Tubby Clayton and Stoddart Kennedy build up a great spiritual family.

14 Blake, ed., *Papers of Haig*, 137; remainder of extract in John Terraine, *Douglas Haig, the educated soldier* (Hutchinson, London, 1963), 174.

15 Blake, ed., *Papers of Haig*, 261.

16 Ibid., 321.

17 It is probably worth noting that, even in these ecumenical times, the Roman Catholic Church only has (and only seeks) observer status at the meetings of the World Council of Churches.

18 Wilkinson, *The Church of England and the First World War*, 160–165.

19 Brigadier-General John Charteris, *Field-Marshal Earl Haig* (Cassell, London, 1929), see Index.

20 Brigadier-General John Charteris, At GHQ (Cassell, London, 1931), 219.

21 Ibid., 314.

22 Cooper, *Haig*, 281.

23 Ibid., 282. Foch was a very devout Catholic and would attend mass every day if at all possible. Whilst commanding the French Army in the North (based in Cassel) in the early months of the war, it was noted that he would also spend considerable periods of time in meditation

24 Lieutenant-General Sir Hastings Anderson, 'Lord Horne as an Army Commander', *Journal of the Royal Artillery*, Vol LVI, No. 4 (1930), 418; Geoffrey Powell, *Plumer: the Soldier's General* (Leo Cooper, London, 1990), 321; Field-Marshal B. Montgomery, *The Memoirs of Field-Marshal the Viscount Montgomery of Alamein, K.G.* (Collins, London, 1958), 542. Certainly not a man to fall into this category was Ludendorff, whose last years were taken up with almost unceasing abuse against Jews, Freemasons, Jesuits, Catholics and Christians. Roger Parkinson, *Tormented Warrior: Ludendorff and the Supreme Command* (Hodder and Stoughton, London, 1978) 223–225.

25 The Countess Haig, *The Man I Knew* (Moray Press, London, 1936), vii–viii.

26 Gerard J. De Groot, *Douglas Haig 1861–1928* (Unwin Hyman, London, 1988), 12.

27 Ibid., 118.

28 For a full discussion of this and related matters see John Hussey, 'Of the Indian Rope Trick, the Paranormal, and Captain Shearer's Ray', *British Army Review* Number 112, April 1996, 78–88.

29 Quoted in ibid., 20–21.

30 Smyth, *In This Sign Conquer*, 192.

31 Quoted in G.J. DeGroot, The Rev George S Duncan at GHQ, 1916–1918, *Military Miscellany I* (Sutton Publishing, Stroud, 1996), 277. The Introduction to the papers bear a close resemblance to an article Dr De Groot wrote some years earlier, 'Haig's Secret Weapon', *Army Quarterly*, January 1992, 60–67.

32 Terraine, *Douglas Haig, the educated soldier*, 173.

33 De Groot, *Douglas Haig 1861–1928*, 17–18.

34 Haig, *The Man I Knew*, 13.

35 It is not quite clear what is being proved here. So, Haig played golf on Sunday – is there anything so unusual in that for a man whose week would be extremely busy? Certainly going to church and playing golf on a Sunday are not mutually exclusive occupations. As regards Church attendance, it is noteworthy that there are several references in Haig's pre-war diary, which was intermittently kept and filled with short entries – seldom more than a hundred words, often as short as ten for any particular day. But he does refer to religion in his entry for Sunday 1 May, 1892; 11 September, 1892; 15 July, 1906 and 26 August, 1906, to take several

examples – and usually comments on the text taken and the quality of the sermon. I am grateful to John Hussey for these references.

36 Cooper, Haig, 282.
37 Denis Winter, *Haig's Command: a reassessment* (Viking, London, 1991), 164–165.
38 DeGroot, *Revd George S. Duncan at GHQ 1916–1918*, 271.
39 Winter, *Haig's Command*, 165.
40 Nigel Cave review of DeGroot, 'Revd George S. Duncan at GHQ 1916–1918', in *Stand To!* Number 53, 14.
41 Haig of Bemersyde, 'Haig at Bemersyde: A Memoir', *Records* (Journal of the Douglas Haig Fellowship), 9.
42 Cooper, *Haig*, 415.
43 DeGroot, *Revd George S. Duncan at GHQ 1916–1918*. Revd John Simms to George Duncan, 378.
44 Blake, ed., *Papers of Haig*, 341.
45 G.S. Duncan, *Douglas Haig As I Knew Him* (Allen and Unwin, London, 1966), 90.
46 Cooper, Haig, 327–328; for a marginally different transcription of this letter, see DeGroot, *Revd George S. Duncan at GHQ 1916–1918*, 292.
47 Winston S. Churchill, *The World Crisis 1911–1918* (Odhams, London, nd), Volume II, 947.
48 Lieutenant Colonel LH Thornton and Pamela Fraser, *The Congreves* (John Murray, London, 1930), 331, 332–333.
49 Charteris to Liddle Hart, 11 Oct 1935, Liddell Hart Centre for Military Archives, LH 1/162/1.
50 DeGroot, *Revd George S. Duncan at GHQ 1916–1918*, 364–365.
51 Duncan, *Douglas Haig As I Knew Him*, 126.
52 Ibid., 138. There is an important article for students of Haig by Lord Reith, written shortly after the publication of Blake's edition of the Haig Papers. It is important both because of Reith's experience in the Great War and his intimate knowledge of the Church of Scotland. See Lord Reith of Stonehaven, 'Into Proper Perspective', *Blackwood's Magazine*, December 1954, Vol 276, No. 1670, 481–489.

Index

Army, German (*continued*)
   losses at the Somme 35n
   morale 73, 114
   strategy 22
   veterans' movements 232
Army, Indian
   discipline 210
Army, Italian 107, 138
   discipline 209
Army, New Zealand
   discipline 210
Army, Portuguese 137
Army, Russian
   decline after 1917 70, 72
   discipline 209
Army, South African
   discipline 210
Army Acts (annual) 208–9, 210
Army and Religion (report) 246
Arnold, Thomas 242
Arras (battle) 8, 83–4, 89, 92, 94,
   149
Arthur, Sir George 228
artillery 24, 56, 64, 68, 71, 83,
   151, 161–4, 166
Asquith, Herbert 64, 107, 115,
   176, 179
At GHQ (Charteris) 247
Atbara (battle) 226
Auchinleck, Field-Marshal Sir
   Claude 213
aviation 24, 165–7

Babington, Anthony 197, 209,
   213–14, 215–16, 219
Badsey, Stephen 55
Barnes, George 116
Barrow, Maj. Gen. Sir George (later
   Gen.) 38
Barry, F.R. 244
battlefield stress 206
   see also shell shock
Baynes, John 8
Beach Thomas, William 181, 183
Beaumont Hamel (battle) 89, 149
Beauvais Conference (1918) 120

Beaverbrook, Lord 177, 178, 186,
   187, 189
Beckett, Ian 2
Bernhardi, Friedrich von 54
Bible 18
Bidwell, Shelford 5
Birch, Maj.-Gen. Sir Noel (later
   Gen.) 16, 25, 35n, 83
Birdwood, Gen. Sir William (later
   Field-Marshal Lord) 91
   appointment as commander 5th
      Army 79, 93
   relations with Haig 93, 95, 96
Blackburne, Harry 249
Blair, Col. Arthur 38
Blake, Robert, Lord 9, 176, 256
Blackadder Goes Forth (television
   series) 217
Bleasdale, Alan 197
Boer War 44–7, 54, 55, 181, 208
Bonar Law, Andrew see Law,
   Andrew Bonar
Bond, Brian 2
Boyle, Capt. C. 45
Braithwaite Maj.-Gen. Walter (later
   Gen.) 28
Briand, Aristide 133–4, 139
Bridges, Maj.-Gen. Sir Tom (later
   Lt.-Gen.) 80
*British Butchers and Bunglers of
   World War One* (Laffin) 13
British Expeditionary Force see
   Army, British
British Legion 225–36 passim
   establishment of 229–30
   in politics 231–2
British Soldier on the Somme
   (Liddle) 216
Broodseinde (battle) 81, 93
Brown, Ian 8
Buchan, John 184
Budworth, Maj-Gen. Sir Charles
   35n
Bullecourt (battle) 89, 93
Buller, Gen. Sir Redvers 53
Byers, Pte. 203

Winter, Denis 2, 3–4, 251, 252
wireless telegraphy 159
Wolff, Leon 51
Wood, Field-Marshall Sir Evelyn 40,
    53
Woollcombe, Lt.-Gen. Sir Charles
    92
Wootton, Graham 228, 230

World Crisis, The (Churchill) 145,
    151

Ypres, First (battle) 25, 55, 130,
    226
Ypres, Third (battle) see
    Passchendaele